Marginal Catholics

Ex Libris

Derek Turnham

Marginal Catholics

ANGLO-CATHOLICISM:
A FURTHER CHAPTER OF
MODERN CHURCH HISTORY

Ivan Clutterbuck

First Published in 1993
Gracewing
Fowler Wright Books
Southern Avenue, Leominster
Herefordshire HR6 0QF

Gracewing Books are distributed

In New Zealand by
Catholic Supplies Ltd
80 Adelaide Rd
Wellington
New Zealand

In Australia by
Charles Paine Pty
8 Ferris Street
North Parramatta
NSW 2151 Australia

In U.S.A. by
Morehouse Publishing
P.O. Box 1321
Harrisburg
PA 17105
U.S.A.

In Canada by
Meakin and Associates
Unit 17, 81 Auriga Drive
Nepean, Ontario, KZE 7Y5
Canada

© Cover design by Gill Onions
Cover illustration, Oriel College

ISBN 0 85244 234 3

Typesetting by Action Typesetting Limited, Gloucester
Printed by The Cromwell Press,
Broughton Gifford, Melksham, Wiltshire SN12 8PH

Contents

Acknowledgements

The publishers would like to thank Yale University Press for permission to quote the *The Stripping of the Altars*; SCM Press Ltd for permission to quote from *A History of English Christianity 1920–1990* and also from *The Bible Without Illusions*.

All efforts have been made to check the copyright of material quoted. Any omissions will be rectified in any future editions.

Foreword

The Preface to the Declaration of Assent begins with these familiar words:

'The Church of England is part of the One, Holy, Catholic and Apostolic Church worshipping the one true God, Father, Son and Holy Spirit. It professes the faith uniquely revealed in the Holy Scriptures and set forth in the catholic creeds, which faith the Church is called upon to proclaim afresh in each generation. Led by the Holy Spirit, it has borne witness to Christian truth in its historic formularies, the Thirty-nine Articles of Religion, the Book of Common Prayer and the Ordering of Bishops, Priests and Deacons.'

There are here a number of significant implications about the nature and character of the Church of England. First, that it is a part of the world wide universal church. Next, it maintains the Christian faith grounded in the Scriptures, and its witness and sacramental life are in continuity with the church across the centuries from the earliest period. Thirdly, its historic ministry is entrusted with the apostolic commission to baptize, teach and preach; to nurture the faithful and provide pastoral care; to offer worship with and for the people of God, and to safeguard the divine word and sacraments.

In the 1830s and '40s the leaders of the Oxford Movement strongly reaffirmed the Church as a divine institution, its bishops ordained in the apostolic succession, and its rule of faith contained in the Prayer Book. They upheld the corporate and sacramental character of the Church's life, and the faith embodied in the catholic creeds and taught by the ancient fathers. They saw this faith and life as being lived out in a tradition of teaching and worship in continuity with the undivided church of the early centuries.

What to many seemed novel doctrine was for the Tractarians a recovery of the true inheritance of the English Church, of which Richard Hooker and the Caroline divines were the classical witnesses and exponents. Although in our own day we have become more aware of the persistence of Caroline theology and devotion during the second half of the eighteenth and early part of the 19th centuries, yet the impact of the Oxford Movement's 'revolution by tradition' upon the Church of England's self-understanding has been profound and enduring over the past one hundred and fifty years.

One important outcome of the Oxford Movement was the development of the Anglo-Catholic wing in the Church's life, though originally Anglo-Catholicism meant the catholic continuity and identity of the whole Church of England. Yet the distinctive character of what we know as Anglo-Catholicism is not the sole legatee of the Oxford fathers. The influence has been marked throughout the whole of the Church of England. Those in the more moderate form of the catholic tradition (known until a generation ago as Prayer Book Catholics), as well as liberal catholics, and those classical Anglicans who eschew party labels, are all in some degree children of the Oxford Movement. However, none would deny that the Anglo-Catholic tradition has been a powerful element in the life of the Church, particularly up to the middle of this century, and its influence today is still very apparent.

Father Ivan Clutterbuck tells the story of the Anglo-Catholic movement. In doing so he draws not only on the familiar histories and biographies of the period, but also on the minutes of the Church Union of which he was once Organising Secretary, as well as on his own long experience and ministry.

It is generally recognised that since the second Vatican Council and in the current period of liturgical renewal, there has been some uncertainty about the continuing role of Anglo-Catholicism as an organised entity. Following the decision by the General Synod in November 1992 to ordain women to the priesthood the future has become still less clear. However, the distinctive quality of Catholic faith, devotion and practice in the Church of England is of great and continuing importance. And I would emphasise three aspects.

First, holiness. The primacy of God; the call to love and adore Him in the perfection of His own being and in response to His love for us. 'Abide in me, and I in you'. The living Christ is present and at work in the human soul, seeking to transform it into His own likeness. The quest for holiness requires a disciplined and orderly framework for our prayer and life, which should be marked by penitence for our sins and joy in God's love and forgiveness.

Next, Catholic life is sacramental. The world is God's creation, and within its beauty and wonder we see intimations of the beauty and mystery of God Himself. The world itself is a sacrament of God's presence and love; and our response in worship is sacramental. Through the water of baptism and the gift of the Spirit we are united by faith through Christ to God. In the offering of the bread and wine in the Eucharist we celebrate and plead the sacrifice of Christ and invoke the Holy Spirit to empower us as agents of God's Kingdom.

Thirdly, our belief is incarnational. Our Lord becomes at one with us in the flesh, and his work of redemption includes the whole range of our social and political relations in life. Set free from the bondage of sin by the redeemer, we are called to love and serve Him in the needs of the poor, and challenge the forces and structures which oppress people, and demean the human spirit.

In the 1830s the Tractarian reformers were confronted by enormous challenges. Yet under God they were the instruments of the renewal of the Church's life and witness. We may learn much from their courage and commitment, their adherence to the heritage of the Catholic faith, their quest for holiness, their recourse to the sacraments, their steady teaching and their zeal for souls, and their strong belief in the catholic character of the Church and its ministry. May we in our generation be granted a like courage and faith.

+ Colin Winton

Author's Note

I have two main reasons for writing this book. The first can be found in a recent work, *Anglo-Catholicism, A Study in Religious Ambiguity* by WSF Pickering.[1] In his introduction he writes, 'There is a dearth of historical studies of Anglo-Catholicism. It is quite remarkable that no definitive book has ever been written on the subject: as John Kent says, nothing serious has been published for the period after 1845 – the year of Newman's conversion to Roman Catholicism. It is remarkable because the movement has exerted no mean influence, not only on the Church of England but also on churches separated from it.'

Pickering does not presume to give a serious historical study but concerns himself with the sociological aspects of the movement. Likewise Francis Penhale also writes as a sociologist in his book *Catholics in Crisis* (Mowbray 1986) and so a conclusion might be reached even before the pages of these books were opened that here was some kind of social phenomenon which had lost its way. I do not see it like that as will appear in this book and I hope it will be seen that Anglo-Catholics are a positive set of people who from the beginning have given a new spiritual dimension to their church in England and then elsewhere.

I cannot claim to be the professional historian Pickering wants, but in recent years I have taught modern church history from 1800 to an advanced level in two public schools and also tutored privately in the subject. In this I have been handicapped by a lack of books on the Catholic movement within the Anglican Church and so I have put together

material which I hope will bridge the gap between the early
Tractarians and the present day. The first leaders have
been well documented. Dean Church's book *The Oxford
Movement 1833 – 1845* is a contemporary chronicle and later
biographies of men like Keble, Pusey and Newman must
to some extent depend on this writer. Keble has had his
excellent biographer in Georgina Battiscombe[2]; Liddon's life
of Pusey has been brought up to date and corrected by a set
of essays *Pusey Rediscovered*[3] and by David Forrester in his
Young Dr Pusey.[4] Books on Newman continue to pour forth
and David Newsome's *The Parting of Friends*[5] brings to a
close the first stage of the Oxford Movement.

It would not be true to say that all is silence after
that because Anglo-Catholics, Tractarians and the Church
Union flit through Victorian history and emerge triumphant
at the beginning of Roger Lloyd's The *Church of England
1900 – 1965*[6] only to be written off by Hastings in English
Christianity 1920 – 1990.[7] One has, however, to search hard
to discover how Anglo-Catholicism developed from being an
academic affair to penetrating every kind of parish. There
are interesting portraits of the first ritualists like Lowder,
Mackonochie, Stanton and Tooth and these have helped
me trace Anglo-Catholic progress. Peter Anson's *Church
Furnishings 1840 – 1940* is a mine of information about Victorian and Edwardian church life and fills in a number of
gaps. However, the sixth former who is studying this period
of church history does not have the time or the facilities for
making such research and needs to have the facts presented
more conveniently. Such students are often not very religious,
but have been attracted to the subject as one might choose,
for instance, social life in British India. Their background
has not enabled them to grapple with the niceties of church
parties and titles such as High and Low, Catholic and Evangelical and useful tuition time can be wasted explaining these
to them when a book giving the background would help.

More seriously, the ordinary Catholic churchman has suffered from a lack of information about the history of his
faith. If it is true that a nation which forgets its history
loses its soul then this can also apply in the field of religion.
As I shall mention later in my book, when I started to go

round the country in 1966, talking about the work of the Church Union, I found a profound ignorance of the background of Anglo-Catholicism. Even the great names of the Oxford Movement meant nothing and I had to begin from scratch. I have no doubt that in the last twenty five years or so the story of Anglo-Catholicism has faded further into oblivion and this cannot be good in the continuing struggle to maintain Catholic faith and practice in the Church of England. At a recent Festival of Faith I looked round the vast Wembley arena and wondered how many of the thousands of Catholics gathered there had heard about the sacrifices and the hardships of their predecessors which had made such a solemn concelebrated Mass possible. I hope, therefore, that I can uncover something of this past church history for the ordinary church member as well as for the student.

After I had finished this book, the General Synod of the Church of England voted to ordain women priests. This has presented Anglo-Catholics with their greatest crisis and challenge. If my book had been about the future, I would have delayed its publication until the situation became clearer. My main object in writing, however, was to describe the contribution which Anglo-Catholics have made in the past and are still making to the spiritual life of their Church. If they should now be forced out of their church, much of this heritage will be lost to the main body. It seems, therefore, the more urgent that this book should see the light of day as soon as possible.

It is also important that the place of the Church Union should be understood in the revival of the Catholic faith in the Anglican Church. Its work still goes on, although hampered by lack of resources because people have little information about it. Catholic pressure groups and societies rise and disappear but the Church Union goes on. Since 1859 it has made possible the work and aspirations of faithful priests in the parishes first by shielding them from litigation and then by taking over the promotion of that spirituality which was the inspiration of the founding fathers of the Oxford Movement. In all the changes and crises of the last hundred years and more, this society has held together by sound teaching in the different strands of Anglo-Catholicism and enabled action to be taken when the life of our Church has been threatened. I have in my possession the council minutes of the English Church Union from 1859 until 1894 and from these I have been able to write about the extent of its contribution to Catholic church life.

As I shall also show, from 1966 until 1974 I was its organising secretary and not only organised the last Congress in 1968 but travelled widely on its behalf. I have, therefore, been able to see from close at hand the work which has quietly continued from its offices in London. When I joined those offices in 1966 we had a large staff, but now this is depleted in numbers although not in its enthusiasm and dedication. In recent years it has underpinned other Catholic societies such as the Confraternity of the Blessed Sacrament, the Guild of the Servants of the Sanctuary, the Society of Mary, the Catholic League and others which for many years have cared for the different aspects of Catholic devotion and service. Through the publications of the Church Literature Association it has enabled church people to keep in step with the best of modern and ancient spirituality. Anglo-Catholics have been accused of becoming fossilised and of failing to keep up with new religious developments. This cannot be said of the Church Union which, for example, prepared its members for the changes of Vatican II. Professor Ratcliff's lecture on liturgical development at the 1958 Eucharistic Congress organised by the Church Union explained why there had to be a reformation and the 1968 Congress at the Royal Festival Hall took Anglo-Catholics further along the road of 'all things new'. All this will have further treatment in later chapters. This is not a book about the Church Union, but it is impossible to write about the story of the Catholic movement since the middle of the last century without its appearing regularly.

My second reason for writing this book is duty; I was brought up as an Anglo-Catholic from my earliest days so carefully and soundly that this faith has been the mainstay of a very varied and demanding life. From an early age I was taught by my parish priest to love God and hate sin and was shown the discipline by which this way of holiness might be gained. I soon learnt that God made me to know, love and serve him on earth and to be happy with him for ever in heaven and that such a vocation made me a very special person. To quote St Ignatius of Antioch, I was stamped with the coinage of God and not of the world. So it was a privilege to attend Mass regularly, to examine my conscience, to keep Lent strictly, to know that there was no crown without the cross, to say my prayers well by rising early and going to bed early. In time, I was taught the art of mental prayer and learnt from the example of the saints. Serving at the altar was a great privilege and had to be done with reverent care. None of these things was important in itself but as part of a vocation to holiness to which all Christians were called. In this I was not singled out for special treatment because all my contemporaries in the congregation were given the same vision. If all did not take advantage of such training that was no fault of the clergy. When I went up to Cambridge in the middle '30s, I found friends from parishes round the country who had been put on the same road to holiness so I came to the con- clusion that this was the legacy of an Anglo-Catholic way of life. Over the years I have been plunged into situations where I have not been able to worship so richly as in my younger days, but the essentials have remained and these have pre- vented me from changing entirely the divine coinage into something less worthy.

The background to this religious life style in which I was brought up is more fully described in the portrait of a parish which can be seen as the centrepiece of this book. If I have chosen just one parish it is because it is one which I remember very well and there are still enough of my contemporaries living to support my memories: yet there are senior citizens alive who will say 'It was like that in our church in Plymouth, in Sheffield, in Manchester, in Birmingham and in Brighton and elsewhere.' Time is catching up with us and the story of this high noon of Anglo-Catholicism must be told while there are still wit- nesses to it. Inevitably there was a dawn and forenoon and these must be outlined for those who feel perhaps that they are now living in the afternoon or evening of a great movement.

When I went to church in the years between the wars I believed that I belonged to the mainstream of Anglican church life. This was not unreasonable because I did not have a general view of Christian churchmanship. In those days we were very insular and there was no TV to show us what went on in other parts of the country. If we joined with other churches it was always with those who did the same things. Mostly, we drew all our religion and entertainment from our parish church and did not venture far beyond except, perhaps, for the annual holiday to the seaside where churches of our own ilk could be found. When I went up to university and then further into the world I discovered I was out on a limb and that most people, if they went to church at all, followed a different kind of faith and practice. In other words, I was in the margins and they were the main body. For this reason I have entitled my book *Marginal Catholics* because I have learnt that socially – to use the word in its true meaning – Anglo-Catholics have been relegated to the margins of religious life in England. This happened to the first leaders of the movement in Oxford for they were pushed to the edge of academic life and this kind of isolation has been suffered in some way or another by those who followed them, up to the present day. Yet this has not deterred them from their purpose which they saw as being to recall their fellow citizens to a vision of holiness. Anglo-Catholicism, as I understand it, is a spiritual phenomenon in the first place. This mission may have been misunderstood by some of its members at times who have been happy to retreat into a ceremonial conscious ghetto but this has been a betrayal of the principles of the movement. Always the sheep must be sought and fed and this duty is shown in the early chapters of this book.

By my title I do not wish to call in question the quality of the faith of Anglo-Catholics. Two notable marginals were St Athanasius and St John Chrysostom in the early Church for they were banished for their orthodoxy. Catholics believe that our Church of England, whether by accident or design, stands firmly within the universal Catholic Church which stretches back through the early Church to the apostles and then to Christ himself. The object of the founding fathers of the Oxford Movement, Keble, Pusey and Newman, was not to make their Church Catholic, but to show it was so already. In the words of an Anglo-Catholic scholar, N.P. Williams, the task of Catholics in the future was to remember the lesson of the first Tractarians and 'reawaken the Church of England to a consciousness of its true splendid position as a historic representative of the one, holy, Catholic and apostolic Church'. From the onset of the movement there has been an appeal to the Scriptures and the primitive Church and later generations have been on dangerous ground, if they forget these two authorities.

This, then, is a story of marginal churchmen and it is told by somebody who is a marginal of the marginals, geographically speaking. For my ministry has been carried out almost anywhere but from within vicarage or parish walls. It happened all too easily and in a way recognisable by earlier generations of Catholic priests in the Church of England. I was ordained priest by a very Evangelical bishop at the beginning of the last war and served in a Catholic parish on the edge of London. My vicar departed soon afterwards and I was left in charge. I obviously overstepped the mark because the new vicar, who was not so High, was not sorry when I looked for another job. I was all set to be the chaplain of a leading public school when I was summoned to the presence of my bishop in Rochester. He sat, red-faced and aggressively Low, and considered me. 'You are not going to school,' he said, 'I am sending you into the Army as a chaplain to learn better manners'. It seemed exciting at the time to be sent into the front line but I quickly learnt I was entering a kind of purgatory. Only six months a priest and the youngest chaplain in two great wars, I was stunned by the sheer unbelief and indifference of the British soldiery. I felt useless as I followed the flag and dodged the shells. Early, too, I realised I was entering an area of church life which was run on strictly Protestant lines. No vestments were allowed and any High Church behaviour firmly discouraged. Regular Army chaplains, suddenly promoted over the amateurs, patrolled the armies to enforce the party line.

However, I saw from close at hand what war meant to those who had to fight far away from home and how little prepared spiritually they were to meet this experience. If I had difficulty in practising my faith, church laymen were in a worse position. My bishop had pushed me to the edge of my Church just as surely as the Tractarians were sent to the margins of university life a century before and as the first ritualists had to face Protestant malice alone in the slums. It was, I suppose, a mini-martyrdom which has been shared by a succession of priests until the present day. Such persecution could mean the imprisonment of priests who would not give up that Catholic faith and practice which could be found enshrined in the Book of Common Prayer. It could mean the hindering of a parish priest from carrying out his pastoral duties as in the case of a Dolling or Mackonochie in the last century or a Bernard Walke in this. The Bishop of Winchester in 1841 refused to ordain priest John Keble's deacon because of his 'bad' connection and in recent years priests have been denied promotion or even a place in their Church because they could not accept a Methodist reunion scheme or the ordination of women. For over one hundred and fifty years there has been a penalty for being an Anglo-Catholic and my experience in 1941 can be seen as a minor example.

On the edge of the Church I remained because, after being blown up in Italy and invalided from the Army in 1944, I found no parish niche and was offered a school job as chaplain and classics master. Catholic externals were rationed here, but there was a chance of teaching the faith. I also gained professional experience because it was important for my pupils that they should pass their examinations. From here I wandered almost accidentally into the Navy where I had some of the happiest days of my life. In this service there are many opportunities for teaching in what has been called the finest educating system in the country. Sea commissions took me east to some of the furthest corners of the world – extremely marginal! I have found myself in many strange corners: I have sat round a sheep's carcase at a sheikh's banquet, tried to explain the Holy Trinity to Hindu professors in Jaffna, viewed close at hand people suffering under the Communist regime in Poland and Czechoslovakia and organised a week of sport and entertainment in East Africa. More seriously I had experience of mission work at the outposts of the Empire, have been flown into the first oil villages in the Persian Gulf and administered the sacraments to our people there; have said mass in isolated embassies and in the oddest of places; have tried to lead back into the Church those who have lapsed and strayed. Back in this country as organising secretary of the Church Union for eight years I travelled a quarter of a million miles round the country and saw at first hand what was happening in the Catholic parishes of every diocese.

All this, no doubt, could provide material for an autobiography but I have mentioned my life in the margins because, as much as possible, I shall use my experience in describing the modern religious scene. In some cases I have not needed to consult books because I have seen events unfolding before my eyes. This is especially true of the impact of Vatican II changes on parish life, of the Anglican/Methodist reunion scheme and not least of life in the classroom of which I have had many years experience in state and private schools.

I can best describe what I have learnt about Anglo-Catholicism, by relating what happened a few years ago when I was conducting a pilgrimage in the Holy Land. When my party was in Galilee we were invited to a kibbutz, not far from Nazareth. Our coach took us along a dusty and rocky road until suddenly we entered an estate full of beautiful flowers and trees heavy with fruit. The leader of the kibbutz told the story of that commune. Twenty years before, a number of British Jews had come to Israel, offering their services. They were given that part of the country. 'But', said the leader, 'it was all rock and nothing would grow'. So the immigrants, men, women and children went to work on the land, tearing out the rock with their bare hands until they uncovered the earth below. This was done for two years and then they planted. 'Now you can see the result of our labours', said the spokesman and so we could.

This seems to be an illustration of the revival within the Church of England from the earliest days of the nineteenth century. It was not only the Tractarians who did the hard work, for others were building new churches and reforming the clergy but they were the people who suffered most and are still suffering. Yet in one detail, my illustration does not tell the full story, because Anglo-Catholics have never been given the ground to work alone. They have had to camp on the edge in outposts and come in as day workers, labouring hard but never admitted as full citizens. In this respect, they may have a certain advantage because they can provide local places of salvation to which those in search of God may come without being committed to the full bureaucratic Anglican system. Religious man has simple needs and generally he is little concerned with synods, reunion schemes or diocesan blueprints for education or evangelism. Growth of the Church to him is when another person or family joins the parish Eucharist. The really dedicated parish priest knows this and is impatient of meetings and committees which take him away from his pastoral work. The much-maligned ritualist priest of the last century took roots in his parish and rarely left it and there are still men like that today.

My book begins with the needs of ordinary people and when I come to assess the achievement and contribution of marginal Catholics up to the present day, my criterion will be whether the local flocks have been cared for. To return to that kibbutz. Gardens and estates never stand still and have to be constantly tended so that the weeds and rock do not return. So the work of Catholics in the Church of England is never finished and at no time can they sit back and feel that the battle has been won. It may be that soon they may be banned from labouring in the Anglican vineyard at all and may become a church in their own right. This could give them a new lease of life and, unfettered by modern liberalism, they will be able to give once again the clear message of holiness which is found in the Scriptures, in tradition and the early Fathers.

I end this note by saying that I shall use the words Catholic and Anglo-Catholic in an Anglican context and Roman Catholic for those who allegiance is to Rome.

References

1. SPCK 1989
2. Constable 1963
3. Pusey Rediscovered Ed. Perry Butler SPCK 1983
4. The Young Dr Pusey Mowbray 1989
5. John Murray 1966
6. SCM 1966
7. SCM 1992
8. Faith Press 1960

Chapter One

Unfair to the Sheep

'Let us now praise famous men and our fathers who begat us.'

So wrote Ecclesiasticus, but at the same time noted that there were some who had no memorial. This book is mostly about the latter, because many of the heroes of the movement I will mention have in some way been celebrated. Later I shall be describing what happened between two great wars in a suburban parish where ordinary church people could take part in a well-ordered ceremonial backed by a programme of sound teaching. Rich and poor alike were able to have a disciplined way of life based on the duty of worship and an examination of their personal religious needs. All this was made possible by a resurgence of church life which began in Oxford in the first half of the nineteenth century. This Oxford (also known as Tractarian, High Church or Anglo-Catholic) Movement took place in two stages and on two levels. It began with the meeting of several great minds in a college common room. There, a resolve was made that the spiritual life of the Church of England should be revived by rediscovering its place within Catholic Christendom. At this first level we find notable scholars like Keble, Pusey and Newman engaged in a battle of ideas, a battle which made them unpopular in a university which feared enthusiasm of any kind among its members. At some cost this struggle was won and the fruits of the victory extended to a wider public. For, as Owen Chadwick has written, a great historical process does not depend upon the choices or minds of single individuals, however eminent or however

1

original. These must take hold of the imagination of social development and public opinion which far transcends the isolated contribution even of a genius.[1] This happened in Oxford when ideas which a few men worked out in private conversation became the subject of wider debate and were finally distilled into the minds of ordinary people. For far too long the Church of England had ignored the needs of the common people and treated them as if they had had a theological training. The gap between the scholar or religious expert and the common worshipper is age-old and continues to this day.

An early Biblical example of this can be found in the Old Testament where the simple commandments given in Exodus are elaborated to such an extent in Deuteronomy and Leviticus that it needed professionals to show how they could be applied in everyday life. In this way a division arose between the ordinary people 'who knew not the Law' and others who did. The sheep were left behind by those who were meant to look after them – this was the charge Ezekiel brought against the spiritual leaders of Israel: they were fat and well-clothed shepherds who left the weaker sheep to perish.

Jesus took up this accusation against the leaders of his time: 'they bind heavy burdens and grievous to be borne and lay them on men's shoulders but they themselves will not move them with one of their fingers'. This abandoning of weaker sheep by shepherds who have more interest in weaving their own patterns of salvation has been repeated throughout Christian history. In the Middle Ages the laity were often looked upon as second class Christians and a barrier inside and outside the church erected between them and the clergy. Professor Duffy has recently shown that there has been an exaggeration of medieval injustice but differences of status certainly existed.[2]

At the Reformation these barriers were removed only to be replaced by a system of weighty sermons and long prayers. Church decorations, which had provided lessons in stone as well as in wood and paint for the illiterate, were ruthlessly destroyed and gave way to bare churches and a Book of Common Prayer. The latter although presented in a rich language must have meant little to farm hands and labourers of no education. Today we have simplified the language but multiplied the rubrics; anybody who has wrestled with the authorised versions of Rites A and B Communion Service will know what I mean!

It was part of the genius of the Oxford Catholic reformers that they recognised that not every Englishman was middle or upper class and that peasants and slum dwellers had souls to be saved. So the second stage of the movement began when the scene moved from the college common room to the parish life of the nation. This development took little time. There was a need to change quickly from the elevated level of academic debate to the more practical catechising of simple souls in the parishes. As we shall see, John Keble soon exchanged life at Oriel College for his country folk at Hursley, Newman devotedly mixed his university career with pastoral responsibility and Pusey never forgot the need for churches in the cities.

All this no doubt would have delighted the heart of that great sixteenth century saint, Francis of Sales who wrote about the spiritual life with much common sense. He teaches that 'the practice of devotion must differ for the gentleman and the artisan, the servant and the prince, for the widow, young girl or wife. Further it must be adapted to their particular strength, circumstance and duties'. He continues by saying that a devotion which conflicts with anyone's state of life is undoubtedly false. If he could have seen labourers and servants struggling with the barren religion of Georgian England, he must have held up his hands in horror!

The needs of ordinary Christians have too often been forgotten and this can be seen in other religions as well: so, before we look at what was happening in England in the centuries leading up to the Oxford Movement, we might ask: What are the religious needs of mankind? In my opinion, these are very basic indeed and can probably be summed up by saying that man, either in fear or need, has sought to tie himself back to the source or origin whence he came. Sociologists and students of comparative religion may consider this is too simplistic, but I believe it is the starting point of man's dealing with God; surrounded by a vast universe, he has sought for most of history a simple formula for guiding his short stay on earth and for dealing with the problem of his mortality. It has been said that religious man needs salvation to be available at the local level and simply too. Thus, when you have the action of God meeting the willingness of man, there is religion.

This religion can vary in quality. It may consist of the handing of simple gifts to Hindu priests at the temple gate or the daily offerings made to household gods by the Greeks and Romans when libations were poured on the ground in front of a shrine. A Biblical parallel can be found in the twenty sixth chapter of Deuteronomy where a Jew is ordered to put produce in a basket and lay it before the altar of Yahweh, his God.[3] The quality of worship will deepen in proportion to the knowledge a people may have of their god. The Jew of the Old Testament made his offering aware of the greatness of his God and the many benefits he had received from Him: in time this act was surrounded by the more elaborate temple worship, but the ordinary citizen was catered for by a simple thanksgiving at the family evening meal.

The Jews remained ever mindful of their place as God's special and privileged people and this remembrance was taken up and deepened by Christians when they gave thanks at their Eucharist for even greater blessings received. Here was an approach which all could understand because it has been a general custom to celebrate a great event with a meal. The greater the benefit received, the more fervent the thanksgiving and the early Christians certainly showed their joy at the salvation brought by Jesus: the Eucharist (or the liturgy) carried out into the world at large not only the proclamation of the mighty works of God through the life, death and resurrection of his Son, Jesus Christ, but also showed how it should be regularly celebrated with the meal of the Last Supper. It was a celebration of all the family of the Lord.

This early enthusiasm evaporated in time and the reason for Christian joy was not so clearly seen: yet, although worship could become perfunctory, it was just as necessary, for human needs remained. Christians continued to be pilgrims in a transitory life and wanted help when the going was rough. The parish priest might be foreign,

the Scriptures and the Mass might be in Latin but the Englishman knew there was merit and help to be gained from
the Eucharist sacrifice.

Medieval religion has had a 'bad press'and has been seen
as the reason for a swift transition to the church of the
Reformation. 'For historians convinced of the bankruptcy
of the late medieval Catholicism there is nothing here to
surprise, certainly no historical problem. A rotten structure
crumbles when kicked, institutions embodying ideas whose
time has passed can be dissolved with impunity.'[4] So writes
Eamon Duffy in a new book, *The Stripping of the Altars*,
but he shows by copious documentation that the traditional
religion showed no signs of exhaustion or decay and was
proving itself well able to meet new needs and conditions.
With examples from the England of that time he gives a
vivid picture of the way the ordinary layman was instructed
in his faith. The ceremonies of such days as Candlemass,
Holy Week and Corpus Christi were extended into social
life so that the utmost teaching could be drawn from them.
Duffy shows the great care which was taken both to train
the clergy and to catechise the laity.

For those who could read there were simple primers and
books of devotion, but for those who could not there is
plenty of evidence to show the care with which they were
taught. Round the fourteenth century font in the parish
church of Bradley, Lincolnshire is carved the inscription:

> PaterNoster, Ave Maria, Criede,
> Leren the childe yt is nede.[5]

and this sums up the basic instruction which every person
had to be given.

There was an elaborate catechetical programme for the
laity which had been decisively formulated at Archbishop
Pecham's Council of Lambeth in 1281 and this included
the Creed, the Ten Commandments and Christ's summary
of these in the command to love God and neighbour – also
to be learnt were the seven works of mercy, the seven virtues
and the seven sacraments: altogether, the clergy were ordered
to give comprehensive instruction in Christian belief and
practice – and wherever the eye wandered round the church

building there were lessons in stone, glass and painting to illustrate them.

This, then, was the English way of life when the Reformation overtook it. The change could scarcely have been more devastating: the visual aids on which simple souls had relied were swept away and replaced by a torrent of moralising words (these were, admittedly, in their own language – but barely comprehensible to them). In an essay, The Englishman's View of the Clergy, Gareth Bennett describes the situation so well that I quote him at length:

'It is hard now to enter into the mental world of four hundred and fifty years ago. In the countryside most people were illiterate and they thought in pictures rather than theories. Their stories, customs and rituals were vital to their community existence. They did not require from their priest elaborate theology or explanations of scripture but an affirmation of their existing view of the world. They saw it as a place of conflict, danger and testing; it was full of powers and forces, good and malign. Devils, evil spirits and witchcraft abounded. If one's child was ill or the cow ceased to give milk, or the crops failed, one looked for some agent which had caused it; some old woman living alone with her cat might be suspected; one might resort to some other "cunning" man or woman to reverse the spell. And over against all these evil forces were the good ones, many of them within the charge of the Church: saints and angels came to one's aid, Our Lady had immense power to heal and protect, and there was a great armoury of forces in the sacraments. The priest above all was the one who said mass for the community, bringing God among them, offering a sacrifice of propitiation for the living and the repose of the souls of the dead. Above all the priest was the man who warded off the fear of death. Death was the close companion of mediaeval people. Most children died in their first year, a man who reached fifty would have lost not only parents but his wife, most of his children and probably most of his contemporaries. Epidemics could wipe out whole villages. And death was a terrible prospect. Mediaeval churches had "doom" windows depicting the souls in hell in eternal torment or the souls in purgatory enduring cleansing fires. The priest was the one who could provide the ceremonies of grace and power: he blessed and cleansed with holy water; he confessed and he absolved; he brought the last rites and he said repeated requiem masses. In the 15th century, when the Black Death subsided there was an enormous phase of church building: even small villages built large choirs and naves, and many chapels and altars. Brotherhoods were set up to tend the altars, pay for the masses and pray for the dead. Recent research has shown how much ordinary people shared in this cult; it was they who tended the lights, cared for statues and roods, provided the labour to build and repair. A priest might be severely criticised but always for failing to do his work; being absent, refusing the sacraments, not taking part in accustomed ceremonies'.[6]

Bennet adds that although some of the younger, better-educated clergy of the 16th century rebelled against the role assigned to them, nevertheless until the break with Rome the old order remained intact. The Reformation, therefore, came as a terrible shock to ordinary people: a new generation of clergy and laity came into being who had been better educated in the universities and grammar schools; they appreciated the new Protestant theology, became preachers rather than priests and they attracted the attention of those who were able to read and write. Bennett, however, describes the plight of the ordinary citizen who of course remained in the majority:

'But the effect when the Reformation was imposed on ordinary villages was to destroy much of what had given the community coherence and identity. The statues, the lights, the altars, all so carefully tended, were destroyed, the guilds and the brotherhoods of lay people were dissolved and their funds confiscated. The whole cult of the dead, of prayer and commemoration was suppressed. The mass with its mystery, colour, movement and song was abolished: a quarterly communion service took its place ... The greatest problem was the relationship of people to the new Protestant minister. More than we realise, he was a kind of vacant space. There was a great difficulty in finding really competent and informed Protestant incumbents and many fell into the position of neither doing the old ceremonies nor preaching the new gospel: in such cases there was often a simple loss of religious interest shown most notably in a new problem of church repairs; people would not give money or labour to a church from which they had been in some manner excluded'.

After this the sermon became the main weekly religious event. Although the better educated professional person may have taken some profit from this, there is plenty of evidence that Elizabethan congregations hated the long discourses and mostly could not understand them. Altogether the ordinary citizen found himself excluded from the vicar's inner circle and although he was obliged to attend church, could not have taken much benefit from it. Worse was to come after the Civil War when Non-Conformity imposed its Puritan ethic on all and sundry. When the Anglican Church returned after the Restoration it brought with it only a slightly amended Book of Common Prayer and although some priests like Parson Woodforde could work devotedly within that framework, generally the gap between clergy and the lower classes remained and even widened.

In fact the parish clergy found their friends and closest acquaintances amongst the gentry and other clergy. In such circles a High Anglicanism could exist in theory although not in practice. This meant that the Church of England could be seen as more than a mere department of the State and its ministry and sacraments respected because they came from Christ. The 'High and Dry' clergymen were described as reverent, reticent and practical and these are adjectives which John Keble would have applied to his father. They were in the minority

Earlier I referred to Duffy's re-assesment of religion in mediaeval times. A 19th century labour leader, Joseph Arch, gives us a picture of churchgoing in his time and there is no reason to suppose Georgian times were different. He writes:

'One Sunday my father was going to stop to take the Communion and I, being a boy, had of course to go

out before it began. I went out of the church, closed the
door, placed my eye at the key-hole and peeped through
and what I saw will be engraved on my mind till the
last day of my life. First, up walked the squire to the
Communion rails, the farmers went up next, then went
up the tradesmen, the shopkeepers, the wheelwright and
the blacksmith and then, the very last of all, went the
poor agricultural labourers in their smock frocks'.[7]

Communion services, of course, were infrequent and we
also have a picture of what the normal worship was like from
a former Earl Nelson. 'The services were dreary to an unbe-
lievable extent; there were only six hymns at the end of the
Prayer Book and these, with the Tate and Brady Metrical
Psalms, were all the congregation could sing. The service
began with the interesting announcement that the Poor Rate
was 1/6d or 2s in the pound. This was intoned by the clerk,
who thereupon called us to sing to the praise and glory of
God from verses of one of the Metrical Psalms. Then followed the Parson and Clerk duet ... Confirmations, once
in three years in large towns, had become holiday outings
with many of their worst evils. Church building was at a
standstill and churches were neglected and in a state of
dilapidation.'[8]

It is possible to multiply horror stories of church life in
England before the Tractarians started their good work and
some have done so. Later, I mention that Clifton Kelway
used to give illustrated talks on the Catholic movement and
I can remember my indignation when he showed a picture
of a so-called altar or holy table covered by hunting clothes
and surrounded by buckets and cleaning material.[9] On the
next slide he showed the same altar beautifully refurbished
by the Tractarians. I also read a report of a church inspection
which found 'a W.C.contiguous to the holy Altar itself, nay
occupying the place where the altar ought to stand'.[10] Much
of the trouble was caused by the practice of clergymen holding
livings in plurality which enabled them to amass a considerable income: this meant that such parishes, and there were
many, did not have proper supervision. It should be said that
this evil was solved, not only as the result of the Oxford

Movement, but also through the efforts of Parliament which passed the Pluralities Act in 1838. This forbade clergymen of the Church of England simultaneously to hold more than one benefice, except in cases of livings of limited value close to each other.

In fact, just as we must not judge mediaeval religion by modern standards so we should not do the same to eighteenth and nineteenth century Anglicanism. We have the evidence of Dean Church who was born in 1815 and who has given us a well-balanced account of the Oxford Movement 1833 – 1845 that all was not gloom. He notes, 'the customs of daily service and even of fasting was kept up more widely than is commonly supposed: the Eucharist, though sparingly administered, and though it had been profaned by the operation of the Test Acts, was approached by religious people with deep reverence'. He describes the typical clergyman as a 'kindly and respectable person but not alive to the greatness of his calling'. Nevertheless when communication was so difficult and infrequent he filled a place in the country life of England which no one else could fill'. He was often the patriarch of the parish, its ruler, its doctor, its lawyer, its magistrate, as well as its teacher before whom vice trembled and rebellion dared not show itself. The idea of the priest was not quite forgotten; but there was much – much even of what was good and useful – to obscure it.[11] The villains of the piece in the eyes of many were well-born or scholarly bishops, furnished with ample leisure and splendid revenues, who presided in unapproachable state over their clergy and who held their own among the great county families. These men allied to the government of the day were more political than religious figures and often incurred the anger of the common people.

Dean Church softens the picture of clerical corruption but he has to say that 'the fortunes of the Church are not safe in the hands of a clergy, of which a great part take their obligations easily. It was slumbering and sleeping when the visitation of days of change and trouble came upon it'. Indeed the Church of England was like a fire which had lost its heat and appeared to be almost out. It

would be the task of the Anglo-Catholic movement to discover any warm embers and fan them into a flame again.
Any person who attempted this was likely to find intense
opposition because he would have to be a man of passion
and enthusiasm and these were qualities unwelcome to the
English scene. Across the Channel the evidence was only too
clear where too much enthusiasm could lead, for the French
Revolution was turning society upside down. Many were
aware that the ingredients for a similar conflagration were
present over here in the masses of underprivileged workers.
There was no lack of firebrands, either, who would gladly
light the blaze. That they had not done so many knew was
due to the moderating influence of church authority. The
bishops and clergy might be unpopular but they managed to
keep a tight hold on public opinion. The last thing anybody
wanted was that they should be infected with enthusiasm! A
frenetic fear of Rome was a further restricting obstacle to
any departure from the status quo. It is difficult today to
understand the violence of this feeling, but memories of religious conflict in previous centuries still lingered in English
minds. England was Protestant and proud of it. As Professor
Linda Colley has shown in a new book, *Britons, Forging the
Nation 1707–1837*, the English nation grew and prospered
on a fear and hatred of Catholics. England was in a perpetual state of alert against an invasion by Catholic France
or Spain on behalf of the Stuart dynasty:

> 'Protestantism, broadly understood, provided the majority
> of Britons with a framework for their lives. It shaped their
> interpretations of the past and enabled them to make sense
> of the present. It helped them identify and confront their
> enemies. It gave them confidence and even hope. It made
> it easier for them to think of themselves as a people
> apart.'[12]

So far, monarchs from abroad had been conveniently Protestant but this might be reversed. With a flow of Roman
Catholic immigrants from France and Ireland increasing,
there was a risk of a change of direction. The Pope's efforts
to get Britain back into his fold had been unceasing and few
Englishmen wanted an open back door ... If the Church

was paralysed by such phobias, the nation was on the move, carried forward by the Industrial Revolution. People flooded into the cities from the country, posing many problems, not least for the Church. If all had wanted to attend church on Sunday, there would have been no room for them. A report in 1811 said that the parish of Marylebone whose population was 60,000, had only one church with a seating capacity of 900. By 1824 it was estimated that over four million souls in England had no place of worship. It is to the credit of Blomfield, Bishop of London 1828 to 1857 that he set about the task of building more churches. For this he had to find money and this meant reforming the clergy and their salaries.

The new town and city folk, however showed few signs of keenness to continue the churchgoing they had endured in village churches (it has already been noted that worship here was more suited to the upper classes). The building of more churches in expanding cities was in vain if the services remained uninspiring. Blomfield, for all his reforming zeal, was no High Churchman.

Change was taking place in every area of national life, and both government and governed alike were impatient with any institution that could not adapt. It should be remembered that most people considered the Church of England to be part of the Establishment, a mere department of the State. A picture of the pace of change may be gained from the experience of two men whose lives spanned the nineteenth century, Gladstone and Newman. In their early days they would have travelled the country by horse or coach, but by the time they died an efficient railway network had been created. The appearance of the motor car at the end of the century together with other technical advances, meant that most people were being brought out of the isolation in which they had so far lived. All this development of national life was done at the expense of the working class, who must have viewed the hardship endured by labourers on the land as a paradise compared with the dreadful conditions which their mass invasion of the cities had created. These were the sheep whose spiritual welfare had largely been neglected by the village vicar. They were not likely, therefore, to be bothered overmuch by the lack of churches in their new life.

This, then, was the challenging situation which Anglicans faced in the years prior to 1833, the beginning of the Oxford Movement. If the more prosperous sheep were satisfied with their weekly ration of religion, the weaker sheep were left out in the cold. It would be wrong to suggest that the first Tractarian fathers were primarily concerned with such pastoral matters, because their field was the college common room. However without their concern for sound teaching, the Catholic movement in the Church of England could not have enjoyed any popular success.

References

1. Secularisation of the European Mind in the 19th century (CUP 1975) p.73
2. Stripping of the Altars (Yale 1992)
3. Deuteronomy Chap 26 vv 1-4
4. Duffy op. cit. p.478
5. Duffy op. cit. p.53
6. Churchman 1988 pp.111 seq
7. Quoted: Hibbert, The English p.641 (Wm Collins)
8. Quoted in Fight For The Faith (Church Union)
9. Story of Catholic Revival – Kelway (Philip Allen 1914)
10. Fashions in Church Furnishings p.48 (Faith Press 1960) p.48
11. Church – Chapter One (Macmillan 1891)
12. Yale 1992 p.55

Chapter Two

A Fire Rekindled

The Church of England at the beginning of the 19th century was a fire which had been neglected and unstoked for many decades. Someone looking at the dead coals and ash might say, 'It has gone out', but another might see a few sparks remaining and get down on his knees to blow them into life. Soon a flame appears and finally the fire is blazing away and warmth returns.

This is what happened to Anglicanism under the influence of the Oxford reformers. Some would date the beginning of the movement from the Assize sermon preached by John Keble in 1833 but this might give the wrong impression. From the influence of this sermon we might form an image of a fiery preacher arousing an eager congregation to heights of emotion by denouncing present evils and calling for future action. Yet this picture would be both simplistic and false. John Keble was no great preacher and, it is said, sometimes deliberately made himself almost a bad one. According to Newman, he was not above borrowing a friend's sermon which had been well-received. He feared that if he preached a good sermon people would praise him rather than his sacred subject. This was part of a modesty which must have infuriated those friends who wanted him to show some leadership. In fact, the congregation on that 14th July, 1833 were unlikely recruits for a new Catholic movement, for they were mostly lawyers and judges weighed down by too many past good dinners and looking forward to the next.

To change a metaphor. That Assize sermon was more like a first probing broadside from a warship which had been brought into position by hard work in the engine room. So, before saying more about the actual sermon, we should study the events which led up to it. For this we need to go into one of most exclusive clubs in the world, an Oxford common room.

Here life has not changed very much over the centuries for, although today it is less cloistered and clerical, the patterns of life there remain the same. Good food and drink are part of the privileges of those elected to fellowships. These stimulate the tongues and the brains of the nation. Colleges vie with each other to keep a good high table. Here conversation is confined to one's neighbours, but when the courses are finished and the traditional ceremonies attendant upon eating and drinking have been carried out, the president calls all to 'combine' in an adjacent combination or common room. Here a circle is made, claret, port or other wines are served, pipes, cigars or cigarettes are lighted and matters of moment are thrown around with all the intensity and abandon which scholars can show. On a good night, argument may continue into the early hours but today's dons have many diversions which take them away early. Wives, college societies and even TV may cut short a promising conversation.

This is today's common room. At the beginning of the 19th century when our story begins, there were few diversions to interrupt the nightly entertainment of stimulating discussion. Fellows not only had to be in Holy Orders but unmarried, and were often elected as much for being clubbable as intellectual. In those years there was no shortage of topics at the nightly combining because changes in most departments of life were sweeping through the country and even beating upon the doors of the two ancient universities.

The demands of the Industrial Revolution, which was now in full swing, made studies in technology and the sciences essential for universities if they were to keep up with the times. These no doubt intruded upon common room talk. Yet dons in Holy Orders whose education had been mostly in the classics would not easily understand their part in this new age. The country wanted more than classics and theology from its educational establishments, yet the nineteenth century went past with both universities and public schools concentrating on turning out Christian gentlemen.

'Just as German technical high schools existed to turn out engineers to run German industry, so mid-Victorian Oxbridge existed primarily to turn out clergymen to run the Church of England, or to become public school-masters and dons, while late Victorian Oxbridge (in particular Oxford) came to exist to turn out public servants.' (Correlli Barnett)[1]

For this the common rooms of an earlier Oxbridge were largely to blame, for their members huddled together as the storms of reform blew violently around them. Like their fellow clergy in the outside world they looked upon attempts by the government to put their Church's disordered affairs in order with alarm. They expected their bishops in the House of Lords to oppose even reasonable measures for reform. Dean Church, a contemporary of that age, describes the situation:

'The official leaders of the Church were almost stunned and bewildered by the fierce outbreak of public hostility. The answers put forth on its behalf to the clamour for extensive and even destructive change were the work of men surprised in a moment of security. They scarcely recognised the difference between what was indefensible and what must be fought for to the death: they mistook subordinate or unimportant points for the key of their position; in their compromises or in their resistance they wanted (lacked) the guidance of clear and adequate prin-ciples and they were vacillating and ineffective.'[2]

So as Oxford dons wined and dined each night there was much to occupy their attention. Plans would be formed to defeat proposed reform bills in Parliament. There would be time in plenty during the day for political manoeuvrings, for, apart from giving lectures, a fellow would have few duties. He might be called a tutor but this could involve the minimum of contact with his pupils. Edward Gibbon, the historian of the *Decline and Fall of the Roman Empire*, who entered Magdalen in the middle of the 18th century met his tutor only once. He describes fellows as 'decent, easy men who supinely enjoyed the gifts of the college founder; their days were filled by a series of uniform employments: the chapel and the hall, the coffee house and the common room, until they retired weary and well-satisfied to a long slumber'. There is no reason to suppose that fifty years later the situation had improved. Thomas Hughes, writer of the novel, *Tom Brown's Schooldays*, went up to Oriel in 1842 and found only fifty or so undergraduates in residence, including half a dozen gentlemen commoners who paid double fees for the privilege of dining at the fellows' table in silk gowns and velvet caps. They were absolved from the need to attend lectures. In fact the real work of the college was carried out by four scholars and one or two studious men. The remaining undergraduates were strenuous athletes, sport being 'the main object of residence at the university'. It can be noted that among Cambridge gentlemen commoners were noblemen and sons of noblemen. Since 1786 they had been entitled to a Cambridge degree without the need to take an examination and it is unlikely that Oxford acted differently.

Competition for this exclusive academic life was fierce. This was especially true for fellowships at Oriel College which in the early 19th century was top of the merit table. To be elected a fellow there after both written and oral examinations was like being awarded an All Souls fellowship today.

To this Oriel senior common room came by different routes three men, Keble, Pusey and Newman, who were to change the face of Anglicanism. Their relationship and interchange of ideas provided the intellectual engine room of the Oxford Movement and established the Church of England again as a respectable part of the universal Church. The first to arrive was John Keble. At the age of fourteen he became a precocious undergraduate at Corpus Christi College and despite being little more than a sixth former gained a double first degree by the time he was eighteen. He had avoided the brutish public school education of the time by being taught at home by his father in the vicarage at Fairford in the Cotswolds. He became not only well-versed in four languages, in history, and in English but had also been given a sound grounding in Church doctrine. The Reverend John Keble, senior, was a High and Dry Anglican who found in the Anglican Book of Common Prayer all that was necessary for a traditional faith based on the Bible and the early Fathers. John Keble junior inherited this same clearsighted faith and took it to Oxford with him. In April 1811 just before his nineteenth birthday he was elected to a fellowship at Oriel and despite his youth quickly established a reputation throughout the university. He was described as the 'first man of Oxford'. He might have been attracted by the free-ranging and sceptical ideas which surrounded him, but instead of Oriel influencing him, he influenced Oriel. Ordained deacon by the Bishop of Oxford in 1815, he found it difficult to decide between parish life and a college career. Keble was modest to a fault and by no means a natural leader – and in the end chose the life of a country vicar, where he taught the Catholic faith with a minimum of outward ceremonial. Fortunately, before that, he answered a call to return to Oxford as a college tutor in 1817 and in this position was able to pass his ideas on to a new generation of pupils, including a young man, Hurrell Froude, who was to force the pace of the movement.

The office of tutor today has become very important. A senior tutor is in loco parentis to his pupils and both supervises their work and helps them to develop their characters. In the early 19th century this was not so. As we have learnt, a student might not see his tutor throughout his college years. If he did, he might be overwhelmed by sheer scholarship. Another Oriel fellow, Dr Whateley, would batter his pupils with remorseless argument and repartee, 'holding them up', as he said, 'by one leg like dogs of the King Charles' breed to see if they squawk'. Keble's approach was more gentle because he was aware of his pastoral responsibility toward those under his care. He treated his pupils as equals and was followed in this by Newman, of whom it was said, 'with such youths (serious students) he cultivated relations not only of intimacy but of friendship and almost equality, putting off as much as might be the martinet manner then in fashion with College tutors and seeking their society in outdoor exercise and in Vacation. When he became Vicar of St Mary's in 1828, the hold he acquired over them led to their following him on to sacred ground and receiving directly religious instruction from his sermons'.[3] This was also Keble's approach although he worked through reading parties at the vicarage at Fairford during vacations rather than through sermons. The result of these intimate tuitions meant that a number of future priests were sent out into the world with a similar religious enthusiasm and became eager contacts when the movement gathered strength. This, I believe, was an important link between academic Tractarianism and its development in the parishes.

While Keble was settling into his tutoring at Oriel, a young man came into residence as an undergraduate at Trinity in 1817. This was John Henry Newman who was to be the second member of the Tractarian trinity. His background was different from Keble's because he was not a son of the vicarage. His father was a banker, later a failed banker and then an unsuccessful brewer who died when his son was beginning his Oxford career. The young Newman, like Keble, also missed the corrupting influence of public schools by being brought up privately. He fell under the influence of an extreme Evangelical clergyman in his youth and, although he was not completely 'converted' or born again, nevertheless took Protestant views to Oxford with him. These were gradually eroded within his new circle of friends and tutors and he began to develop sound traditional ideas about his Church. However, he retained a respect for the power of the pulpit which he used to good effect later on when he became vicar of the University church. If Keble shunned the limelight, Newman could revel in it. Despite a disappointing degree (caused through overwork and tension) he was seen to have promise, and was elected to a fellowship at Oriel in 1822. Here he shared the common room with Keble who was now at the height of his power in Oxford. This success scared him and he was preparing to return to an unobtrusive Oxfordshire country parish. Newman's next relationship, therefore, was with Edward Bouverie Pusey who was elected to an Oriel fellowship in 1823.

Here was another destined to play a great part, perhaps the greatest, in the continuing Catholic movement. Yet

Pusey also came from a different background from the others. He was an aristocrat and this no doubt gave him a certain amount of protection in a snobbish world: at Eton, as an Oxford undergraduate and later as a member of the unpopular Tractarian party. His relationship with Keble was fleeting because the latter left for Fairford in the same year as Pusey's appointment to his fellowship. However, he shared lodgings with Newman and went for long walks with him. Both were struggling to come to terms with the basic facts of the religious life, Newman with his Evangelicalism, Pusey with his problems of unbelief and agnosticism.

We now have our three leaders, Keble, Newman and Pusey in position. Keble's links with the others were tenuous because he overlapped with them for a short time at Oriel. Yet he had clearcut ideas about the Church of England which were to stimulate the others. To see how a stronger tie was forged we need to introduce a fourth person, Hurrell Froude, who in the end was to give a kind of kickstart to the Oxford Movement.

In 1821 one of Keble's friends in a letter commended this young man, Froude, the son of a Devonshire arch-deacon. His attractive bearing and Etonian self-assuredness disguised a certain unhappiness within. Yet he could be a charming companion, despite a cutting tongue. Dean Church, who knew him, describes him as having a 'keen, logical mind, not easily satisfied, contemptuous of compromise and evasions', qualities which he was to use with some effect in the Tractarian cause.

Keble immediately took him under his wing and included him in the reading parties which he held at the Fairford vicarage during vacation time. Froude was looking for authority in his religious life and this he found in Keble's teaching about a Church of England founded upon Christ and his apostles. Keble swept away the irrelevances of the history of that Church since the Reformation and showed that its Book of Common Prayer provided a priesthood and spiritual discipline based upon the early Church and the Fathers. Froude became an avid disciple of these ideas and took them back to Oxford and injected them without compromise into college life. Church notes that 'in Froude he had gained a disciple who was to be the mouthpiece and champion of his ideas and who was to react on himself and carry him forward to larger enterprises and bolder resolutions than by himself he would have thought of'.

In 1826 Froude was elected a fellow of Oriel and joined Newman there. Newman was now emerging from a liberal period and Froude was able to introduce him to Keble's ideas about religion and the Church. In 1828 through Froude's good offices it was arranged that Newman should stay with Keble at Fairford and thus began a famous friendship. Froude remarked shortly before his death, 'if I were asked what good deed I had ever done, I should say that I had brought Keble and Newman together'. Pusey had also been helped by Keble during these years, but after being elected to his fellowship he had been sent to Germany to learn what was happening in Biblical scholarship there. At first interested by this, he later saw the dangers inherent in it and repudiated his optimistic first impressions. In view of the upheaval which such critical speculations had for Bible study in this country, we must be grateful for this rejection. If the authority of the Church was to be essential for the future of Catholicism within the Anglican Church so also was the authority of a Bible which supported it.

In case it is thought that all this was done in a man's world, it should be said that the beginnings of the Oxford Movement were fraught with domestic affairs. Despite his self-effacedness and saintly character, Keble was not adverse to the opposite sex and after some adventures married Charlotte Clarke in 1835. Her health was not good and although Keble would not have admitted it, her illnesses were a hindrance to his activities. In the years to come he would need to take her away for a holiday by the sea when he might have been occupied elsewhere. The sombre figure of Pusey which we may have must be balanced by that of a man besotted by a young girl at an early age. Indeed his health was at risk because her parents forbade his advances. In the end they gave way and he married Maria whose temperament seemed the opposite of his. Their marriage appears to have been a happy one despite this, and when she died he was devastated and went into almost perpetual mourning. If any Anglo-Catholic priest today has a conscience about his married state he may reassure himself by considering that the Tractarian movement in Oxford was accompanied by much domesticity. Even Newman, who never married, had his own family problems and after the death of his father had to provide for his mother and sister.

So, despite illnesses and domestic diversions, friendship between Keble, Newman, and Pusey matured. As Dean Church puts it, 'each mind took fire from the other'. We must not forget Hurrell Froude, for without him the movement might never had taken off. What were ideas to the others became a cause for him. He was the impatient reformer, possibly because he knew that his bad health might not give him many more years of useful service. In the event, after 1830 he could only keep going by wintering abroad and he died in 1836.

In view of the controversies which were to develop later in the century over matters like confession, the Eucharist, and ceremonial, we might ask exactly what these friends discussed. Their chief subject was the nature of the Church in this country. It was clear that the Church of England had failed its people and a strong current was flowing against it. Amid all the violent changes of the early nineteenth century something more was expected than a crippling attachment to the State where its policies were determined by the political party in power. Since the Tractarians were to be accused of leading their Church to Rome, it must be said that the Roman Catholicism in England at that time provided little inspiration for a strong doctrine of the Church. After past persecution Roman Catholics were lying very low and treated their religion as a private matter. They were very anxious to show their loyalty to the king and treated papal claims with indifference, even hostility. Catholic priests were more dependent on the country houses of their lay people than on the Vicars Apostolic, and the Catholic gentry often treated their clergy as some species of superior servant. Since a priest was often unavailable on a Sunday, the laity were thrown back on their own resources. Where Mass was celebrated it was done with a minimum of ceremonial, and music was exceptional. Religious practices found on the Continent, such as Exposition of the Blessed Sacrament and the rosary, had no place among English Catholics. Devotions to Our Lady were dismissed as 'Continental' and quite unsuited to England.[4]

Within twenty-five years the scene for them would change dramatically and the Roman Catholic Church in this country would enjoy what Newman later described a 'second spring', but while the Church of England was wrestling with its identity it had little inspiration to offer. The salvation of the Anglican Church had to be found from within its own resources and this is what happened.

The big question, then, was What is the Church in England? There were several answers on offer in those days as Dean Church tells us. Some followed Hooker, who was the theologian of the Elizabethan settlement: he identified the Church with the nation and in this he was supported by the Eastern Orthodox Church. But this link with the Establishment had already brought the Anglican Church into disrepute. 'It was an invisible and mystical body', said the Evangelicals, whose call to personal conversion had not found general support and whose influence was on the wane. It was the aggregate of separate congregations, said the Non-Conformists, but this was a recipe for further division. It was the parliamentary creation of the Reformation, said those who believed in the supremacy of the State over religious matters, but few sound churchmen in the nineteenth century would have found this acceptable. The true Church was being in full communion with the Pope, said Roman Catholics, but as we see above, this was by no means accepted in England.

There were those who recognised that the Church of England was more than any of these and who viewed it as a special religious society; but they had not developed the idea. Perhaps they could not go further without taking the path which made the Tractarians unpopular.

Keble and his small group argued their case with the Book of Common Prayer in front of them and here they found plenty of evidence for a Church basing itself on the Bible, the primitive Church, and the Early Fathers. Here was prescribed a disciplined spiritual life of prayer (public and private), Eucharistic worship, abstinence and fasting, together with a ministry of bishop, priest, and deacon which followed the example of the first apostles. It is almost incredible that the Tractarians should have been persecuted for putting into practice what the Bible and the Prayer Book ordered, but in modern times we see our Church doing exactly the same thing when it proposes to adopt a female priesthood. If you want to do something illegal it is inconvenient to study the small print too closely! John Keble had studied this small print carefully and was under no illusions about the nature of his Church. 'To him the thought of the Catholic and Apostolic Church was a warming, steady fire, not the sudden burst of illuminating light that it was to Froude, Isaac Williams and, above all, to Newman. This was to be the difference between him and the other Tractarian leaders: he saw the Oxford Movement as the defence of something dear and familiar to him since childhood whilst they saw it as the spread of a new revelation.'[5] (Battiscombe: John Keble).

With a belief such as this he could but note with alarm the way his Church was being treated as a mere department of the government, to be reordered and reduced to the status of one sect among many. The last straw was a proposal to reduce the number of Anglican bishoprics in Ireland by eight and archbishops by two. Now this was not unreasonable because the bulk of the Irish population was Roman Catholic, but to Keble it was the final betrayal of his Church by the nation and he made this the subject of his Assize Sermon in 1833.

At this point Pusey held the prestigious office of Regius Professor of Hebrew in the University and was also a Canon of Christ Church. Newman and Froude had been joined by two more pupils of Keble, Robert Wilberforce, a fellow of Oriel, and Isaac Williams, a Fellow of Trinity. Newman had become vicar of St Mary's University Church in 1828 but more significantly he and Froude had just returned from a Mediterranean cruise which included a visit to Rome. Newman had been both fascinated and repelled by religion there. Whilst in Sicily he had almost died from a violent fever but had made such a miraculous recovery that he saw this as a sign that God had more work for him to do in England. Keble had been made Professor of Poetry in 1831 and this gave him an excuse for commuting from his country parish to Oxford. On July 14 he climbed into the pulpit of his friend Newman's church and delivered the Assize Sermon which has been considered the first shot fired in the Oxford Movement. Newman had landed from his Mediterranean adventure just a week before.

Keble had no idea that he might be starting a religious revival in what might be called a routine sermon, but when his words on national apostasy were printed they reached followers who were waiting for a battle signal.

Keble addressed himself to the issues of Church and State and made it clear that he saw them as separate and even opposing forces. To the question what can the Church of England be if it is not the English nation in its spiritual aspect, Keble gave a clear definition in his sermon. The Anglican Church is the representative in England of the whole Church Catholic and Apostolic, built upon the Apostles and prophets, Jesus Christ being the chief cornerstone. Its authority is the authority of Christ, handed on by him to the apostles and their successors. This Apostolic Church is a greater thing than the Church of England, although the Church of England is certainly a true part of it, and it is to this Church that a man's loyalty is ultimately due. This glorious Church had been betrayed into the hands of libertines but, even if it should perish, still the great Catholic and Apostolic Church would go on undefeated. Such a sermon set men thinking and planning further action.

This action began when a number of clergymen met soon after Keble's sermon in H.J. Rose's vicarage at Hadleigh in Suffolk. Neither Keble nor Newman was present at this important meeting which discussed what the next step should be. One gets the impresson that those who were there were an ill-assorted group and not the persons for the job in hand. They decided, however, to send a petition to the Archbishop of Canterbury protesting against the State's interference in Church affairs, but Keble thought this petition was not strong enough – 'skim-milkishness' he called it. One possibility discussed at Hadleigh was the forming of a defence association, 'like the English Church Union or Church Defence association of our days,' writes Dean Church many years later.

But this idea was turned down, although it was to surface when life became more difficult.

Newman disliked committees and organisation and preferred a series of tracts setting out matters of concern. So were born Tracts for the Times which were to give the Oxford reformers the name Tractarians. They are dull reading today, and we can only be surprised at the furore they caused at the time, but then the style of the media in those days was solid rather than racy. Newman wrote the first tract in which he called his fellow 'Presbyters' to remember the dignity of their calling. He reminded his readers that their bishops were successors of the apostles and that they must be defended. 'Exalt our Holy Fathers, the bishops, as the representatives of the apostles and the Angels of the Churches; magnify your office, as being ordained by them to take part in their ministry.' He went on, 'to remain neuter much longer will be to take a part. Choose your side'.

One tract followed another on subjects ranging from the authority of the Church to the length of prayers and proposed liturgical change. Sound teaching had been missing from church life for many generations and now it was poured out in short papers which could be easily digested. Dean Church sums up the sad state of religious scholarship: 'But custom, and the prevalence of other systems and ways, and the interest of later speculations, and the slackening of professional reading and scholarship in the Church, had made their readers (of the Tracts) forget some of the most obvious facts in Church history, and the most certain Church principles: and men were at sea as to what they knew or believed on the point on which the Tracts challenged them.'[6] He adds: 'There were many whom the movement forced to think, who did not want such addition to their responsibilities.' It is impossible to read such words and not draw a parallel with what is happening in today's Church, one hundred and fifty years later. As then, unwise schemes of reunion and ministry flourish in such ignorance.

The early Tracts were meant to compel attention and this they did. They were the more powerful because they came from distinguished university scholars and they received a fresh impetus when the much respected Dr Pusey joined the authors and the movement. Eager hands distributed the tracts round the country and here the careful tutoring by the Oriel dons bore fruit. There were many clergymen in the parishes waiting to get on with the good ideas they had learnt first from Keble, then from Newman, Froude, and other tutors.

As long as the Catholic reformers merely dealt in ideas, only minor irritation was caused to the unconvinced, but when they started to apply their principles to university and national matters they drew fire down upon themselves: there was also a fear that the Church of England was being led along the road to Rome. This was not helped by tactless remarks from Froude, and when he indicated that the Reformation had not been entirely beneficial to the Anglican Church and that the Roman Church was more right than many had been prepared to admit! His words shocked many people. As we shall see the publication of Tract 90 confirmed the authorities in their worst fears.

Meanwhile the movement gathered pace in the devotional field. As Dean Church notes, there was a deep earnestness on the practical side of genuine Christian life. Newman's sermons in the University Church drew large congregations anxious for spiritual guidance. Holiness was a theme which he emphasized. There was an increased concern with the Gospels where there could be found a living Master who could teach as well as save. There was also an increased sense of the need for self-discipline. Oriel College had given the money for a Church at Littlemore on the edge of Oxford and here Newman brought some ground for a community house where the Christian life could be lived more intensely. More and more he stayed there taking companions with him. It was the beginning of the revival of the religious life in the Church of England although it lasted only while Newman remained in it. In 1838 Newman, with the support of Keble, had a book published about the intense religious life of Hurrell Froude who had died in 1836. It revealed heart searchings and austerities which were foreign to the English mind. Many were shocked and offended by this book and, in retrospect, its publication can be seen as a mistake.

Suspicion that a strong Romanising element was at work in the Church of England was confirmed by the appearance in 1841 of the last of a long series of Tracts for the Times. This was Tract 90 written by Newman himself. In it he examined the Thirty Nine Articles of Religion which set out the faith and practice of the Church of England and which were supposed to put up an insurmountable barrier between it and all things which savoured of Roman Catholicism. The Tract dealt with all the Articles showing that although corrupt practices of Rome were condemned, yet they could be interpreted in a Catholic sense. Looking back from a distance we know that Newman had a good case to make, but his contemporaries did not think so, and met Tract 90 'with panic and wrath', to quote Dean Church again.

So far the Tractarians had been on the attack, chiefly because, as we have seen, they had taken the university by surprise, but now they found themselves on the defensive. Universities have their own way of exacting revenge on those who step out of line. Just as degrees and academic distinctions can be awarded, so they can also be withdrawn and this is what happened. An outspoken follower of Newman, a layman, W.G. Ward, was first dismissed from his Mathematical Lectureship at Balliol and then stripped of his degree. Isaac Williams, another follower, failed to be elected to Keble's Poetry Professorship in 1841. Pusey was reported to the Vice Chancellor for a sermon on the Eucharist and condemned by a select committee. To make matters worse, in the Church outside, an agreement had been reached to create a joint Protestant bishopric with the Lutherans in Jerusalem and to this the Tractarians protested in vain.

The bishops now began to take action. At first they had been puzzled, even flattered by the nice things which had been said about their apostolic authority, but Tract 90 was too much for them. Newman was summoned to explain his position to the Bishop of Oxford and was asked to withdraw it. He began to have doubts about the Catholicity of his Church and gradually removed himself from vulnerable positions in the university. More and more he exchanged his simple suite of rooms and little oratory in the first court of Oriel for a semi-monastic headquarters at Littlemore on the edge of Oxford.

Even Keble who had withdrawn from university to married life in the vicarage of Hursley, not far from Winchester, felt the effects of unpopularity. In 1841 after the publication of Tract 90 he wished to have his curate, Peter Young, priested. This worthy young man was put through a searching inquisition about his beliefs by the Bishop of Winchester. As a result the Bishop refused to ordain him and he had to wait sixteen years until another, more friendly, bishop accepted him. Such episcopal reprisals were to become a weapon against the Catholic movement right into the 20th century.

In 1845 after many heart-searchings Newman was received into the Roman Catholic Church and this confirmed the suspicions many had about the intentions of the Oxford reformers. Others followed him, and since Froude had died nearly ten years before and Keble was now totally engaged in his country parish, Pusey was left to fight alone in Oxford. This he did with great effect and became the leader of the movement. But, for the time being, the battle scene moved elsewhere. The Oriel common rooms under the old library had played their part in being the engine room of the movement: as debate there was silenced, it was taken up in parishes round the country, and especially in the cities.

References

1. Macmillan Papermac p.220
2. Church op. cit. p.2
3. John Henry Newman − Ian Ker p.38 (Oxford 1988)
4. Cardinal Manning − Robert Gray (Weidenfeld and Nicholson 1985) pp.144−5
5. Op. cit. p.156
6. Church op. cit. p.106 fol.

Chapter Three

The Sheep Remembered

Anglo-Catholicism begins with the Oxford story and its three leading characters, Keble, Newman and Pusey. Here the fight was started to restore the Church of England to its true position within Catholic Christendom. The important lesson quickly emerges that sound teaching must always precede the finer points of worship, such as ceremonial, vestments, and the like. Neglect of orthodox theological reading had left the clergy of the early nineteenth century uncertain about what they believed. After all, they received no special training for their ministry and were accepted for ordination merely after a degree course. Therefore much spadework had to be done to re-establish the very reasons for going to church. Generally people did this to be uplifted and edified. Sunday Morning Prayer has been described as the Englishman in his best moment. Keble would have none of this and at Hursley laid great emphasis on the duty of churchgoing, whether it was to the daily office or the Eucharist. When this lesson had been learnt, the number of Communion services were increased without necessarily any extra ceremonial. In our modern age when simple altars are the fashion, we might find it strange to learn that coloured frontals became a priority for some Tractarians and even became the subject for legal action. There were, however, good reasons for this.

First it was important to make the altar the centre of attention in any church so that what took place at it might be seriously understood. Secondly a change of colours could teach the different seasons of the Church's year. In this way people could easily learn that purple meant penitence, white rejoicing, and red the flame of the Holy Spirit. These were the first steps only in the process to teach spiritual lessons. It could be said that the Oxford Catholic pioneers prepared the ground into which later generations planted the seed. Anyone who has inherited a waste piece of ground as a garden, knows that first a design has to be worked out and only after this can it be filled with beautiful flowers. This, then, was the state of affairs in the early days of the movement. The heroes of the Oxford common rooms had tilled the waste land and had proved that the Church of England was worthy of loving attention. The Catholic outlines had been restored; it now needed willing hands to decorate them. There were influences at work which conspired to make this possible.

It has been said that the Tractarians wrote the Oxford Movement, and Cambridge men illustrated it. It is certainly a useful coincidence that while a battle of ideas was raging in Oxford, there was a growing interest at Cambridge in church building and decoration. The Cambridge Camden Society was founded in 1839 and after being renamed the Ecclesiological Society in 1846, continued in existence until 1868. Whilst there had been widespread vandalism of churches throughout the land during the Reformation and Cromwell's Commonwealth, the buildings themselves were still standing and neglect alone could not efface superb mediaeval stonework. The novels of Sir Walter Scott revived people's interest in the distant past and there developed a desire to rescue our architectural heritage before it was too late. The Camden Society at Cambridge was able, therefore, to attract many interested members and, under its founders John Mason Neale and Benjamin Webb, it quickly established itself as an authority throughout the country. It sent out directives about the building of new churches and their decoration and it was brave man who could ignore them.

It is an interesting fact that while priests were being persecuted for ritualist practices in the second half of the nineteenth century, the ecclesiologists were sending out a stream of advice about all manner of church decoration to church builders, churchwardens and even 'to Workmen Engaged on Churches'. Peter Anson's *Fashion in Church*

Furnishings 1840–1940 gives an amusing account of the activities of the Camden Movement:

> 'Writing as if with the authority of the Roman Congregation of Rites, they laid down that the Lord's Table should be raised two or more steps from the floor of the chancel, which should have a step or two up from the nave. No seats must be placed between the chair stalls and the altar rails between the north and south walls, so that as much room as possible be left for the access of communicants'.[1]

In 1842 the Society started to give published recommendations on church plate and ornaments including altar candlesticks. In the same year Bishop Blomfield of London tried to put an end to liturgical novelties but he had no idea of what was allowed and what was forbidden. One of the boldest of the Tractarian pioneers was the Revd. J.W.E. Bennett who became vicar of St Paul's, Knightsbridge in 1840: he cautiously raised the tone of the services in this fashionable church first by wearing a surplice for preaching, then by dressing his choir in cassocks and surplices and making them chant the psalms. He then took an eastward position at the altar, bowed to it and then added a cross, candlesticks, flower vases and frontals. His bishop was shocked and condemned such practices! It must have been a perplexing time for incumbents, with the Camden Society waging war on the slovenly state of many churches and recommending all manner of furnishings and ornaments, while their bishops were trying to resist emblems of popery. As Peter Anson says, by 1850 church furnishers were wondering what ecclesiastical goods it was safe to make and put on the market, so great was the terror in episcopal circles that the services of the reformed Church of England were being assimilated to those of the Church of Rome.[2] In fact a ritualist wave was surging through the established Church and the bishops were powerless to stop it. An interesting story from that time illustrates how this wave could affect even a rural parish. A young Cambridge man, influenced by the Camden Society, was ordained and sent as curate to a church in the Oxford diocese. His vicar, after seeing him installed, absented himself abroad for six months. During that time the new curate put over his views so well to the churchwardens and congregation that they overhauled the church and put a stone altar against the east wall. Imagine the surprise of the vicar when he finally returned to find a transformed building! That story does have a moral, however, for it shows the importance of careful instruction before any changes. So often resentment has been caused over the last one hundred and fifty years by priests sweeping into a parish and changing things overnight without proper preparation.

Other influences were also at work in the cause of ritualism. By turning Anglican attention toward the small print of the Book of Common Prayer, the early Tractarians showed that there was legal sanction for a return to Catholic worship and ceremonial. For, was there not a rubric at beginning of the Order for Morning and Evening Prayer which said '*And here it is to be noted, That such ornaments of the Church and of the Ministers thereof, at all times of their Ministration, shall be retained and be in use as were in this Church of England, by the authority of Parliament, in the second year of the reign of King Edward VI*'? Now this Edward came to the throne in 1547 and in his second year the vestments and ornaments of churches had altered little from what was used before the Reformation. This therefore gave great scope to those who wished to breathe new life into Anglican worship.

For the style of vestment there was no need to look over the shoulder to see what Roman Catholic priests were doing at Mass because a study of the early Church Fathers showed what had been the liturgical wear of that era. There was plenty of illustrations in the ancient mosaics in Italian churches. The Roman Church, however, was growing in strength and number as a flood of Irish and Continental immigrants entered the country. Their priests would bring with them the baroque vestments which were characteristic of the Counter Reformation age. All this was good material for jokes in the pages of Punch and the magazine did not hesitate to use it. In drawing rooms and boudoirs, as Anson remarks, ladies and gentlemen argued heatedly over details of ceremonial – the design of a dalmatic, the cut of a chasuble, the shape of a stole. There are different claims for the first use of a chasuble in the Oxford Movement. In 1840 the vicar of Morwenstow in Cornwall, R.S. Hawker, wore a 'distinctive vesture' which might have been a chasuble. The first definite use, however, was in the chapel of Wilmcote, Warwickshire in 1849 and this was followed by J.M. Neale at East Grinstead in 1850. Whoever it was who first established the custom, the practice, like the redecoration of churches, quickly caught on and by the 1860s Anglican priests could throw themselves into their pastoral duties not a whit worse clad liturgically than their Roman Catholic counterparts.

All this was far from the very restrained practices of Keble and Newman who were content to celebrate the Eucharist in hood and scarf. It was the service which mattered, not the vesture of the celebrant. There is an interesting picture, dating from the 1850s, of a celebration of Holy Communion in Margaret Chapel (later All Saints', Margaret Street) showing three priests in academic dress of surplice, hood, and scarf, kneeling before a well-decorated altar.[3] This image probably illustrates most accurately the first steps in ritualism. If Keble, Pusey and Newman did not show the way to ceremonial, they certainly gave an example of pastoral care for those who passed through their hands. We have seen how Keble and Newman set a new standard for private tuition by caring for the souls of their pupils as much as their brains. Keble was to transfer this care for every individual to country parish life where he dealt not only with the squirearchy but more especially with simple farm labourers and their families. Every human soul was precious to him and he agonised over every sheep who went astray. At Hursley his care for his people became proverbial, and late at night he would go out through the lanes to instruct some farm hand whose work had kept him from ordinary confirmation classes.

Such care communicated itself to his disciples and resulted in a new generation of priests who felt themselves called to the mission field of English slums. Already their Roman Catholic counterparts were at work in these overcrowded, deprived areas and they were joined by men like Lowder, Mackonochie, Stanton, Dolling and many others whose hearts bled for the sub-human lives which many were forced to live in East London, Portsmouth and other cities.

Through Charles Lowder we may trace a continuity with the Oxford reformers into the further margins of the Church. From a letter to his parents in about 1840 we know he was influenced by the preaching of Newman. After ordination he took this inspiration first into Somerset parish life, and then via the church of St Barnabas, Pimlico into the slums of deepest London dockland. He had wanted to be a missionary in New Zealand, but instead found himself engaged in a project twice as demanding: for there is nobody more difficult to convert to the Christian faith than the person who has taken a look at it and decided it was not for him. By the early part of the nineteenth century English cities were packed tight with families who had come from the country hoping to make their fortunes in industry and commerce. These were the sheep who had in the main been neglected by the clergy in the rural areas and now were left to their own devices in the terrible slums which clustered round cities like London, Manchester, Birmingham, and especially the dockland areas. Not even the modern film industry has been able to reproduce adequately the appalling conditions of Dickensian times. Conditions were bad enough in the early part of the twentieth century; in those days they were far worse. Observers of the social scene like Henry Mayhew and the Booths describe overcrowded houses, inadequate sanitation, brothels in profusion, drunkenness, unemployment and all manner of vice. In such squalor went priests who had, in the words of William Booth, turned their backs on privileged social life to minister to the outcasts of Darkest England. Pusey talks about his academic bondage which prevented him from living and working in the slums of England. He said, 'If I had no duties here (in Oxford) ... I would long ago have asked leave to preach in the alleys of London where the Gospel is as unknown as in Tibet.' He did what he could, and provided money to build churches in deprived areas.

It was mostly the Catholic priests of the Church of England who devoted their lives to working in the slums. It is said that the Evangelicals worked for the poor but the Catholics worked with them, and this is, I believe, a fair estimate of the two parties. The Evangelical approach was mainly through biblical exposition and this was not entirely appropriate in the circumstances. If they showed preaching ability there was the temptation to move into larger and better-attended parishes and to prosper in the Establishment. They did noble 'ambulance work' especially through their missions, but they did not 'muck in' with the poor as, for example, Roman Catholic priests did with the Irish, and the Ritualists did with the slum dwellers in their parish. The fact is that the Ritualists – for this is what the Tractarians came to be called – identified themselves with the lives of the poor in a way that other groups in the Church failed to do. This tradition has continued until the present day. Their use of ceremonial in presenting the Gospel was essentially a means of bringing vividness and colour into the drab courts and alley-ways of the slums. General Booth was later to use the same technique with his brass bands and ceremonies in the Salvation Army.

When Charles Lowder moved into Wapping and the dock area he set about building mission churches furnished as much as possible for Catholic worship. Inspired by the example of St Vincent de Paul he also founded the SSC, Society of the Holy Cross, which provided a discipline for priests engaged in work among the poor.

The task facing these priests was a daunting one, but many dedicated their entire lives to the service of the slums. While Lowder and others were tackling the problems of East London, Fr George Rundle Prynne was serving the slums of St Peter's, Plymouth: elsewhere through the land similar devotion was being given. The brave men had a further, crippling, obstacle to face because persecution had broken out against ritualism. Protestants inside and outside the Church, alarmed at the advance of the church improvers, went on the attack, first from the pulpit, then by letters of complaint to the bishops and, when they failed to stop the Anglo-Catholics by legal action, mob violence and Parliamentary opposition, I am indebted to L.E. Ellsworth's book, *Charles Lowder and the Ritualist Movement* (DLT 1982) for a table showing how complaints changed from the 1840s onwards:[4]

G.R. Prynne in late 1840s

Surplice when preaching:
Use of Prayer for Church Militant when no Communion:
Bowing at name of Jesus:
chanted psalms:
intoned prayers:
omission of prayer before sermon:
collection of alms in bags:

Liddell in mid 1850s

Credence table:
stone altar:
rood screen:
an altar cross:
altar cloths of seasonal colours:
altar lights:

Mackonochie in 1868
----

elevation of the sacrament:
incense:
mixed chalice:
kneeling during Prayer of Consecration:
altar lights:

Down in the south west of England Fr Prynne's heroic
efforts among the povery-stricken of Plymouth were interrupted by the opposition of his fellow clergy and mob
violence. However, his work and that of the Devonport
Sisters of Mercy during the cholera epidemic of 1849
won the affection of the people of Plymouth. In 1854
a churchwarden of St Paul's, Knightsbridge brought an
action against his vicar, Robert Liddell, over illegal ornaments. After a messy hearing and three years of argument,
judgment was given in favour of most of the subjects of complaint. In 1859 action of a different kind was taken against
St George's-in-the-East at Wapping. There, the vicar Brian
King and his curate Charles Lowder had to withstand the
attacks of a rent-a-mob (there were plenty of unemployed

willing to earn a bob or two by disrupting church services).
Such attacks followed Lowder when he established his own
mission churches in dockland and there were times when it
was almost impossible to celebrate the Eucharist because of
the interference. A drawing of Lowder's Chapel of the Good
Shepherd shows the kind of setting which would be thought
moderate today, an altar with frontal at the east end, two
altar lights, a simple emblem of a cross on a simple reredos
and stained glass windows. He started to wear plain linen
vestments but gave them up for a few years in deference to
his bishop.

From here it was a simple step to gild the lily, and soon
full Catholic cermonial was established in London and elsewhere. Fr A.H. Mackonochie, after serving under Lowder,
was offered the new living of St Alban's, Holborn and here
he set up a famous partnership with Fr Arthur Stanton. High
Mass with incense became the main Sunday act of worship
and the parish flourished with its full Catholic faith and
practice. Unfortunately he was dragged through a number
of court actions and finally died, exhausted, in the wilds of
Scotland. When his body was brought back to London for
burial, crowds lined the streets and many could not get into
the Solemn Requiem in St Alban's. Stanton's work went
on unabated until 1913 when thousands paid homage at
his funeral. While all this was going on in London the
ritualist movement was spreading throughout the country
and the bishops were hard-pressed to stop it. They were
under constant pressure from Protestant societies to take
action and yet they had to concede that these priests were
doing valiant work in areas which nobody else would touch.
They could cajole, threaten, or even inhibit, but this did not
stem the ritualist tide. It was difficult to take legal action,
for ecclesiastical courts in the nineteenth century were confused. Although the Court of Arches (Canterbury) and the
Chancery Court (York) could hear cases, there was a final
right of appeal to the Privy Council whose members might
not be churchmen, or even Christian. It could contain men
who had had no legal training. The tragedies within the
Church in the late nineteenth century were caused by the
inabilities of lawyers to deal with religious matters. In this

situation it was possible for Catholics within the Church of England to be treated unfairly and, to counter this, unions of churchmen began to be formed round the country. These, as we shall see in the next chapter, finally became one large Union.

Meanwhile pressure was rising for a commission to inquire into variations in ceremonial practice. In 1867 a Royal Commission was appointed and this led to the passing of the Public Worship Regulation Act in 1874. It was presented by Disraeli and was meant to put down ritualism. The Church had little say in it because Convocation was not consulted and it was finally amended in a Protestant direction.

The Act provided for the appointment by the two archbishops of a single lay judge to try ritual cases. Final appeal could be made to the Judicial Committee of the Privy Council with a provision secured by Archbishop Tait that a bishop could veto proceedings under the Act. As a result a number of priests were brought before the courts and five were imprisoned for offences such as eastward position, incense, vestments, mixed chalice, and altar lights. They were:

Arthur Tooth of St James', Hitcham, sent to Horsemonger Gaol in London for 28 days
Pelham Dale of the City church of St Vedast, sent to Holloway Gaol for 49 days
Richard Enraght of Holy Trinity, Bordesley, Birmingham, sent to Warwick Gaol 49 days
Sydney Green of Miles Platting, sent to Lancaster Gaol 595 days
J. Bell Cox of Liverpool, gaoled for 16 days.

All this made the average Englishman very uneasy and when the saintly Bishop King of Lincoln was also prosecuted by the Protestant Church Association for the same kind of ritualism, the matter had gone too far. Edward King appeared before a court of his fellow bishops and was exonerated of almost all the charges. When the Church Association tried to appeal to the Privy Council they were refused and this unhappy chapter of Anglican history came to an end. Further suits dealing with cermonial were fewer in number and dealt with by the bishops' spiritual authority. It should be said that while these legal suits were taking place there were many parishes which pursued their ritualist way untroubled.

The second stage of the Anglo-Catholic movement had been completed, albeit with some suffering. Men had been thrust to the furthest margins of the Church for their beliefs but, like the first apostles, were filled with joy because they had been counted worthy to suffer dishonour for Christ's sake. By the end of the nineteenth century the Catholic outlines of the Church of England could be clearly seen and it was being filled with the beauty of worship.

An uneasy peace now settled over the Church of England, uneasy because the Establishment had never really come to terms with its marginal Catholics who have provided the church's traditional conscience. Bishops have had their own methods, some subtle, others more harsh of trying to tame these stormy petrels. These measures have failed and today Catholic clergy speak out as fearlessly as did their Tractarian and ritualist predecessors. In one important point the ritualists differed from the first Oxford reformers and that was in their attitude to episcopal authority. Keble, Newman and Pusey had gone to the university with the slogan of apostolic succession. The bishops were successors of the apostles who derived their authority from Our Lord himself and therefore, they must be obeyed. This posed problems for Newman and some of his friends and in the end they decided to leave the Church, but Keble and Pusey stayed and worked within the Church of England's constraints. Keble was not primarily concerned with the question of authority although he regarded it as a matter of importance. '. . . He found himself held to the Church of England not by the authority of the bishops or Councils but by the example of her saints' (Battiscombe).[5] To people's arguments for and against the Church of England he could reply in two simple words, 'It works'. The ritualist attitude to episcopal authority was bound to be different because they saw their fathers in God actively obstructing work which they knew had to be done. They knew also that the imprisonment of Catholic priests could have been prevented by the bishops' veto. Lowder and his colleagues were too fully occupied in the daily wrestling with the problems of slumland to agonise overmuch about such matters, but Stanton and Dolling were more forthright. Stanton believed authority rested in the whole Church, not in the office of its administrative officers. He wanted bishops elected by people of the Church, not appointed by the state — a system which came 'perilously near blasphemy'.

There was something of a Hurrell Froude about Stanton in his daring remarks. He claimed to be 'politically socialistic, in faith papistical, in Church policy a thorough-going Non-Conformist'. Perhaps that sums up the ambiguity in the position of Anglo-Catholics which Pickering talks about throughout his book. Although there has been a papalist group within these marginal Catholics, I do not think that the Pope played too great a part in the history of Anglo-Catholicism until recent years; certainly the matter of authority has never been clearly resolved. Many have been content to seek refuge in the phrase 'the authority of the universal Church'.

Father Stanton was a very powerful preacher, so much so that he was feared by the bishops and was inhibited from preaching anywhere but at St Alban's where he drew great crowds. Here was an Evangelical side to the ritualist movement. Their desire to bring the Gospel to the slums through their preaching and their enthusiasm has led some to identify them with the Evangelical movement rather than with the Tractarians. In later years it became the custom for Anglo-Catholic churches to hold missions, especially in Lent, and this gave scope for the development of a further generation of fiery preachers. Open air processions also drew the attention of the world at large to the fact that the Church was at work among them. Although the day of the great preacher seems to have passed, street processions still make a witness to the Catholic faith. What shall we say about the success in numbers of these slum priests? It is sometimes said that the poor loved their priests and would do anything for them but go to their churches. Certainly the congregations worshipping at the churches of these devoted men could be numbered in hundreds rather than thousands, yet Lowder's results were steadily impressive. Into his mission church in

Wapping came an increasing flow of candidates for baptism and confirmation. In one year there were 160 baptisms, and fifty to sixty were prepared for Confirmation each year. Communicants rose year by year and by the end of 1859 Lowder could say that several hundred people more or less attended the mission chapels on a regular basis. Counting heads is always an unsatisfactory business, and it is better to say that through the efforts of dedicated men the Church was shown to a mass of deprived humanity as a sign that God was at work among them still.

The real significance of the ritualists is that they identified themselves with the lives of the poor in a way other groups in the Church failed to do. They realised that for the Gospel to mean anything to people in the slums, it had to be effective in their material as well as in their spiritual lives. Clubs were formed to provide clothing and food, rescue homes for reclaimed prostitutes were opened, and education was organised at all levels. Since that time there has never been a lack of Catholic priests and laymen to tackle the nation's social problems.

In fifty years we have seen the Church of England go a long way along the road to recovery. In 1833 the first signal was given and a fire was re-kindled. Round the country eager priests provided parched fields where the fire could take hold and quickly spread. Other influences were at work, not least the 1846 Pluralities Act which prevented clergymen holding more than one living at a time, unless they were adjacent.

There was, it is true, a programme of church building carried out, by bishops like Blomfield of London but these new churches needed to be filled with something more inspiring than the religion of the early 1800s. This need being gradually supplied by the Tractarians and their followers.

Stanton said that it was the poor parish at St Alban's which was persecuted while 'rich parishes where the same ritual was being used, were left undisturbed'. This was true except in one or two cases. Certainly my parish of St George's, Beckenham was left undisturbed, as we shall see. Perhaps the lesson which can be learnt from this chapter in the Church's history is that Catholics in the margins of the

Church of England were willing to endure almost any privation, in their determination to bring the message of the Incarnate Christ to the ordinary people of this country. This resolve was demonstrated in the nineteenth century and is still being shown today.

References

1. Anson Church Furnishings p.49
2. Anson op. cit. 167
3. Good and Faithful Servant – Galloway and Rawll p.22 (Churchman 1988) p.22
4. Charles Lowder and the Ritualist Movement – Ellsworth p.56 (Darton, Longman and Todd 1982) p.56
5. Battiscombe p.239

Chapter Four

Protecting the Marginals

Peter Anson in his book on fashions in church furnishings notes that 'Never had so many new churches been built in England or old ones restored as in the year 1857'.[1] But he adds that this extensive programme attracted only limited interest, the general public being more concerned with the Indian Mutiny which broke out in that year. This picture is not entirely accurate, however, for in that year Lowder was fighting to keep the vestments and ornaments he had introduced in his Chapel of the Good Shepherd. In fact the struggle for Catholic worship was to continue for many years, and at times it could become extremely nasty. The belief that the Church of England was being steered towards Rome was reinforced by the secession of men like Archdeacon Manning around the year 1850. Churchwardens and others (not always parishioners) took action against their vicars, and bishops were urged to stop this Romish rot. Later Protestants organised campaigns against ritualism. In 1865 the Church Association was formed and this was responsible for bringing Catholic priests into the law courts. Later the Kensit family took over the Protestant attack. No action could be taken without episcopal consent, and some bishops were determined to put down ritualism. Others hesitated to go against a Catholic tide which was gathering strength.

New churches require architects and there was no shortage of these in the middle of the 19th century. Names such as Pearson, Sedding, Gilbert Scott and Butterfield come to mind at once. Such architects were likely to be influenced in some way by the Ecclesiological Society, and they

44

prepared buildings which cried out for appropriate interior decoration and ceremonial. There was an increasing number of priests anxious to provide this, and from 1859 they could be armed with a book, the *Directorium Anglicanum,* published by the Revd John Purchas. This was the first attempt to provide practical directions for the decent performance of ceremonial in accordance with the ancient usage of the Church of England. In 1865 a second edition was even bolder and directed that cassocks and surplices must be bought for choirmen and boys; every church should be provided with at least one thurible and incense; candlesticks and crosses should be put on the altar or rood screen; there should be processions, vestments, much bowing to the altar, sign of the cross, and other reverences. In 1866 a popular version of these directions was published for laymen, called The Ritual Reason Why. This remained in print well into the next century. For all churchmen who wanted the best for their churches, there was no lack of instruction and information.

Not every priest was bold enough to implement all the advice given at once. Where Catholic changes were introduced, however, persecution could break out in any part of the country. This was more likely to happen in towns and cities because rural areas have their own methods of imposing religious sanctions on practices they do not like. Yet despite this oppression, there was an increasing number of lay people who wanted both faith and worship improved, and these began to form groups or unions to protect their clergy. Alarm was felt at the attempt by the State to take over religious education in church schools and in 1844 the Bristol Church Union was formed to combat this. Archdeacon Denison, who was to become a powerful champion of the Catholic cause in every department of church life, was one of its first secretaries.

Soon the fledgling organisation found itself involved in other protests and during 1848 and 1849 more unions sprang into existence around the country. These both sought to defend the Church against the assaults of its enemies, and to promote the restoration of Catholic doctrine and discipline. These various Church Unions became affiliated with the Bristol Church Union which thus can be called the mother of the Church Union system. Efficient organisation was lacking, however, and this meant that it lacked power or 'clout', as we would say today.

With the secular Judicial Committee of the Privy Council trying to usurp power from ecclesiastical courts, it became a priority to forge a stronger weapon with which to protect the Church. On 23 July, 1850 two meetings were called by the London Church Union to try to re-establish faith in the position of the English Church. Further events convinced the different Church Unions that they were now facing desperate challenges. Archdeacon Denison had been prosecuted for teaching the Real Presence, Liddell of St Paul's Knightsbridge had been condemned by a secular court, and riots were being organised against St George's-in-the-East. The existing Church Unions were too isolated and lacked the means for common action. So, on the initiative of the President of the Metropolitan Church Union, on 4 November, 1859 two delegates from each union came to London to find a way forward. Five associations responded, the Bristol, Exeter, and Chester Church Unions, the Church of England Protection Society, and the Guild of St Alban. There was no response from Unions in London, Coventry, Gloucester, Norwich, Southchurch and Yorkshire, but the convener, the Hon Colin Lindsay, persevered and put forward ideas for a new association which would be incorporated in the Church of England Protection Society. On 11 January, 1860 a provisional meeting was held, but this was poorly attended. It was decided, however, that all Church Unions should be incorporated within the Church of England Protection Society. This latter amended its rules so that it could take action for the defence of the doctrine and discipline of the English Church and in May 1860 its title was changed to The English Church Union. The objects of the Society were as follows:

1). To defend and maintain unimpaired the doctrine and discipline of the Church of England.

2). To afford counsel and protection to all persons, lay or clerical, suffering under unjust aggression or hindrance in spiritual matters.

3). In general, so to promote the interests of religion as to be, by God's help, a lasting witness in the land for the advancement of his glory and the good of his Church.

The means by which the Union hoped to achieve all this was by combining with other similar societies, by parish associations, by meetings (one annual, eight ordinary), by publications of different kinds, by petitions, and by grants of money.

It was to be a predominantly lay society although clergy could be members. All had to be communicant members of the Church. I am fortunate to have a bound copy of the minutes of meetings over a period of thirty-four years and these provide an interesting commentary on church affairs in the second part of the last century.

The final business of the Church Protection Society in the summer of 1859 was to deal with the case of a priest whose licence had been withdrawn by the Bishop of London for hearing a confession, to try to stop the rioting at St George's-in-the-East, and to appeal to Parliament against any alteration of the Prayer Book. Among new members of the Society was the name of John Keble, who five years later joined the council of the new English Church Union. It is interesting to see also the name of Archdeacon Randall with the note that he became the Bishop of Reading, which indicates that being in such company did not entirely disqualify a man for higher office. Matters discussed at this meeting and many more were to be included in the agenda of the new English Church Union, which came into being on 2 May, 1860 at newly acquired offices in Leicester Square. Church Unions round the country had been consulted and the Union went from strength to strength. The Hon Colin Lindsay became the first President and the Council contained both priests and laymen. Personalities changed through the years and some very notable people threw in their lot with the Union. J.M. Neale was there from the beginning, and in 1866 Dr Pusey became a member. He explained that his slowness in joining was through fear that ritual might be more important than sound teaching — to use his own words, 'that externals might be taken at the expense of internals' and so the whole movement should become 'superficial'. He had been afraid that 'clergy should exercise anything that should seem a tyranny as by modelling the services of the congregation according to their own will'. He was assured that the Union did not stand for this sort of thing and so gave it his full support. Indeed throughout its long history the Church Union has always been concerned above all with sound teaching, and with building 'externals' on this foundation. In time it developed Six Points of ceremonial and supported priests who tried to implement them, but this has never been its prime concern.

In 1860 its members numbered 205 but this steadily increased through the years. By 1863 it had passed one thousand and from here onward members flooded in, sometimes reaching five thousand in a year. When my records end in 1894 there were over 35,000 in the Union. Branches round the country also increased rapidly from 35 in 1864 to 387 in 1894. No doubt improved rail travel allowed more and more delegates to travel to London for council meetings, but accommodation in the city might have been a problem for those who had no club or could not afford a hotel. What is impressive is the number of noblemen who took part in the Union's work. For instance at a great meeting in London on 31 January, 1873 the Marquess of Bath presided, supported by Earl Beauchamp, Earl Nelson, the Hon Charles Wood (later Lord Halifax), and others. But for illness, the Duke of Marlborough would also have attended. In 1888 a protest by the Union against ritual prosecutions was signed by the Marquess of Bath, Earls Nelson, Limerick, Strafford, Strathmore, Manvers, Yarborough and Wharncliffe, Viscounts Halifax, Molesworth and Melville; Lords Egerton, Addington, Clinton, Sackville, Cecil, Crewe, Lamington, and Northbourne. Who could resist such a noble barrage as that! Of course it was the enthusiasm of the rank and file which made the Society flourish and this has always been the case.

For anyone who wants to know about the history of Anglo-Catholicism in the second half of the nineteenth century, the minutes of English Church Union meetings make compulsive reading.[2] They show both the crises which arose and the methods used to meet them. In similar situations, to the present day, the Church Union has employed sound argument in trying to deter the Church of England from unwise action. It was, and has continued to be, a predominantly lay society although it has included many priestly members. Its purpose has been to enable clergy to get on with their spiritual duties and preach the Catholic Faith. Beside it, societies have sprung up to promote the devotional needs of both priests and laity. In 1855 the SSC was created by Fr Lowder for priests; in 1862 the Confraternity of the Blessed Sacrament was founded, followed by the Guild of All Souls. Through the years other fellowships were formed for special needs. It would be true to say, however, that all these societies were made possible through the work of the Church Union, whose work was mostly political. This method of action was necessary because political measures were being taken against those trying to revitalise the Church of England. As we have seen, bishops did not hesitate to use Parliament and the law courts to enforce their authority and the Church Union met them on their own ground. Always action was taken on sound theological and legal grounds. With such men as Keble and Pusey among its members it was a formidable body. Nevertheless there were times when it had to admit failure.

The Church Union stood foursquare on the Bible and the Prayer Book and this meant sometimes taking a conservative line which we would think strange today. For instance, for over thirty years the matter of the Deceased Wife's Sister Bill had a regular place in the minutes, until it was finally thrown out by the Lords in 1894. The Union opposed such a marriage firmly on the grounds that Scripture and the Canons of the Church of England forbade it. More seriously in 1861 the Unions attacked a book, *Essays and Reviews*, which contained liberal views about the Bible and asked the bishops to condemn ideas expressed therein. We might think it went a bit far in trying to uphold the historical facts of Genesis, but

Darwin's books were only beginning to circulate in that year and evolution was a little-known theory. Pusey, however, would have known how dangerous such a book was, for he had studied German biblical criticism with growing alarm. Not only did it damage the credibility of miracles but it dimmed the inspiration of the Holy Scriptures, the Virgin Birth and other facts of Our Lord's life. Newman had seen Christianity as being revelation, a 'definite message from God to man distinctly conveyed by his chosen instruments and to be received as such a message' and the Church Union members would have said Amen to that. Strangely enough the bishops did condemn this book, but failed to stem the tide of even more radical criticism, some of which has been irresponsible to say the least.

Of more regular concern was a continuing attempt in Parliament to alter the Prayer Book. It was clear that this was a device to stop ritualists appealing to the Ornaments Rubric. Indeed in the House of Lords in 1865 the Bishop of London (Tait) said that he strongly disapproved of certain ritual observances and 'that he was perfectly ready ... to promise his support to any measure introducing any alterations (in the Prayer Book) which would tend to remove this difficulty'.

To change a Prayer Book was bad enough, but to have it changed by a Parliament which was now no longer composed of Anglican members (for example since 1858 Jews could be MPs) was a terrible thing. The Church Union formed a Prayer Book Defence Committee and then prepared the following memorial to be signed by clergy and lay communicants:

> We the undersigned, clergy/lay communicants of the Church of England, respectfully object to any alterations being made to the Book of Prayer respecting the 'ornaments of the Church and of the ministers thereof' and the mode and manner of performing Divine Service 'according to the use of the Church of England'.

The total number of those who signed was 41,620 and and the petition was presented to the Archbishop of Canterbury at Lambeth Palace on Saturday, 3 February,

1865 by a deputation of 140 persons among whom were the Earls of Carnarvon and Devon and other notables. The Duke of Newcastle and the Earl of Dartmouth were among other well-known people who signed but could not be present. Such a weighty body of opinion swayed the Archbishop and he promised that he would not consent to any alteration. The Church Union record of the event notes that all classes of people signed the petition including professional men and 'churchwardens, tradesmen, farmers, mechanics, and parish clerks'. This indicates the great variety of people who belonged to the Union five years after its foundation. It should be said that this was not the last time such concerted action was taken to preserve the sound doctrine of the Church of England.

This was not the only attempt at changing the Ornaments Rubric in Parliament, but in 1879 another proposal was defeated and the matter was finally dropped. As we have seen, prosecution of ritualists finally burned itself out with the case of Bishop King of Lincoln in 1890. The Prayer Book, then, was a satisfactory manual for Catholics. If it had any limitations these could be overcome by the different books of devotion which appeared. For instance the bleakness of the Prayer of Consecration in the Communion service could be enriched by a quiet saying of the Roman Canon which was the practice of Roman priests anyway. The Church Union not only defended the ritualists but also produced what was called the Six Points for worship. It was careful not to impose them on the Church but stated at the annual meeting in 1875 'in order to bring about a generally satisfactory settlement of the present ritual controversy in the Church of England, there should be no prohibition of the following usages when desired by clergy and congregations – viz: a) The eastward position b) the vestments c) the lights d) the mixed chalice e) unleavened bread f) incense'. These points of course were not generally accepted by the Church at the time but they found their way increasingly into parish life.

They were in fact already topics of conversation in the clubs and drawing rooms of society, and in April 1871 Punch had

produced an ABC for Youthful Anglicans which contained
such letters as:

> C is a Chasuble, hung on a peg
> And useful to hide defects in the leg.
> D's a Dalmatic, for festival use
> Embroidered all o'er by an Anglican goose.
> E is an Eagle which serves as a desk
> In part mediaeval, in part arabesque.
> F is a Frontal, which gracefully fell
> O'er the altar, affronting the people as well.
> O is the Orphrey, a piece of embroidery
> Worked o'er the vestments to make them more
> tawdry.
> T is the Thurible, whose very smell
> Incenses the people, and makes them rebel.[3]

(It is said that the English like to make fun of the things
they respect, so maybe the Catholic movement was finding
a place in the nation's life.)

In the final pages of the minutes of Church Union meetings
which form a well-documented history of the society, the
editor, the Revd Bayfield Roberts, denies that the Church
Union is a ritualistic society and asserts that the primary
object of the Union is not to propagate ritualism but to
defend Doctrine and Discipline. This it certainly did in the
second half of the nineteenth century. Nothing was too great
or too small for its attentions. We find concern for fasting
Communion and protests when Dissenters were allowed to
take part in the Eucharist. It opposed a Clergy Relief Bill
which was to provide for those who abandoned Holy Orders
because it said that those Orders were indelible. To show
the diversity of interests, we are told that a meeting in 1864
action was taken on the unsatisfactory state of the Church
in the Navy without Episcopal supervision, on evening
Communions encouraged by the Chaplain-General of the
Army, on Good Friday desecration, the better observance
of Ascension Day, the treatment of the homeless poor and
other matters. It fought for the reform of Convocation and
for the increase of bishops and also for the evangelisation
of the masses. This last was prompted by pressure from the

branches which said that the interests of the Union would be better served if they understood that the objects of the society included active work and that the promotion of the knowledge of the Faith went side by side with defence work. It asked that a programme of teaching of Catholic Doctrine, Disciple and Ritual should be given round the branches. This is a subject which has recurred throughout the later history of the Union until the present day.

Education was becoming a major problem for Church and State alike and we find the Union expressing concern at the State's interference with religious education in schools. In 1871 the Church Union council warned churchmen to defeat the attempts of Secularists and Dissenters to deprive the Church of the education of the people. The fight for church schools has again been a matter of continuing concern for Catholics.

It will be seen, therefore, that from the time of its foundation in 1860, the Church Union took an important part in the affairs of Church and country and that this was possible because of ground roots support. The advance of the Catholic faith in the Church of England over the last one hundred and fifty years is due first to the Oxford Tractarians, who were prepared to go into the wilderness for the sake of their convictions, but credit must also go to the rank and file, the tradesmen, farmers, mechanics, and others who were prepared to work at the committees, meetings, and demonstrations in the margins of the Church. There were setbacks for the Union, not least when its first president, the Hon Colin Lindsay went over to Rome in 1868, but since this made way for the future Lord Halifax the damage was soon repaired. As one thumbs through these minutes of the Union over thirty years it is impossible not to understand that many of the issues which Catholics face in today's Church were experienced by their predecessors a century ago. The lesson is clear that unity is strength if the marginals are to be protected.

References

1. Anson op. cit. p.161
2. History of English Church Union – Bayfield Roberts 1895
3. Anson op. cit. p.215

Chapter Five

Further into the Margins

All this liturgical and doctrinal skirmishing was far from the intentions of the first Catholic reformers who wished to uncover for all, rich and poor, the spiritual treasures which already existed in the Book of Common Prayer. The difficulties which they and their successors suffered were mostly caused by those who found it very inconvenient to look below the surface of Anglicanism. All the first Tractarian leaders, Keble, Newman, Pusey, and Froude were intent on opening up the way to true holiness which they saw as the goal of every Christian believer. When Keble said of the Church of England, 'it works', he meant that it offered means of holiness through its worship and discipline. Newman had much to say about the pursuit of holiness, which he knew was something different from being good. Goodness was something which man could attempt on his own with varying success. Holiness depended on creating a relationship with God which he himself had made possible through revelation. For Newman, Christianity was revelation and the religious and good life flowed from that. In a sermon he says 'We dwell in the full light of the Gospel and the full grace of the Sacraments. We ought to have the holiness of the Apostles.' As Gabriel O'Donnell has shown in his essay on Pusey's spirituality in *Pusey Rediscovered* he had an intense spiritual life based upon the Bible, the Fathers, and tradition. The last included post-Reformation piety, much of which was gained from French writings. O'Donnell sees the Oxford Movement as being primarily concerned with a renewal of the spirit of holiness within the Church of England. For this the Evangelical revival in the previous century made its contribution and Liddon notes in his long biography of Pusey that the 'Oxford Movement was a completion of the earlier revival of religion known as Evangelical'. O'Donnell sums it up when he says, 'They, through the fusion of Evangelical fervour and sound Catholic doctrine created a spirit, an atmosphere, a movement which had a deeper significance than any revival which might be simply doctrinal on the one hand or merely enthusiastic piety on the other'.[1]

It is not surprising, therefore, that following the ritualist battles of the second part of the nineteenth century there were a number of men and women who tried to put this 'deeper significance' into practice within the Church of England. This they did by reviving the monastic life which had mostly disappeared at the Reformation. Since that time there had been attempts to live a religious life in community like that of Nicholas Ferrar and his group at Little Gidding in the seventeenth century but no attempts had been made to create more formal directives. The desire to give up everything and follow Our Lord has never been absent from the Christian Church and through the centuries there have been a variety of monastic foundations, hermitic, Benedictine, Dominican, Franciscan, Oratorian, and many others. In some cases men and woman have come together in order to carry out a special task in the Church, teaching or caring for the poor, but there have always been those who have just felt called to separate themselves from the world to pray and serve God more perfectly. Such were the men who pursued St Benedict until he set up an organised community life. Benedict's community has been one of the most formative ways of life for western Christianity, indeed for western civilisation itself. Knowing well the frailty of human nature he produced a rule which was both spiritual and practical. Everything great and small in daily life was to be done in order that God might be glorified.

With this way of life Benedict 'proposed to establish a school of the Lord's service' for those who had taken vows of stability, obedience and perseverance in a Rule. It was a design for holy living under an elected abbot who was 'to act in the place of Christ in the monastery'. The very name 'abbot' came from the Hebrew Abba meaning father and the intention was that he acted in a fatherly way to those who had renounced completely their natural family in favour of another. They were not to be completely enclosed and should be open to guests. Each day was to be made holy, or sanctified, by the reciting of the Divine Office which revolved round the Psalms and readings from Scripture. It started in the early morning and continued at intervals through the day until Compline. Entrance to the community was by slow stages and final vows were not taken until the brother was certain that he wanted no other way of life. In addition the abbot and the other monks had to deem him worthy and suitable. This last point was important, as monasteries were sometimes thought of as waiting to pounce upon unsuspecting young men and women and imprisoning them against their will. Certainly this fear was not far from the public mind in Victorian times when religious orders began to be founded. No community of any kind could have happily existed against the will of its members.

This diversion into the earlier history of monasticism has been made because St Benedict's Rule to some extent influenced most of the later foundations. It would have stood as a kind of model for the revival of the religious life in the Church of England. It should be remembered that although monasteries were dissolved at the Reformation, yet their ruins and their survival in some cathedrals and parish churches were reminders.of the past. Once the Tractarians began to raise the banner of holiness it was not long before some men and women felt the same kind of call to the religious life which fellow Christians had heard from the earliest days of the Church. Newman made a tentative beginning when he formed a small community of like-minded friends at Littlemore on the edge of Oxford. Yet this was more to facilitate devotion than to create a permanent monastery. It followed the Oratorian way of life founded by St Philip Neri in the sixteenth century. Newman was to continue with this semi-monasticism after he had gone to Rome, and it has also found a place eventually in the Church of England with the Oratory of the Good Shepherd and to a lesser degree the Company of Mission Priests.

It is always invidious to say who was first in any endeavour but the distinction of having been the first to re-establish a religious community in the Anglican Church seems to go to the Park Village West sisterhood in London. This was founded in 1845 by a Miss Priscilla Sellon.[2] We should not, however, forget that in 1841 a Miss Hughes with the help of Pusey had taken life vows in Oxford and she played an influential part in the first sisterhoods. These began to spring up everywhere like mushrooms. Devonport, Wantage, Hastings, Oxford, London Colney, Windsor, Brighton, East Grinstead and many others were all founded in the space of ten years. More were to follow in the next ten years until by the end of the century there were fifty communities established throughout the country from the south coast to Edinburgh and beyond.

Progress was slower for the men. In 1863 a Father Ignatius Lyne had the vision of re-founding the Benedictine way of life but after a series of adventures it petered out. More solidly in 1865 the Society of St John the Evangelist, later called the Cowley Fathers, slowly took shape in a drab and uninspiring suburb of Oxford under the leadership of Richard Meux Benson. This priest became vicar of Cowley in 1850 and lived unobserved in prayer and labour among the poor. He felt called to missionary work and had set his heart on North West India where he had hoped to set up a group of priests and laymen who would live on a common fund. However, Wilberforce, the Bishop of Oxford, persuaded him to stay among the poor of Oxford and even gave his blessing to a community of priests and laymen. Those entering the community vowed to give up the world and to live by a simple rule, devoting themselves to prayer, study, and mission. A programme of action for the future was made which included missions for a week or fortnight in any parish at the invitation of the vicar, a mission house in London for boys and young men, a house in Oxford for scholars living under a rule, a chapel in London where 'they could address the educated classes upon the dangers of the fashions and scepticism of the present day', foreign missions and retreats. Over the next few years the Cowley Fathers achieved all these objects. The community began quietly in 1865 when Father Benson and an American priest, Charles Grafton, began to live under a rule in a little house within the parish. They were joined by others including Charles Wood, a young man, who hoped to be a lay brother. This did not happen, but he became instead Lord Halifax and had a considerable influence on the Anglo-Catholic movement. On the feast of St John just after Christmas three priests, including Benson, took vows of celibacy, poverty, and obedience. There was very little glamour in this religious community, for they worshipped daily in an ugly iron church. Here the community gathered daily for the Eucharist which the Bishop had insisted should be strictly according to the Book of Common Prayer without any liturgical additions. The chapel has been described in H.F.B. Mackay's book, *Saints and Leaders* (1928) as 'an embodiment in brick and wood of poverty and detachment, like St Damiano and the Carceri but planted in an ugly English midland suburb with none of the Italian charm'. Perhaps that sums up the Cowley style, which has always had a reputation for austerity. Even when full Catholic worship was introduced it still retained a certain bleak but well-polished elegance. It has been said that you could not get any more austere than lunching in a SSJE house on Friday in Lent! I would add from personal experience that it was even more severe in wartime. For the daily office, Morning and Evening prayer supplemented by Day Hours of the Church of England have been used until this day.

Here then was a monastic life which owed little to its Roman counterparts except the threefold vows. The rest of its elements were derived wholly from the Church of England. The driving force was Father Benson himself who was distinguished only by a tranquil shining spirit which shone from his short-sighted eyes. The community flourished and soon a proper church was built, dignified but still restrained. It spread out from Oxford to St Edward's House in London where it attracted all manner of men and a few women. It went further to America, Canada, India, and South Africa.

By the end of the century two more 'home-made' communities were started, the Community of the Resurrection, and the Society of the Sacred Mission. Each, like the Cowley Fathers, had its own ethos. The former, with founding fathers such as Charles Gore and Walter Frere, who both became bishops, could not fail to be academically based, and over the years it has produced some notable scholars. However side by side with these academics have been ordinary priests and laymen who have taken their vows.

The community which was to be known as the Mirfield Fathers grew out of a 'holy party' held in the Isle of Wight about 1875.[3] It was influenced considerably by Christian Socialism which was the result of a new emphasis on the doctrine of the Incarnation which some theologians, Gore among them, were making. Christian Socialism inevitably was a subject for Catholic churchmen as a result of the work of ritualist priests in the slums, and this group of priests felt that by living the life of the first Christian community, they would be able 'to study in common how to apply the moral truths and principles of Christianity to the social and economic difficulties of the present time'. There was an interest being felt in the English workman and it was suggested that this modern religious order might live as regards food, house, and furniture on the scale which would be desired for an English artisan. On St James Day, July 25th in 1892 six men made their professions at Pusey House, Oxford. Two lived with the Cowley Fathers for a time to gain practical experience of the religious life and then the community moved to a vicarage at Radley where Gore had been offered the living. Here a few students read for ordination, a foretaste of what was to come. From here Gore moved to a canonry at Westminster and the group followed him. Gradually a pattern of living was worked out which was based on democracy and simplicity. The brethren vowed to stay in the Community for life and this vow was retaken annually. There was a fear that one man might dominate the rest, so obedience was promised to a common rule rather than an individual. A Superior was to be elected for a period of three years. Each member retained his private capital but handed over the income to the common fund and so it could not be said that poverty was practised. Soon it was clear that the Community needed a proper centre rather than following their founder round from job to job, and it was decided that the ideals of this Community of the Resurrection would best be served by living in the heart of industrial Yorkshire. So they moved once again to a small town on the edge of Huddersfield in 1898 and have remained there ever since. By now it was seen that many young men were barred from becoming priests because they had not got the money for their training at Oxford or Cambridge and so it was decided to build a college for training priests in this place. Since then it has looked after a constant flow of ordinands.

When Gore became bishop of Worcester in that same year, Walter Frere took over as Superior and under his guidance Mirfield flourished. In 1923 Frere became bishop of Truro but remained in the Community and took two brethren with him, forming a branch house in the bishop's palace. From Yorkshire the Community has spread throughout the world and taken its educational and pastoral work with it.

If Cowley is associated with the deepening of the spiritual life of the Anglican Church, the Community of the Resurrection has become well-known for education. Yet at Mirfield there was great emphasis also on the discipline of the spiritual life and the day revolved round the Mass and an office which, like that of Cowley, centred round Prayer Book Mattins and Evensong joined to smaller day hours. In 1872 a Priest's Book of Private Devotion was brought out by the Revd. Joseph Oldnow which contained Prime, Terce, Sext, None and Compline, and this became very useful for those who were monastically minded. Also at Mirfield there were prescribed times for mental prayer and over the years the Community has contributed greatly to the prayer life of the whole Church through books and missions.

In the last decade of the nineteenth century another community emerged from the Church of England. Inspired by missionary zeal, its monument stands on the banks of the River Trent, two miles from Newark. This is Kelham Hall, ornately designed by Sir Gilbert Scott, built around the year 1860. It was taken over in 1903 by the Society of the Sacred Mission for the training of poor students for the ministry.

In recent years its sheer size has made it impracticable and the community has split up, but it stands as a memorial to a great priest, Father Herbert Kelly. He also was called to missionary work abroad but instead was persuaded to train a number of young men for overseas work in 1890. This he did first of all in a house within the parish of St John the Divine, Kennington, just south of the Thames. The motto 'per ardua ad astra' would be fitting to describe the life which was followed because there were few of the romantic externals of monasticism. Mattins and Evensong with day hours and a daily Mass formed the basis of the spiritual life. All the inmates took their share of the domestic work and the day was fully occupied with study and manual labour. Even after the move to the more elegant house at Kelham this routine was followed by all, and it was reckoned that if an ordinand survived his years there he must be keen. The successful training in Kennington of young men for the mission field led to the widening of the community's work at home and abroad, but always the main object was 'to increase the number of those who give their lives to the divine service, especially by training those of whom at present use cannot be made or is not made, whether through their lack of means or of education, or through other causes'. Kelham became a religious household of members whose ages ranged from sixteen to eighty. Many a priest today can look back with gratitude to the community, because without it he might never have been ordained. In time the size of the community made it possible for parishes like St George's, Nottingham and St Cecilia's, Parsons Cross in Sheffield to be taken over and run from priories. Today shortage of vocations has led to a retreat from many of its activities.

Here, then, were three new religious communities of men rising within the Church of England, basing their organisation only on a general monastic ideal. But the Benedictine way of life beckoned to others and after a number of incredible diversions the Order of St Paul was finally established at Alton in Hampshire. It all started improbably with a sea-faring family called Hopkins in the middle of the nineteenth century. Charles was born in 1861 and as a boy he accompanied his parents before the mast in windjammers on long voyages.

After the family settled in Falmouth, Charles Hopkins chose a career in music and qualified in Germany and London. He became the organist in Rangoon Cathedral and began doing mission work among the many sailors who had nowhere to go for their runs ashore. So began his life work for God and our sailors. He was very successful in this apostolate and was subsequently ordained. But his efforts for seamen's unions made him unpopular with the authorities and he returned to England where he had his first taste of the religious life in the slum parish of Holy Trinity, Shoreditch. Here a Father Jay had started a Society of St Paul and in this Charles Hopkins took his vows with the name of Michael. He then went to Calcutta as seamen's chaplain and started a small order among sailors where the Day Hours of the Church of England were said. But again his work with the unions made him persona non grata and he came back to England again. A priory was started in the seaport of Barry in South Wales and then the community moved to a piece of land near Alton. Here, with great hardship, a monastery was built from the local flints. Father Michael divided his time between the community, where retired seafarers were looked after, and the different ports. When he died in 1922 there were just three members, two men and one woman but they refused to admit defeat. A novitiate was started, the Rule was revised and brought in line with that of St Benedict, and in time a fine Abbey was built. Today the Benedictine way of life flourishes there.

Meanwhile a more direct attempt to revive the Benedictine way of life was made by a young medical student, Benjamin Carlyle who in 1893 drew up a constitution for the 'Oblate Brothers of the Holy Order of St Benedict'. He envisaged the establishment of three groups of Benedictines; oblates living in the world, active monks engaged in mission work, and an elite leading an enclosed contemplative life. He took his model more from the Church of Rome than from the Church of England and this was to bring him into confrontation with Anglican bishops, even Gore. Slowly he gained a following and took his men round the country: the Isle of Dogs in East London, the Cotswolds, Iona, Milton Abbas in Dorest, to mention a few places. Finally they came to rest on

Caldey Island off the coast of Pembroke and, after one other interlude in Yorkshire under the eye of Lord Halifax, they started to build. Carlyle had now become Abbot Aelred and in 1906 he put into practice the full rule of St Benedict with few concessions to the Church of England. It all was very exciting for many Anglo-Catholics and within a year many were making pilgrimages there, thus disturbing the strictly enclosed and contemplative life which the community sought. There was no doubt that the abbot had achieved much within ten years, but some wondered if he was not attempting the impossible, even within the broader limits of Anglicanism. He had no official standing within the Church of England, except that of a clergyman in colonial orders — for he had been ordained in America. He attracted large congregations when he toured the country begging for money and this brought dangerous publicity. He was, in fact, one of those individualists who have enriched the Anglo-Catholic scene. The lure of Rome was never far away and when the Church of England refused to give him official recognition, except on impossible terms, he and most of his community made their submission to the local Roman Catholic bishop. Of the thirty-three brethren who made up the Community in 1913, only one monk and two oblates continued as a faithful remnant within the Church of England and later joined a new Benedictine community which was founded at Pershore in 1914.

The failure of Abbot Aelred's experiment was a great disappointment to those Anglo-Catholics who expected much from the revival of professional monasticism within their Church. Cowley, Mirfield and Kelham were slowly learning their trade, as it were, whereas the Benedictine way of life was almost fifteen hundred years old. Lord Halifax was still optimistic that the 'waste places' might be rebuilt and encouraged the faithful remnant to accept the offer of the Abbey House at Pershore in Worcestershire. There was even official support for this from the Archdeacon of Worcester who, although a moderate churchman, saw that unless the needs of men who felt called to the religious life were met, the 'choice lay between rejecting their vocation and transferring themselves to the Roman obedience'.

So the only professed monk, Dom Anselm Mardon, was installed on 1 May as Superior by the Bishop with the Revd. Denys Prideaux as chaplain. Fr Prideaux had lived at Caldey as an oblate without taking full vows. A few other men joined the Community as postulants. The Bishop allowed the use of the monastic breviary but insisted that only the Prayer Book Communion service should be used. This had been the chief bone of contention with Abbot Aelred but this time the condition was met. It can be seen that the spring of 1914 was not exactly a good time to be born, for the First World War soon broke out. More trouble was to follow for the new Superior went over to Rome, leaving Fr Denys and a handful of novices and postulants. Cometh the hour, cometh the man, and Fr Denys after his full profession was installed as abbot. He was a man of many parts, not least a scholar, and he attracted like-minded men to the Community. Soon Pershore became too small and in 1926 a house was taken over at Nashdom. This had been built by Lutyens for a Russian princess. Dom Denys died in 1934 and was succeeded by Dom Martin Collett as second abbot. In the words of the Community, for the next fourteen years 'he established its unsteady foundations, amplified its worship, established its finances upon a sound basis, founded the first daughter house and guided it safely through troublous years'. When he died in 1948 he was succeeded by Dom Augustine Morris whose abbacy lasted for a quarter of a century and stability was assured. The Benedictine miracle had happened and Nashdom was accepted generally within the Church of England, even though by now both Mass and Divine Office were entirely Roman.

More religious orders, both of men and of women came into being with only an occasional Protestant skirmish. Some failed but others remained. Strangely the Francisan Order was not refounded until 1921 but it has prospered more than most.

These thumbnail sketches of the revival of religious orders in the Anglican Church are important for any account of Anglo-Catholicism and teach several lessons. If the first Tractarians and then the ritualists worked within the margins of the Church of England, the religious communities took it to the very limits of Christian devotion. The British have never been given to excessive piety and certainly the Victorian Church was turgid, to say the least. Here, however, were small centres of men and women who were prepared to give up all to follow their Lord and although, no doubt, they made some uneasy, nevertheless they held up a banner of what might be possible in Christian discipleship.

It might be thought, after reading these accounts, that God works in a mysterious way his wonders to perform, because some of the communities had very precarious beginnings and at times almost collapsed, and yet they took root and have flourished.

More seriously, the revival of religious orders illustrates the text 'by their fruits you shall know them'. From the beginning Anglo-Catholics had faced stiff and, at times, unpleasant opposition. They were accused of being a subversive influence in their Church and even in their country and were seen as an evil force which had to be destroyed. How else could one explain the chain of court cases brought against them and the mob violence used to disrupt their worship? Now, however, they had produced men and women who gave up material possessions, family, and their own wills not only for a deepening of the spiritual life but for the service of their fellow men. Possibly the reason there was so little opposition to the men's communities as they arose was that they were trying to meet a special need in society. The first convents did rouse considerable feeling but this was quietened when sisters were seen braving disease and terrible living conditions. By the time communities were started because men and women wanted a deeper prayer life, they were no longer seen as a threat.

But the inner life of the different communities could be shared with their fellow church people in the world because each order had its system of association or oblation. This meant that priests and laity outside could undertake some kind of spiritual discipline and also could be entertained for retreats and quiet days. The whole Church in the end profited by this flowering of Catholic spirituality. If there are few Anglican churches untouched by the ritualist movement, the devotional life of every Anglican has been enriched in some way by this fruit of the Oxford Movement.

St Benedictine delineates very carefully the kind of man the abbot should be, and teaches that the health of the community depends on sound leadership. The story of the revival of the religious life within the Anglican Church (the Church overseas also owes much to this) is that of a few great men who felt a call to the cloister and let nothing stop it from being fulfilled. We may think of Father Benson of Cowley, distinguished only by the fire which shone from him. Then there were men like Gore and Frere of Mirfield, Fr Herbert Kelly of Kelham who guided his community through the first half of the twentieth century (he was ninety when he died), Fr Michael of Alton, the abbots of Nashdom, and Father Algie and Father Douglas of the Society of St Francis. The women's orders also had their notable superiors, Mother Kate of Haggerston and Mother Lydia of Plymouth, to name but two.

When Anglo-Catholics were enjoying their high noon between the wars, the religious communities also prospered. The large Victorian buildings which had become monasteries and convents at Woking, Haywards Heath, East Grinstead, Nashdom and Cowley were filled with those who had taken vows. These were to be a problem when vocations became fewer but there has been no decline in the number of ordinary lay people who use them as places of spiritual refreshment.

References

1. Pusey Rediscovered p.244 (SPCK)
2. Peter Anson gives comprehensive list of Anglican monastic activity in Call of the Cloister (SPCK 1955)
3. A full account of the Community of the Resurrection is given by Alan Wilkinson (SCM 1992)

Chapter Six

A New Generation of Marginals

During the 1920s when I was a young boy of nine I was taken by my parents in a parish outing from Beckenham to Otford Court near Sevenoaks for the annual Corpus Christi procession through the school grounds. I remember it chiefly for the unworthy reason that we had a very good tea of home-made bread and cakes. There also remains in my mind the image of a very old priest in biretta and cassock who sat in the corner of one of the rooms. 'That's the great Father Tooth,' I was told, 'He went to prison for the Faith'. Here indeed was the last survivor of the ritual persecutions in the last half of the previous century. When he came out of prison in February 1877 he found his church at Hatcham locked against him, and he devoted his long life to an orphanage and a sisterhood.

Yet he had made his stand, together with other priests, for Catholic faith and practice; and this paved the way for the richness of Anglican church life which was to follow. Randall Davidson, Archbishop of Canterbury over the very important years 1903–1928, tried to hold back the growing wave of Anglo-Catholicism, but wrote in a memorandum in 1905:

'It is impossible in my judgment to exaggerate the importance of these imprisonments, I believe they did more than any single thing that has occurred in the ritual controversy to change public opinion upon the

67

whole question of litigation of this sort; it may have
changed for good or evil, but that the change was
largely due to those imprisonments I personally have
no doubt.[1]

The Archbishop was writing at a time when further action
was being urged by many in Parliament against increasing
ceremonial in the Church of England. Most of the great
Catholic figures of the previous century had died, Keble
in 1866, Pusey in 1882, and Newman, at the age of eighty
nine, in 1890. A new generation of priests, trained more pro-
fessionally in Tractarian theological colleges like Chichester
and Cuddesdon, were no less keen, however, and they were
to pose a problem for the Archbishop who so much wanted
peace in his Church.

In the new Edwardian age of Elgarian elegance and tran-
quillity the Catholic movement might well have been
accepted by the nation. A broad churchman, the Revd.
H.L. Jackson, vicar of St Mary's, Huntingdon, had written
in a parish magazine in 1899 that although he did not like
the High Church party, yet he had to acknowledge that they
were now in a very good position. He writes:

'The High Churchman has, I think, deserved to win.
Very patiently, very courageously, has he worked. Most
of the opposition he has met has been fatuous to the last
degree. The High Church position is largely warranted by
our Church's formularies. It is, so it seems to me, only
malice and ignorance that can determine otherwise.'

As a result of this conclusion, he determined to live more
faithfully by the Prayer Book and this meant more regular
worship and even the wearing of vestments, in accordance
with the Ornaments Rubric! Conversion indeed.

This cameo is reported by Roger Lloyd in his book, *The
Church of England 1900–1965*, which has become a very
useful text book for the teacher of modern church history. He observes that probably many fair-minded church
people were ready to accept that the Anglo-Catholics had
won, for they had out-thought, out-lived, and out-suffered
their opponents.[2]

The very change of monarch also favoured the Anglo-Catholic party. Queen Victoria was known to have an intense dislike for them and did not hesitate to show it. Although she appears never to have found out what they really taught, she hated them with a passion, and when she had to write about them, venom poured from her pen. By 1900 she had become a legend to the nation and people almost worshipped her. To hold opinions contrary to hers was anti-social, even unpatriotic thinking. Now in 1901 the country had a king who, when Prince of Wales, was known to have worshipped with his wife at the Anglo-Catholic shrine, All Saints', Margaret Street.[3] There was hope that the nation might begin to accept the Catholic movement. Yet it did not, and it must be said that Anglo-Catholics continued to be very unpopular. The late Queen's dislike was carried over into the twentieth century and was constantly fanned by papers like Punch, part of the establishment in those days, which pilloried by joke and cartoon the Puseyites as they called them. Week after week, brutally and vulgarly, it attacked them until it managed to infuse into the average English mind that something both Un-English and dangerous was prowling the country. So the Englishman's respect for the little man's fight against the odds was turned into a kind of fear, and Anglo-Catholics were regarded rather like the Moonies today. The harm done by Punch was aggravated by authors such as Compton Mackenzie who wrote a triology of books, *The Altar Steps, Parson's Progress* and *The Heavenly Ladder*, which although they were a good read for the Catholic, were a caricature for the outsider. The story centres round an 'advanced' priest who tries to change a Cornish parish and comes to a bad end. As Roger Lloyd points out the different characters were easily recognisable as leaders of the Catholic movement, Lord Halifax, Fr McKay of Margaret Street, and Fr Dolling of Portsmouth, to mention a few. He adds that the details disclosed were scarcely decent.

Lloyd also thought that the organisation of the Anglo-Catholics by The Church Union did not help, because it was always creating crises and giving the idea that religion was like a party game. In this he argues it was supported

by the *Church Times* which all too often vilified the Protestants and urged the Catholic cause. Bishops were a regular
target for uncharitable attack. Yet we have seen in an earlier
chapter that without the English Church Union the Catholic
movement might not have survived and many priests would
have suffered more severely than they did. It is a sad fact
that such organisation was necessary, but forces both ecclesiastical and political were being directed at ordinary clergymen
who were just too busy in their parishes to take time off
to fight back. Like Nehemiah in the Old Testament, they
might say, 'I am doing a good work and therefore I cannot
come down'. The fact is that they were living in a perpetual
state of crisis and did not know whence the next blow would
come. Catholics could be forgiven for thinking that their
bishops were against them and seeking their undoing, for
their record had not been good from the very beginning
of the movement. The fact that they had stood aside and
let their priests be prosecuted and sent to prison was not
exactly encouraging. No doubt some of the language used
about their fathers in God by Catholic priests was unfortunate, but it was spoken under great provocation. As a
parish priest looked at the sheer mass of unbelief and indifference round him, he knew that only the unadulterated
Catholic faith and practice could make any progress, and
he was prepared to throw himself into the battle without
a thought for himself. He was likely to have little patience
with interference from bishops and influential laymen in
ivory towers.

This attitude, however, raised the vexed question of
authority. It has been said that there was a great difference
between the Anglo-Catholic's insistence on authority and
his actual practice of it. Apostolic succession was after all
one of the main tenets of the Tractarian movement, and
Newman especially did all he could to obey his bishop as
the representative of Christ. When he saw the impossibility
of obedience to bishops who were persisting in holding on
to unprofitable and outdated life styles, he left the Church
of England only to find that there was no easy answer in
Rome. Most of the reformers remained and had to find a
modus vivendi or obediendi. This they found in the witness of

the Scriptures and the world-wide Catholic Church through the ages rather than in the Pope in Rome. There have been papalists, I know, who have seen the Pope as their natural head, but they have had little encouragement for continuing in this allegiance. Although some popes like John XXIII and, to a lesser degree, Paul VI have made encouraging pronouncements about Anglicans, the gap remains absolute. The hardworking Catholic priest in the Church of England has had to improvise in the matter of authority, for there seems no easy answer and a full day's work in his parish has left him little time for the luxury of theological agonising. There has been no solution to this problem and as we shall see in a later chapter this has posed difficulties for the present day Catholic, both Anglican and Roman.

From the bishops' point of view the Anglo-Catholics had turned the Church into a battle field. They were expected to run a smooth organisation and this was made impossible. With hindsight it can be said that this might have been avoided if the bishops had paid heed to the first Tractarians when they uncovered the hidden teaching of the Prayer Book. But they did not do so and a gap was opened up which refused to be healed. Some of the bishops must have realised in the later part of the nineteenth century that they were fighting a losing battle, but they had powerful Protestant voices supporting them, not least in Parliament, telling them not to give in to revived Catholic practices. If they would not take drastic action, they knew there were extreme Protestant organisations who would not hesitate to do so. They were constantly called upon to deal with religious strife, but did not know how to handle it.

Their predicament was further complicated by the sneaking regard some must have had for these troublesome priests. They knew that when they ordained these men they would go out into parishes and work themselves to death for their people. Some might spend the rest of their lives in the slums where they happily laboured in very uncomfortable conditions. This kind of priest was very interested in his people and knew exactly how to deal with them. He identified himself with them and wanted only to bring them all to salvation. This meant dealing with their sins and bringing them to Mass. Such care was taken with Confirmation classes as had not been known within the Church of England. A bishop would know what was going on in his diocese when he was asked to take an increasing number of Confirmations. By careful teaching a priest would build up a faithful congregation of communicants and if any of them were sick or dying he would be beside their bed ministering the Last Sacrament. These priests were professional uniformed priests (they wore cassocks everywhere) who had no time for trivialities or non-essentials. Canon Ollard wrote in his history of the Anglo Catholic revival that 'the Anglo-Catholic Revival began, continued and is today an attempt to preach Jesus Christ as he has not been preached for many years'. In the hands of these dedicated parish priests an instrument of conversion was at work which was something quite new to the country.

The Church of England, then went into the twentieth century in a troubled state. This was a tragedy because the nation was drifting further and further away from it. There had been a great revival of religion in the second part of the previous century. Adrian Hastings notes in his *History of English Christianity 1920–1985* that England in the mid-Victorian age – at least middle-class England – can be claimed as one of the most consciously religious societies that ever existed, but he reckons that religion peaked in 1881 and then fell off steadily.[4] Yet there were more baptisms, confirmations, and Easter Communions, and these were rising. For example in 1881 Easter Communions numbered 1,225,000 and in 1911 2,293,000, an increase of over a million. A major reason for this must be the progress of the Anglo-Catholic movement because under its influence the number of Eucharists was multiplied. Whereas in the past people had gone to Matins and Evensong, now more were getting confirmed and going to the Holy Communion service, no matter how it was celebrated. You might say that in the old days there was quantity, but now there was increasing quality.

Hastings says that what was new in the Edwardian age was not so much the Church's loss of the working class because the poor had never really belonged to it, but the decline in Christian belief of the middle class. He cites Charles Masterman's book, *The Condition of England*, for this;

'It is the middle class which is losing its religion; which is slowly or suddenly discovering it no longer believes in the God of its fathers.' Hastings continues; 'Religion in the Edwardian age was, as it has remained, a wider thing than churchgoing. If you follow the Book, you won't go wrong, was the core of working-class Protestant Christianity and it remained alive for many people who for some reason or another did not favour regular attendance at any service. In the upper class, family prayers, grace and even "the Book" were fading away, but church attendance might remain, while in the working class it could be the other way round: the institutional and social attachment was a good deal less, the religious attachment rather more but for both "one God, no devil and twenty shillings in the pound" was a popular and not unfair summary of what religion had come to mean for the generality of people by 1920, including many a churchgoer'.

Through the changing scenes of life in England, the Bible remained the chief refuge for those who needed religion, but even here they were being cheated. The theories of evolution and historical criticism were undermining this simple faith. As the years went by the speculations of theologians increasingly undermined the Bible's credibility and many people drifted into agnosticism. In vain was the country told that the work of these Bible critics was making the book come more alive. Too often explanations were couched in language the ordinary layman could not understand. All he knew was that somebody had taken the Lord away from the Bible and He could not be found. We shall meet this predicament later in this book.

The Catholic priest, slaving away in his parish, might have been taught something about this scholarship at his theological college, but he might also have learnt that the Bible was only for Protestants and so would not have been unduly worried. Rather had he to learn the techniques for putting over the Catholic system of the spiritual life, and this depended on the authority of the universal Catholic Church.

For this priest was on a different wavelength from those seeking the good life by edifying sermons and Bible study. If he had not gone to the lengths of those who had taken the vows of chastity, poverty, and obedience, he had caught the call to holiness which Keble, Newman, and Pusey had sounded a century before. These men had opened the treasury of devotion which had been started by the early Fathers and continued in the two main branches of the Catholic Church. This enabled later generations to be drawn into a slipstream of spirituality which could lead to holiness. For this, a discipline was required which the Catholic priest was happy to embrace. He was exhorted to be governed by two practical measures. The first was to make a rule of life and to fit into it all other activities; the second was to go to bed early and get up early. This latter advice was essential for the priest who wanted to start the day with Mass. Fasting from midnight was rigorously enforced and therefore parishioners had to come before they went to work. A priest might well need to be in church by 5 a.m. if he was to say his prayers before Mass. After breakfast there would be a full day of prayer and work.

Such a dedicated life became a powerful force in any parish and gave a vivid example to the next generation of priests of which, in time I became one. If at times the demand made for self-examination, confession, and fasting became ultra rigorist, nevertheless it produced an awesome approach to God which was rarely found elsewhere in the Church. Undoubtedly these priests went far beyond the requirements of the Prayer Book but they would have said it was the only effective way of teaching simple souls. The soul was approached through the eye, and the heart was moved by pageantry. This had been the way the pre-Reformation Church operated, as we saw in a previous chapter.

What was the well-dressed priest wearing for this ceremonial in church in those Edwardian days? Fortunately we do not have to resort to guesswork because Peter Anson's book, *Fashions in Church Furnishings*, tell us all.[5] Apparently there were two styles for both vestments and church decoration. The first was promoted by the Alcuin Club under the inspiration of Percy Dearmer whose strange genius stamped a sort of ye olde English label on all that was done in church. He claimed to follow only the Book of Common

Prayer, but surrounded it by elaborate ceremonial which was inspired more by the Sarum use than the Roman. Altars were simply decorated with cross and two candlesticks and enclosed by four riddel posts and curtains. In the sanctuary of this 'English altar', servers moved in apparelled albs and amices and waited upon a clergy vested in very full Gothic vestments. A sort of Christian Socialism governed the making of such vestments for no sweated labour could be employed but only a home-spun craftmanship. Anson amusingly notes that this new ecclesiastical style could be detected in the clothes of the worshippers. Men defied Sunday conventions by wearing baggy suits of home-spun tweed, shirts with soft collars, and often sandals instead of boots or shoes. Women tended to look like the models painted by Rosetti or Burne-Jones in free-flowing liberated floral dresses. The cathedral of this new life style was St Mary's, Primrose Hill in north west London. This remained a sort of period piece until the Second World War and was copied by other churches round the country. It could be seen in its most purist form at Thaxted under its 'red' vicar Conrad Noel. Altogether it was a very distinctive example of English aestheticism.

For those who wanted to go down this road there was a guide, *The Parson's Handbook*, written by Percy Dearmer and published first in 1899. A series of leaflets and booklets was also produced to keep the faithful in touch with the new developments. In time a *Warham Guild Handbook* also appeared and this showed many photographs of rich frontals, altars with riddels and dossals, servers vested in apparelled albs or sleeveless rochets, and clergymen in flowing surplices. All this emphasised a difference from Roman liturgy. Its dogmatism, however, was above the heads of the ordinary Catholic layman, especially in poor parishes.

Many Anglo-Catholics looked upon the Alcuin Club as both heretical and out of date. They turned their eyes on what was going on in the Roman Catholic Church on the Continent. On 24 February, 1911 a meeting was called of prominent Anglo-Catholics to form a body to act as a counterblast to what was being called British Museum Religion. The Society of SS Peter and Paul was started with Mr Samuel Gurney as secretary, assisted by Father

Maurice Child. Among other supporters were Ronald and Wilfrid Knox, N.P. Williams, and the Duke of Argyll. The object of this society was not to return to the pre-Reformation period but to advance to what the Church might have been if the Reformation had not taken place. So the ideal aimed at was to transform the externals of Anglican worship into the closest possible resemblance to those of seventeenth and eighteenth century Continental Catholicism. This meant that a Baroque decor invaded not only church interior design but also printing and publishing. Liturgical books of all kinds, missals, office and choir books and occasional offices, were beautifully produced with florid rococo illustration. Churches were decorated in the same way and the back streets of Soho were ransacked to find furniture of the right Baroque or Rococo styles. Gothic vestments were out and fiddleback chasubles, birettas, short cottas trimmed with lace took over. Younger Anglo-Catholics were now pressing for extra-liturgical devotions of the Roman rite like Benediction and the Rosary. Although the Church of England was not in communion with Rome, nevertheless they thought it should approximate as closely as possible in worship to it, rather than depend on archaeological research and anti-quarian fancies. All this, they hoped, might hasten corporate reunion in God's good time. Anson notes that 1924 saw the climax of Baroque and Rococo in high Anglican churches at the same time as the Diaghilev Russian Ballet was being exotically performed at the Coliseum. So wholesale was the transformation of some churches under artists like Martin Travers that they can still be seen today, albeit adapted to Vatican II requirements.

Such developments were fiercely attacked by the Prot-estant opposition. It is time, therefore, to return to the beginning of the new century when the last fully orches-trated attempt was made legally to stop Anglo-Catholic progress. The storm broke in 1904 when a Revd. Mr Bowen of the Church Association wrote a violent and abusive pamphlet and sent it to the members of Par-liament. This had an explosive effect because many there had also watched with alarm the growth of ritualism and wanted it stopped. They demanded from Mr Balfour, the

Prime Minister, that he should do what the bishops were unable to do. They even threatened to bring down the Government if he refused. They wanted a Select Committee of the House of Commons to consider and remedy clerical lawlessness.

By now Randall Davidson had become Archbishop of Canterbury and, as we have seen, he was convinced that the back of legal action had been broken by those priests who had been prepared to go to prison for their beliefs. He resisted, therefore, demands for a select committee which could have led to further obstinate rebellion. He pressed for a Royal Commission instead. The former, he thought, would have had the authority of the House of Commons and Anglo-Catholics would have resisted it. The latter would have the authority of the King and this they would treat with greater respect.

So a Royal Commission was appointed composed of fourteen members, the Archbishop, two bishops and laymen who were divided into High, Broad and Low. The main Protestant witness was the Mr Bowen who had originated the attack. He produced spies who said what they had seen going on in Anglo-Catholic churches. Vicars of these churches were sent the accusations to which they replied in words carefully composed by the English Church Union. When it was the turn of Anglo-Catholics like Viscount Halifax and Athelstan Riley they went on the attack and produced lists of Protestant churches which neglected some of the requirements of the Prayer Book, especially the Ornaments Rubric, for they did not wear vestments at the celebration of Holy Communion. It was in fact a slanging match between the Church Association and the English Church Union. The Commission met 118 times and produced a vast Report. The main positive good that emerged was that leading laymen now came to see that the secular courts could not be used to force conformity because this only led to an imprisonment from which nobody gained. Archbishop Davidson summed up this matter by saying: 'A court dealing with matters of conscience and religion, must, above all others, rest on moral authority if its judgments are to be effective. As thousands of clergy, with strong lay support, refuse to recognise the jurisdiction of the Judicial Committee, its judgments cannot practically be enforced.'[6]

After 1906 there were no more attempts to invoke secular authority to restrain Anglo-Catholics and they were left free to pursue their own liturgical preferences. Bishops in their diocese might attempt action by refusing to promote rebellious priests and this became their chief weapon.

Catholic faith and practice, therefore, penetrated further into the parishes, especially in the growing suburbs of big cities. Anglo-Catholicism was approaching its high noon and was helped by the increasing number of Catholic ordinands who were coming out of the theological colleges, especially Mirfield. Their dedication was no less than that of their Tractarian predecessors.

In common with the rest of the nation, however, it first had to endure the upheaval of the 1914–18 war. On the home front this meant that attention was diverted from religious controversy and parish priests were left to carry out their duties without hindrance. There was plenty of pastoral work to be done because there were few families without battle casualties. For those pitchforked into the armed forces, both priest and layman, it was a time of great trial. Catholic laymen often found themselves surrounded by dreadful slaughter without the ministrations of their clergy. This was no fault of the latter who were only too anxious to share the dangers of their men. Rather it was worsened by the Army Chaplains' Department which was both badly organised and also a Low Church preserve. Bishop Taylor Smith, the Chaplain General, to quote Alan Wilkinson 'was a naively patriotic and pietistic Evangelical who while being shaved would ask the barber about his soul'.[7] As Roger Lloyd notes he had no sympathy or understanding of the Anglo-Catholic position.[8] Very quickly Lord Halifax, the Church Union and the *Church Times* went into action against him and said that soldiers should have the same religious privileges in the army as they enjoyed at home. 'There must be hundreds and thousands of men who would wish to make their confessions and receive Holy Communion before going into action' (Lockhart: Halifax vol.11 p.247). The response from the Bishop was not encouraging and both the English

Church Union and the *Church Times* started the signature tune, 'the Chaplain General must go'. In the end a more friendly bishop was appointed as Deputy Chaplain General and life became easier for Anglo-Catholic chaplains. Nevertheless, they were working against great odds for most of their men, although nominally C of E, had little real religion. To quote Wilkinson again, they were envious of Rome for producing soldiers who were familiar with the sacramental shorthand so vital for crisis ministry. A naval chaplain, Walter Carey (later a bishop) wrote a letter to the *Church Times* in January 1916 and said, 'ordinary Anglican religion won't do; it doesn't save souls in any volume ... therefore it must be scrapped; the only forms of religion in the Anglican Communion which have any life in them are the Evangelical and the Sacramental ... Dignified Anglicanism has failed'.

As Hastings remarks, there was no genuine religious revival during the war, nor after the war which had unleashed bewilderment and hate. The churches had done very little to help with either. However it finally came to an end and the survivors returned to their homes. It was then that Anglo-Catholics found themselves strong and confident enough to call a series of congresses which set the tone for the years between the wars.

References

1. Bell: Randall Davidson p.466 (Oxford 1938)
2. Roger Lloyd: The Church of England 1900−65 p.120 (SCM 1966
3. Good and Faithful Servant pp. 95−96
4. Hastings: History of English Christianity 1920−1990 pp.35 seq (SCM)
5. Anson: Church Furnishings pp.307−11
6. Lloyd: op. cit. p.141
7. Wilkinson: op. cit. pp.133−4
8. Lloyd: op. cit. pp.214 seq.

Chapter Seven

Congress Days

Early in the summer of 1919 a young curate was sitting in the large, solid clergy house of St Matthew's, Westminster, resting from his labours. The nation was slowly recovering from a traumatic war and this priest might well have been visiting families in the different blocks of flats between Victoria Street and Horseferry Road, who were still mourning casualties. Few households had escaped some kind of loss. The priest's name was H.A. Wilson and he was waiting for the call to dinner when his vicar, Fr M.E. Atlay came into the sitting room. 'Look here', he said, 'next summer there is going to be an Anglo-Catholic Congress.' 'What in the world is that?' asked the curate. 'I am not quite sure,' was the reply, 'but I am chairman of the committee and you are the Congress secretary'.[1]

A meeting had been held that afternoon at which the Executive Committee of the First Anglo-Catholic Congress had been appointed. This was the result of discussions which had taken place before the war in 1914. Some Catholic incumbents who called themselves Friends In Council used to meet once a month to talk about problems affecting many of the Anglo-Catholic clergy who were working alone in their parishes. From the beginning of the century the Catholic-minded churchgoers in England consisted mainly of a number of isolated units which could present neither a united front against attack nor be strengthened by a sense of brotherhood with others in the same situation. In 1915 Fr C.R. Deakin, then vicar of Christ Church, South Hackney suggested that when the war was over a Conference of Catholic priests in

London should be called so that the clergy, at any rate, could get to know each other. Thus were sown the seeds of the First Anglo-Catholic Congress which steadily grew into a plan for a Catholic Congress for Devotion and Conference. This would be open to all clergy at home and abroad, and would be held as soon as possible after the ending of the war. At a later meeting it was decided that laity should be invited as well.

This, then, was the background to the more definite organisation which began to take shape under a committee composed of men like, Fathers Deakin of Christ Church, South Hackney, Leary of St Augustine's, Kilburn, H.F.B. Mackay of All Saints', Margaret Street, A. Montford of the Ascension, Lavender Hill, E.A. Morgan of St Andrew's, Willesden, H. Ross of St Alban's, Holborn, F.L. Underhill of St Alban's, Birmingham and a number of laymen. Fr Atlay had been elected chairman, a churchwarden of St Alban's, Holborn, Mr Sidney, vice Chairman, and a former secretary of the English Church Union, Mr H.W. Hill, Treasurer. Later other members were added but Fr Deakin was undoubtedly the 'Father' of the Congress movement. At a first meeting of the committee it was agreed that 'a Congress for Clergy and Laity be held in 1920 and that it be named The Anglo-Catholic Congress'.

The reaction of the Press in those days is interesting. 'The most surprising feature of the Congress is that it is meeting for the first time' (*Church Times*). 'Not content with the admirably broad platform of the Church Congress which has room for all parties in the Anglican Church, the Anglo-Catholics are to have a Congress of their own' (*The Christian World*). 'Ritualistic clergymen all over the country are looking forward to the Anglo-Catholic Congress. A strong committee of clergy and laity have been formed, representative of schools of thought from the ordinary High Churchman to the very spikiest of Anglo-Catholics' (*The Daily News*). This paper also noted that other important international religious gatherings would take place in that year.

Under the chairmanship of the Revd Dr Darwell Stone, Principal of Pusey House, Oxford, a committee drew up a programme and invited speakers. Almost all the home bishops and foreign bishops who were coming to the Lambeth Conference at that time were written to and asked to be patrons of the Congress. The response was more than disappointing, we are told by the Congress secretary, on whose notes I depend for a blow by blow account of events.

By the end of 1919 the machinery was well in progress. There was a shortage of cash but not of enthusiasm. This latter was needed because there was plenty of discouragement from outside and dismal failure was prophesied. Nothing daunted, the committee pressed on in the new year despite the fact that the secretary, as he himself says, was a very new curate and had never written a minute or organised anything in his life.

Once the Congress had been fixed for the end of June 1920, a search began to find suitable buildings to hold the different events planned. It is clear that in those days it was easier to find accommodation in London than it was twenty five years later when at least two years notice was required. There was a search for a cathedral where grateful members of the Catholic movement could sing a Te Deum and for a bishop who would preside over the greatest gathering of church people ever held in England. One suburban priest thought the Congress should be held in the open air and offered his garden! An enterprising catering firm sent such succulent samples of Belgian pastries to each member of the committee that it was awarded the contract for the garden party which was included in the events. The Congress office was St Matthew's clergy house and this was inundated with people and mail. One press reporter came asking for a story with a 'sob' in it.

The *Church Times* of 23 January, 1920 carried an article by Fr Atlay, the Chairman, which set out the objects of the Congress. These were threefold: 1) to strengthen the faithful 2) to extend knowledge of the Faith 3) to make plain the Anglo-Catholic position and strength. The writer emphasised the missionary aspect by saying that chaplain after chaplain had come back from the front saying that soldiers and sailors had no knowledge at at all of Christian faith and practice. Therefore the Congress had to be evangelical in outlook and witness to the fact that Catholics in the Church of England were going in no other direction than that of our Lord. He ended by saying that while the Modernist was out to destroy and the Protestant to deny and resist, the Catholic was out to uphold and construct. Therefore it was in a very strong position.

These objects were clearly illustrated in the programme planned.

TUESDAY JUNE 29TH AFTERNOON
The Message of the Church

The Faith and Modern Criticism	Prof. C.H. Turner, Early Church historian at Oxford
The Faith and Modern Speculation	Prof. A.E. Taylor, Moral philosopher, St Andrew's University
The Faith and the Evangelisation of the World	Bishop of Zululand
The Kingdom of God	Fr Lionel Thornton C.R.

WEDNESDAY JUNE 30TH MORNING OUR POSITION

Authority and belief	Revd. N.P. Williams, Oxford
Authority and Discipline	Revd. Leighton Pullan, Oxford
The Limits of Toleration	Revd. F.L. Underhill, St Alban's Birmingham
Our ideal	Bishop of Zanzibar

WEDNESDAY JUNE 30TH AFTERNOON
Christian Unity

Roman Catholic Church	Revd. Milner White, Dean of King's Cambridge
Holy Orthodox Church	Revd. Dr Frere C.R.
Other Christian bodies	Revd. G.H. Clayton, Little St Mary's, Cambridge
Witness of the English Church	Revd. C.S. Gillett, Liddon House, London

THUSDAY JULY 1ST MORNING
Corporate Religion

The Sacrifice of the Altar	Revd. C.J. Smith, Ely Theological College
The Reserved Sacrament	Revd. G.A. Michell, St Stephen's House, Oxford
The Faithful Departed	Revd. Arnold Pinchard, Secretary English Church Union
The Saints and Angels	Revd. Dr Darwell Stone, Pusey House

THURSDAY JULY 1ST AFTERNOON
Personal Religion

Prayer and Communion	Revd. G.W. Hockley, Rector of Liverpool

Meditation and Mysticism	Revd. G.C. Rawlinson, St Barnabas, Pimlico
Retreats	Revd. J.F. Briscoe, Rector of Bagborough
The Religious Life	Revd. Fr H.P. Bull S.S.J.E.

THURSDAY JULY 1ST EVENING
The Church and Social and Industrial Problems

Bishop Gore
Rev Fr E.K. Talbot C.R.
Mr G.K. Chesterton
Mr A. Moore (President of the Silvertown Branch of Rubberworkers' Union)
The Tuesday and Wednesday Evening Sessions were repetitions of some of the above papers.

I have given this outline in full because it set a pattern for future Church Union interest and concern in its mixture of doctrinal, devotional and social subjects.

It was, however, one thing to prepare a programme, another to find the kind of buildings which would house an unpredictable (at that point) audience. Incredibly it was not until January 1920 that a serious search for accommodation was begun. Few had heard of the A.C.C. and it was by no means certain that anybody wanted to do so. By the end of January an option had been obtained on the Great Hall of the Church House, Westminster which held 1500 people but it was thought wise to find out how many people were contemplating buying a membership ticket (price 5/-) by a notice in the *Church Times*. Those intending to do so were asked to send a postcard to the secretary. Within less that a week 1500 replies were received and it was immediately obvious that the Church House hall would not be large enough. This made nonsense of a newspaper forecast that 'this Congress will be a gigantic failure, for the Anglo-Catholics are a small band, subject, like the ten little nigger boys, to a process of attenuation'.

An attempt was made to hire the Central Hall Westminster but, as the *Church Times* put it, the Methodists were much concerned over 'misuse of their premises in Westminster' in the words of their official journal. In fact, it appeared to be available for hire for all and sundry except the Anglo-Catholics. This was understandable, perhaps, in view of the stand taken by the Catholics against allowing Non-Conformists to take any part in Anglican Eucharists.

By March 3000 tickets had been sold and still no venue had been found. So the committee considered the largest building in London, the Royal Albert Hall, where speakers could be audible – it was before microphones were available. Before May more than 6000 evening tickets had been sold and it was clear that The Albert Hall would be needed for all the sessions. There was the danger, however, that people might have bought tickets without intending to be present. One editor of a newspaper said, 'Hire the Albert Hall! You must be mad. You won't fill it once, let alone eight times.'

This then was the worry, and although two to three hundred priests had accepted offers of hospitality from London hostesses, there was no guarantee that others would travel to London. It was indeed a gigantic risk.

The first day of the Congress was the feast of St Peter. In the morning nine High Masses were arranged, eight for the laity and one for the clergy. This last was due to begin at 11 am and was to be preceded by a procession through the streets of Holborn. The day had begun with heavy rain but by 9 am the sky was cloudless. This promised well for the Mass at St Alban's Holborn, if any clergy turned up. The Congress secretary, Fr Wilson, was driven by chauffeur from Westminster to Holborn – private cars were still a rare luxury – and when they reached the Strand and Kingsway he saw clergymen everywhere hurrying eastward, carrying brown bags with robes inside. City clerks gazed wonderingly and policemen almost forgot to direct the traffic. Fr Wilson then joined the Chairman at the corner of Gray's Inn Road and later watched a procession of 1200 vested priests and a number of overseas bishops in copes and mitres, headed by a great silver crucifix and two smoking censers, making their way along Holborn, at the busiest time of the morning.

St Alban's was packed to the doors with clergy. Late-comers could not get in, including one indignant bishop. Support for the Congress from diocesan bishops had been poor but the Bishop of Salisbury was brave enough to preach. He referred to the dark days of the 1870s and rejoiced that the Catholic movement had emerged into the light.

Fr Wilson returned to his church at Westminster and found that packed with laity. Similar scenes were being repeated at

All Saints', Margaret Street, St Augustine's, Kilburn, St Mary Magdalene's, Munster Square, St Paul's, Knightsbridge, St Peter's, Vauxhall, St Stephen's, Gloucester Road, and St Michael's, Shoreditch. The adventure of the Congress had succeeded beyond the wildest dreams of the organisers. That same evening the Albert Hall was packed with Anglo-Catholics from towns, cities, and villages throughout the country. At the end of this first session the Bishop of Zululand appealed for money for foreign missions and not only did money pour in but some of the ladies took off their jewelry and gave that. Over £40,000 was given – no small sum in those days – and this had to be guarded in a back room overnight by two perspiring policemen until the banks opened the next day. It should be said that when the Bishop of Salisbury appeared in the Hall he was cheered as being the bravest bishop in England for daring to identify himself with the Congress.

All the speeches were published in a simple hardback volume and it is possible to read and wonder at the scholarship which was poured out. Professor Turner, an Oxford don, opened with a comprehensive survey of the state of Gospel criticism, giving his vast audience a taste of Q and other theories but coming down firmly on the side of John as an early witness to the Lord. This must have been strong stuff for the laity but they came back for more each day and heard on the second day Fr N.P. Williams, also of Oxford, talking on authority. He summed up by quoting Bishop Ken, 'I die in the Holy, Catholic and Apostolic faith as professed by the whole Church before the division of East and West', and this no doubt gave encouragement to those who were wrestling with this problem. When G.K. Chesterton heard that the meetings were to be in the Albert Hall he tried to excuse himself on the grounds that he would be inaudible – which he was at first – but went on to give a typical lecture on the social and industrial problems of the time. The final sermon, given in Southwark Cathedral by another brave diocesan, Bishop Michael Furse of St Alban's, could be summed up in the words, Thank God.

The Congress secretary notes that the Dean and Chapter of St Paul's Cathedral had been approached for this final

Thanksgiving service but had refused the request. However, Southwark came to the rescue. Fr Wilson says it was impossible to remember everything which happened but the emotional singing of Stuckey Coles' hymn, 'Ye who own the faith of Jesus', at one session made the earth shake and the heavens drop. Like all organising secretaries he was overwhelmed by infuriated clergymen or angry spinsters who had lost themselves, their tickets or their relatives, but retired from time to time to refresh himself in a small bar behind the platform which was always full of cassocked priests and ribboned stewards. In the end he could announce a sum of £50 10s 8d as the overall balance in hand. The success of the venture was clearly very much due to him and his vicar, Fr Atlay.

Congresses were held regularly until 1968, but it is interesting to read the Bishop of Zanzibar's summing up of the first a few years later. Although later Congresses had been similarly successful he thinks that the vision faded somewhat. He saw that later there was the tendency to rely on human means to safeguard the Catholic movement and to have the support of some 'pillars' of the Church. It became vital to get more priests promoted to high office. 'This', he writes, 'was not in accordance with our vision of 1920 in which we saw ourselves founded on the Truth, and walking with the Truth, along paths of passion and even loss, to the fulfilment of his purpose'. In brief, he regretted the passing of the years of martyrdom.

My own reaction on reading through all the speeches of this first Congress is amazement at the amount of ground covered and the depth of the scholarship. It must have been strong stuff especially for the laity and one wonders what they made of it. Yet they came back for more and this must be attributed to a desire for sound teaching. If we criticise it for trying to solve too many problems at once, we need to remember that there was no guarantee that there would be any more congresses and that this might have been the only opportunity to debate issues which had been mounting up. I can only say that nearly forty years later we had to set our sights lower!

The success of 1920 made way for a first Anglo-Catholic Priests' convention in Oxford in 1921. The Warden of Keble, the Revd B.J. Kidd, was the President and Fr Wilson again the secretary. The title of the conference was Priestly Efficiency and here again much ground was covered: intellectual efficiency, practical efficiency, personal efficiency. By the time the large gathering left Oxford they would have been instructed not only in theology, dogmatic, moral, and biblical, but in saying Mass, hearing confessions, catechetics, and a rule of life. Fr H.F.B. Mackay of Margaret Street was clearly the right person to talk about the mechanics of worship. After saying there was no longer any problem with vestments, he advocated simple altars, clean linen, and punctuality. This has remained a lesson for all.

I have almost come to the end of the forenoon of Anglo-Catholicism but should include the Anglo-Catholic Congress of 1923 which was held with the greatest confidence after the success of 1920. There is almost an atmosphere of triumphalism shown in the splendidly-printed record of events and speeches published by the Society of SS Peter and Paul. The Bishop of London (Rt Revd. Arthur Winnington-Ingram), threw his support and presence behind the event and gave the opening address in the Albert Hall. He emphasised that the Oxford Movement had taught from the beginning that the Church of England was part and parcel of the great Catholic Church throughout the world. He illustrated this by saying that when he met the idea in America in 1907, that the Church of England started in the reign of Henry VIII, he countered it by asking how the Bishops of London had managed to live at Fulham Palace for 1300 years. The Dean and Chapter of St Paul's Cathedral now welcomed Congress members for a Mass of the Holy Spirit on Tuesday, 10 July. This began with a procession of bishops which included the Greek Archimandrite, Pagonis, and the Russian metropolitan, Eulogios. Messages of respect were sent to the King, the Archbishop of Canterbury, the Patriarch of Constantinople, and to the Pope — the last did not reply.

The title of this Congress was The Gospel of God and under this heading many addresses were given which covered all the main Christian doctrines from Creation to the End of Time. The needs of the world were not forgotten and the soldier's padre of the Great War, G.A. Studdert Kennedy, Woodbine Willie, made an impassioned plea for Anglo-Catholics to take a greater interest in social problems: 'The Christian adapts himself to the world because he cannot adapt the world to himself – and despairs of doing so'. This was followed by the now famous words of Frank, Bishop of Zanzibar:

'You have got your Mass, you have got your altar, you have begun to get your Tabernacle. Now go out into the highways and hedges where not even the Bishops will try to hinder you. Go out and look for Jesus in the ragged, in the naked, in the oppressed and sweated, in those who have lost hope, in those who are struggling to make good. Look for Jesus. And when you see him, gird yourselves with his towel and try to wash their feet'.

The final sermon was preached by Michael Furse, Bishop of St Albans. Once again Fr H.A. Wilson had organised a successful Congress. All went away full of sound teaching. The Congress addresses were written up by two editors, Francis Underhill and Charles Scott Gillet, and published in fifty two booklets at 3d each, or in larger volumes. Such a library provided the Catholic with enough doctrine to last him a lifetime.[2]

So began the high noon of marginal Catholics, and the success of the 1923 Congress carried them forward to further events: from 1927 when the Holy Eucharist was the theme; to 1930 when the subject of the Church was debated, to 1932 when priests discussed Public Worship. There were 28,873 members for the 1930 Congress; fifty seven bishops took part; the Archbishop, Cosmo Cantuar, sent greetings, and the subject of Women in the Church was debated. So the stage was set for the 1933 Centenary Congress which included a massive High Mass at the White City. By this time a promising young people's movement, the Seven Years Association or SYA, had started. Before it had run its course,however, war once more had overtaken the country.

It is possible to draw a conclusion from all this success and enthusiasm that the battle for Catholicism within the Church of England had been won, but there was another side to the coin. Most of the bishops who attended the Congresses came from overseas, where Anglo Catholicism was having a less interrupted progress. With a few notable exceptions diocesan bishops at home boycotted the events, and Catholics felt they had been let down. In 1933 for example, the only diocesan bishop who attended the final service was the Bishop of St Albans and most church dignitaries stayed away. No doubt it did one's future prospects no good to be seen in such company! There were probably tensions, too, even among the High churchmen who flocked to the Albert Hall and other venues. A glance at the speakers, for example, shows a wide range of churchmanship because the organisers had wanted to get experts for the different subjects. The Bishop of London, Winnington Ingram, could do and say the right things up to a certain point but he held his ground in certain matters. Out of deference to him some hymns of Our Lady were omitted in the 1923 Congress. The telegram of good wishes sent to the 'Holy Father' also was by no means unanimous and divided, no doubt, the extreme from those who did not have their eyes in that direction.

Concentrations of lectures and addresses, no matter how brilliant, can be evanescent and leave the hearers with general impresions and emotions rather than with lessons for life. Certainly any churchman who sat through the wealth of subjects in the first two congresses must have been blinded by theological science. As any schoolmaster knows there is a limit to the amount of knowledge which a pupil, young or old, can take in at a time. Back in the parishes, members of the different congresses would have found their priest labouring away and probably too busy to take time off in central London. He would be the one who caught the brunt of his bishop's displeasure if he took one Catholic step too far. The Bishop of Zanzibar had said that Catholics were getting their tabernacles but controversy over Reservation of the Blessed Sacrament continued to rumble on in the inter-war years. I can remember that at St George's, Beckenham we were forced to exchange a tabernacle for an aumbry in the side chapel. In some cases bishops positively forbade the practice of reservation except in case of illness. However when you looked at Anglo-Catholic parish priests in those days you saw men fulfilled. They taught hard and visited devotedly and mostly saw their congregations growing. If there were problems with authority I doubt whether they had time to dwell on them overmuch, and although some might have yearned to have the approval of the Holy Father, they were realistic enough to admit that they might not have enjoyed the tight discipline he imposed.

So the forenoon of the Oxford Movement which began academically in Oxford and ended in a blaze of pastoral care for the country's neglected sheep, ended with the high noon of the 1920s and 1930s. As we shall see the afternoon was not so glorious but this was not entirely due to the fault of the Catholic Movement.

What did all this flowering of Anglo-Catholic activity mean to the ordinary citizen? In this next chapter I will draw on personal experience to show what was going on, not in city or slum parishes, but in a London suburb.

References

1. H.A. Wilson: The Other Half (Knott 1937)
2. Congress Books (SSPP 1923) Three vols. God and His Church, Word and Sacraments, Man and His Future.

Chapter Eight

Portrait of a Parish

As London grew in the nineteenth century there was a steady expansion in all directions. This growth is most clearly marked today south of the Thames by a line of handsome houses which were built along the Brixton Road so that the 'quality' as they drove south would not be distressed by the poverty and squalor of the suburban peasantry who, over the years, had occupied the open spaces. It is not easy to visualise this kind of countryside today because every square yard is covered by a variety of developments. But in those days, once out of London, village life began.

Past Brixton, the middle classes began to build their houses and villas. First Clapham, then Norbury and Streatham became fashionable. As public transport improved the population moved still further south to Dulwich, Herne Hill, Sydenham, and, by the end of the century, the village of Beckenham had been invaded. Building went on apace and soon there was a large conurbation for which the Southern Railway provided several stations, Kent House, Clock House, Beckenham Junction, Beckenham Hill, and others. Twenty minutes and the city worker exchanged country air for London smoke. By 1916 when I was born, Beckenham was a town served by five parish churches, one Roman Catholic temporary church and several Non-Conformist places of worship. The locals, however, still talked about the village and indeed there were plenty of open spaces. One was the considerable garden and grounds which surrounded the large rectory where the incumbent of the main parish church, St George's, lived. Developers failed to get their hands on these until the end of the 1920s when the rector of the day aroused great controversy by selling it all off, and changed the whole landscape. Until then it was possible to walk up a hill to the huge parish church past railings and fences which kept wild life from straying on to the main road. This road led south to Bromley, which was also being steadily developed, and eventually to rural parts where primitive camping was possible, a blessing for Boy Scouts. Northwards within two miles was the extremity of a London tentacle. You could be in Beckenham, Kent, one minute, in London S.E.20 the next. I was born on the very boundary so can call myself both a Londoner and a Kentish man. For a shilling return you could catch a train to the heart of London Town, for sixpence you could go by bus, but for a penny you could catch a tram in Penge and be hurtled on hard wooden seats through Peckham and Deptford to the same place. You could say that Beckenham had been overwhelmed by suburbia, today it has been absorbed by Greater London. I have chosen this setting for my portrait of a parish between the wars for two reasons. It was typical of many parishes on the outskirts of our cities and I knew it personally. I spent the first twenty years of my life there. For a nation which had mostly abandoned religion there was a great selection of churches, High, Low and Moderate. The Low Church was Christ Church which seemed to take its stand on prayer meetings and Bible classes. It was in the hands of a Protestant trust, so continuity was assured. It was not a place people lightly entered, certainly those of a Higher persuasion. St Paul's was the moderate church but was hidden away on the edge of the town and made little impact on the community at large.

My family was High and unlike most of our neighbours went to church regularly. My father came from a family which helped to pioneer the Tractarian movement. He had come under the influence of a great priest, Walter Carey, at Woolwich in the first great war. So definite had been his instruction that he believed it a serious sin even to enter a building of schismatic worship. This posed problems, for he was a consultant engineer and sometimes had to inspect the heating of Non-Conformist chapels. When this happened his conscience could not be at rest until he had gone to confession. This reminds me about the early days of mission work in Ceylon at the beginning of the nineteenth century. A pioneer was the Revd. Joseph Knight who learnt Tamil from a Brahmin priest. Contact with this Christian foreigner made the Hindu priest unclean so after each lesson he had to bath to purge himself of the defilement. Not less careful was my father and this may explain the intolerance of his son!

A Catholic Anglican was spoilt for choice in Beckenham. At the London end was St Michael's, working class Catholic and nearest to Rome. In my early days Fr Eves was vicar before going to St Alban's, Holborn in the wake of those great martyrs for the Faith, Fathers Mackonochie and Stanton. To the south and at the country end was St Barnabas' – respectably Catholic and always shining with polish as befitted a church surrounded by the middle class. There were two mission churches near the centre with devoted priests.

But there was no mistaking the main parish church from which the other parishes had been carved before the first war. This was St George's, standing splendidly on the top of a hill like a small cathedral. It had been rebuilt in mid-Victorian times over an older building and could only have been designed for Catholic worship, for the sanctuary was spacious and lent itself to dignified ceremonial. The focal point was a large altar under a marble reredos on which six brass candlesticks and a heavy crucifix had at some time been placed. Two steps below were two huge brass candle-stands and above, seven lamps suspended from the roof. At either side were sedilia, on the right for the clergy, and on the left for servers. Further down were stalls for a large choir confined within a marble chancel wall. To the right of this was a beautiful side chapel where the Blessed Sacrament was reserved in a handsome tabernacle and to the left another side altar beside which was an expensive statue of Our Lady. Everything was in good taste and it is surprising that no note of it can be found in Peter Anson's book, *Fashions in Church Furnishings 1840–1940*. But then the Catholic Faith blossomed quietly at St George's and this probably left it mostly undisturbed by wreckers, episcopal or otherwise. There was seating for several hundreds and this was needed for the crowds who flocked to its different services. Of these there were many. On Sundays at 7.00 and 8.00 am Communion was received by those who had fasted from midnight, at 10.30 there was a full Sung Matins followed immediately by High Mass at 11.30 at which only the aged and infirm communicated. So it was all go on Sundays and if you added Catechism at 3.00 pm and Solemn Evensong at 6.30 pm people were surging in and out for much of the day. It was all done in a very friendly way and there was no conflict between Matins and Mass. All were proud of belonging to St George's. Add the daily Mass and there was a full programme. At the main entrance there was, very properly, a baptistry and it was here I was made a member of Holy Church early in 1917. From the world's point of view this was not a good time to be born, for wholesale slaughter was contining on the Western Front. It was, however, the beginning of a floodtide for the Anglo-Catholic movement. The reason for this was twofold, the litigation of the past had proved an own goal and people were otherwise too occupied to be involved with religious controversy. The Pope himself might have landed on the Norfolk coast and been treated as a friendly visitor.

The rector who baptised me was Canon Henry Arnott, an interesting man. He started life as a doctor and became consultant surgeon to St Thomas' Hospital in the 1860s. Next we find him at Chichester Theological College in 1876 where no doubt he was grounded in sound teaching, for that college was an early fruit of the Tractarian movement. He became rector of Beckenham in 1909 and undoubtedly laid the foundation of the lavish Catholic faith and practice in which I was brought up. I do not remember him because he retired in 1919. He was followed by an equally interesting man, Father James Tait Plowden-Wardlaw who was a qualified barrister at law. He had earlier been a curate at St George's before returning to Cambridge. Now he was our new rector and I remember him well. He was an excellent preacher, no doubt due to his legal training. He did not cease demonstrating that the Church of England was a lawful part of the universal Catholic Church and our worship faithfully reflected this. I have in front of me a copy of the St George's Service Book printed for the congregation, which he put together in 1923. It is a masterly little work. In thirty two pages not only is the order of service printed simply and without confusing alternatives, but also the history and meaning of the Mass (Breaking of Bread, Eucharist or Communion) is given. Since this little book nourished not only my faith but also that of many others I will describe it in greater detail. It measured only 5″ by 3½″ and was printed in fine style by the Society of SS Peter and Paul. A visitor would read first that 'the Rector would be grateful if new-comers and strangers would kindly place their names and addresses in the box at the end of the Church in order that he might call upon them'.

Then was explained why this service had always been the main act of worship for Christians. After early centuries of persecution, 'churches were built, Church music began its history, ceremonial developed, and all that man could do to surround the Christian Mysteries with beauty and splendour was done'. It went on to give three reasons for this development; the service was unique as being the service of Jesus himself; it was believed that Jesus Christ was present under the forms of bread and wine by virtue of the consecration; the Sacrifice of Calvary, though not repeated, was understood to be perpetuated in this service. It then noted that these three points are laid down in the Book of Common Prayer and are now part of the teaching of the Church of England. English church people therefore had the duty and privilege of joining in this offering of the Holy Sacrifice, of receiving the consecrated elements in an act of Holy Communion and of joining in the service with devotion, even though not actually communicating. Since the universal law of the Church laid down fasting before receiving Communion, celebrations at an early hour were provided. If you attended the full sung Mass at a later hour you would not expect to make your Communion.

The next section explained the use of processions, the Crucifix, altar lights, the sanctuary lamp, vestments and incense. Suitable texts from Holy Scripture were given. The worshipper was now ready to pay attention to the Mass itself.

Here a bare framework of the 1662 Communion service was given, with the opening Commandments being replaced by the Kyries. Apart from that, the order was followed faithfully with the Gloria at the end and the Prayer for the Church after the offertory. After the Sanctus a note is given that the priest now prays privately and this meant for us that he used the Roman Canon which then surrounded the Prayer Book Prayer of Consecration.

The manual concluded with the Angelus and an Office of Devotion Before the Blessed Sacrament. I have described this manual at some length because it was the kind of *pis aller* which enabled Anglo-Catholic churches to flourish without dependence on the Pope in Rome. Why should we look elsewhere when we had all things necessary for salvation within the Church of England? If our Church said little about offering a sacrifice nevertheless we could be sure that the silent prayers of the celebrant during the Canon made good the deficiency. The English Missal published first by the Society of SS Peter and Paul and later by Knott put before the priest all he needed to say and do when he pleaded the eternal sacrifice. It also provided for the holy days and extra ceremonies which the parsimonious Reformers had omitted.

In fact, far from reaching out Romewards the local Roman Catholic church was thought of as an enemy which was lying in wait to snap up faint-hearted Anglicans. When this happened the new convert was sorrowfully mentioned in hushed tones as if he had died or made an unfortunate marriage. There was a Roman Catholic church in the High Street but it was better to pass it quickly before a fatal fascination took hold. The parish priest, Father Byrne, was known to have a low opinion of those apeing the true faith and this made it easier to avoid him. Although Pickering says in his book, *Anglo-Catholicism*, that there were those who wanted complete reunion with Rome papalists, they could not be found at St George's.

I was introduced to this way of life when I was two. I still remember being scolded by my mother for kicking the pew during High Mass and did it no more for I was an obedient boy. Instead I became completely absorbed in the liturgical scenario. This was richly provided for our Catholic family by priests, servers and choir at the fully sung Mass on Sunday morning. It was always High Mass with three sacred ministers and if a priest were lacking then a lay subdeacon obliged. The Western vestments, chasuble and dalmatics were beautifully fashioned, the servers perfectly dressed and trained and the choir capable of rendering the finest music.

I was admitted to an active part in all this splendour at the age of six. It was suggested to my father that I should become a boat boy and one weekday evening I was taken behind the scenes and measured for cassock, linen, and black felt slippers. Then I was put through my paces and finally introduced to the resident thurifer whom I would keep supplied with incense for the next few years. He was a very superior being, always carefully dressed. He had a flourish all of his own and sent waves of scented smoke over clergy and people with the grace worthy of Bertie Wooster's Jeeves. There was a cigarette advertisement at that time showing a butler respectfully proferring a packet on a silver tray with the words, 'Your Kensitas, sir' and it was thought that this described perfectly our man in action. His name was J. Cleveland Allen and, like Melchizedek of old, he seemed to appear on Sunday from nowhere and return there after Mass via the Railway Tavern until the next week. His union rules seemed to prevent any weekday appearances. Much later we learned that he was an assistant in a men's outfitters in London and had an odd wife. Still he was very kind to me and gave me a good start in the sanctuary.

I can still feel the excitement of those early days. Everything was done to create a sense of aweful occasion and one felt that there could be no greater honour on earth than to assist at the sacred Mysteries. But you had to take care not to touch with lay hands things which were sacred to the priests alone. The terrible fate of Uzza in the Old Testament who put his hand out to steady the Ark was a warning to servers who got above themselves. So I grew up with a deep reverence for God and the lesson learnt in those days has remained with me. The fear of the Lord was indeed wisdom and lack of it at the present time is a great handicap to the religious life. Not least it induced a sense of unworthiness which is proper to the human condition and this led naturally to a need for confession and absolution.

I have in front of me a group photo of all the principals of St George's in June 1925. It was taken in the vast rectory garden with the church towering, literally, behind, and is an impressive tribute to the flourishing religious life we enjoyed. Seated in the middle are the clergy, six in number and all birettaed. On either side are the churchwardens and sidesmen, eminent citizens both of the church and of the local community. There is still a touch of Edwardian elegance in the dress of some of these gentlemen who represented success in the City, in the Law, and in local enterprise. Immediately behind them are the gentlemen of the choir, sixteen in number, and sitting on the ground in the front are twenty choirboys. High at the back are the servers carrying the equipment of their trade, banners, candles, Cross and thurible. I am clutching my boat.

The photograph must have been taken just before the departure of Fr Plowden-Wardlaw for he left us in that year to become the chaplain at Cannes. I met him again when I went up to Cambridge for he finally returned there as vicar of St Clement's. Meanwhile Father Morgan from St Andrew's, Willesden took his place at Beckenham and the Catholic tradition was assured. More importantly Father Cyril Smith came as curate and took over my development. He brought youth and an even firmer Catholic discipline to the parish. He was not a good preacher, but oh! how he visited and organised the young! He came from a notable family in Rochester and was typical of the public school boy and Oxbridge graduate who dedicated himself to the Church in those days. He was a convinced celebate and a Benedictine oblate but because of his strong views was not given his own parish until middle age. Here he worked patiently until old age and when he died at the age of ninety we were surprised to hear he had left a large fortune. He certainly did not spend money on himself.

He had chosen the hard way and this he taught me. From an early age I learnt the Via Crucis, Via Lucis or no-crown-without-a-cross approach to life and this was certainly necessary if I was to carry out my church duties. For the first sixteen years of my life we lived some distance from St George's and, since we had no car, had to walk when buses were not available. Since daily Mass had to be at 6.30 or 7.00 am, it meant getting up early and a lonely journey. In time I was given a bike but even then the going could be hard in the winter. In Lent there were extra services but as I peddled through snow, rain and fog I knew I was earning myself a special place in heaven. After several years of this kind of philosophy I became uneasy if the going was not difficult and this outlook followed me for the rest of my life.

I joined the Friday evening Confession queue early in life at the age of eleven. It was important to be one of the first because it could be a lengthy business, and you could be very late home. I was certain of meeting most of my young church friends there and we would often indicate to each other the probable length of our stay in the 'box'. We learnt that middle-aged spinsters were wont to prolong their sessions and uncharitably attributed unworthy motives to them. So there could be an undignified jockeying for position especially after Stations of the Cross in Lent. This besieging of the confessional was not due to missions or emotional appeals to the congregation. Rather it was the result of steady teaching at Sunday afternoon Catechism by Fr Smith. The case for shedding sins as well as gaining grace was so reasonably presented that none of us thought confession and absolution an unnatural exercise. After all, if sin made the soul black and separated from God, no one could afford to miss the chance of sacramental forgiveness. So there was little embarrassment among my contemporaries about confession as we struggled with the increasing temptations of adolescence.

Two sins seemed especially damaging, missing Mass on Sundays and days of obligation, and masturbation. There was little opportunity for me to commit the former because my parents took good care that I always went with them unless I was ill, and if we went away on summer holidays the first thing we did on arrival was to find out the time of Sunday Mass. This might not always be what we were used to but normally we could find somewhere where vestments were used and the Eucharist celebrated. In fact the ease with which we found satisfactory churches certainly left me with little idea of the continuing struggle of the Catholic movement.

Sexual matters were more difficult to organise and tended to come irresistibly upon you. When they did they were manifestations of the devil and had to be dealt with. You could often tell the fierceness of this battle by the number of times a person appeared on Friday evenings or was hurried away to an emergency session. We were all very ignorant of sexual matters in those days because it was never discussed in any kind of suburban company. I certainly understood neither the special temptations of girls nor their sexual equipment and I remained in this ignorance long after I had left home for university. Only the priest in the confessional saw both sides of the problem and he was not telling. So I was brought up without the inhibitions which modern church people seem to have about sin and its treatment. I have never ceased to be grateful for this part of my religious upbringing for it has put me into the hands of excellent directors who have helped me with every part of my spiritual development. The Catholics of old were right to insist on the necessity of the sacrament of penance, and Christians today sadly lack guidance in such matters as prayer by not going regularly to confession. Pickering talks about the painful introduction of confession into the Victorian Church and no doubt it caused much controversy. Yet in less than a hundred years parishes like St George's could teach it without trouble. This leads me on to the matter of sound teaching which is lacking in today's Church. I was very well taught as a boy and this applied to the many young people who went to church with me. Our Sunday school or Catechism was very well organised and our teachers well trained. Faith Press published courses for all ages illustrated by a weekly stamp and absence could easily be seen because you had a blank in your book. We not only knew what our faith and practice were, but also the authority for them. We might not dwell unduly on the Bible like Christ Church down the road, but we studied Our Lord's life and knew that he founded the family of the Church. Here were to be found all means of salvation for all people and this described the word, Catholic. This Church had been the voice of the Lord through all the centuries and must be obeyed. Despite the blip of the Reformation the Church of England had emerged with its resources intact and this made it just as good as St Edmund's Roman Catholic church a little further down the road.

It has been said that religious man needs salvation to be available at a local level and this surely was true of the church in which I was brought up. At St George's the means of salvation were clearly and beautifully made available. Even when the Scouts went away to camp in some lonely spot, the first tent to be erected was the church, and here Fr Smith said Mass daily and celebrated a full Sung Mass on Sundays. It was all very exciting and an excellent lesson in the proper priorities of life.

If the parish priest lacked the gift of teaching there was a steady flow of instructional books designed to teach the faith simply and cheaply. I have before me a thin volume, *Notes of Instruction to Candidates for Confirmation*, written by a Priest and published by the Church Sunday School Union first in 1882. It does not pull any punches. Note what it says under the words Apostolic Church.

'Nothing but ordination by a Bishop whose ordination has come down from the Apostles, can possibly make a man a priest. Dissenters have no ministry.'

Such words today would make even the firmest churchman cringe, but it was the language of that day and it underlay the teaching I received as a boy. In 1906 a paperback was published, *The Congregation In Church* by A.R. Mowbray. The sub-title was, A Plain Guide to a Reverent and Intelligent participation in the Public Services of the Church. It offered 'brief information concerning the six ritual points, the principal rites and ceremonies of the Church; ecclesiastical vestments and ornaments; sacred seasons, feasts and fasts; liturgical colours; ecclesiastical terms and various other matters appertaining to Catholic worship'.

To sum up what Anglo Catholics were being taught between the wars, I could not do better than quote what this small book, written earlier in the century says under the title — No Popery.

'There was a time in the history of the Church when she was one and undivided, when the single main trunk of the Christian tree had not forked off into two great branches, one represented by the Greek Catholics of our time, the other by the Roman Catholics. It is this early age of Christianity that we profess to follow — the age which was nearest to Apostolic times, which necessarily preserved best the personal instructions of the Twelve and which was consequently most likely to think and act in accordance with the Will of our Divine Lord and Master.'

By the time I learnt this lesson, some extra bits and pieces had been added to this primitive Christianity but it did not concern me. I had a local entrance into the One Holy, Catholic and Apostolic Church and that was enough.

I suppose all this bred a certain intolerance in a growing man and I must own up to it. At Cambridge I had friends who had a similar upbringing. We used to go church-crawling in the years before the war with the question on our lips, Is he sound? By this, of course, we meant the vicar. Those were the days when it was safe to leave churches open all day without fear of vandalism and we entered them to apply certain criteria. Was there a Sung Mass on Sundays, were there six candles on the altar, was the sacrament reserved, was there a sweet smell of incense? If all seemed well we decided to stay and worship but woe betide if the western rite was not used! Sometimes we thought we had discovered a gem of a church only to find unfortunate aberrations which revealed that the vicar was not sound. As far as we were concerned there was a right way of doing everything and we expected our clergy to approximate as closely as possible to that. Sometimes we would leave our suggestions in the visitors' book.

This question extended to right belief as well. Is he sound about the Virgin Birth, miracles, the Resurrection, authority? In morals, too, we were judgmental. Birth control was a big issue in those days and not at all approved of by Catholics, even though the younger ones might have a flimsy knowledge of sex. I remember a scathing remark made by one priest about another. 'He used to believe in the Immaculate Conception, but now he believes in the immaculate contraception'. You knocked people like that off your visiting list!

It would be wrong, however, to suppose we were an exclusive elite. As Beckenham grew during those years between the wars, newcomers arrived from round the country and were welcomed. In 1931 yet another rector, The Revd. Francis Boyd, came to use from St Saviour's, Pimlico and once again the tradition was assured. He was a strange mixture of piety and waywardness, but he brought the new dimension of mission to St George's. So far the large congregations had been reinforced by a steady flow of families who had moved into the new housing estates. These mostly had learned their faith elsewhere. The new rector was concerned to reach those who had no contact with the Church and this he did in several ways, not all of them popular with his flock. For instance, there had been fierce controversy over the opening of the local Regal Cinema on Sunday evenings and the Rector of Beckenham was expected to head the opposition. Far from doing this he made a deal with the manager by which he was allowed to give a five minute religious talk on the stage before the film began. He also held a Good Friday service there. He was adept at speaking to unbelievers and kept alive the Church's contact with a world which was drifting away. Looking back, I realise it was a brave gesture and compensated for some of the bad mistakes he made in the parish. We also had parish missions which brought in flamboyant preachers from outside. It also introduced us to religious communities who came to support our efforts at evangelism.

The life of this flourishing parish went on largely undisturbed. You might ask what the Bishop of Rochester thought about this Catholic life style, and I cannot answer because as far as I know he did not interefere. He regularly came for our Confirmations, or sent his assistant, and generally did what we asked him. From 1905–31 it was Bishop Harmer, who at one time had been chaplain to Bishop Lightfoot of Durham and then had been made Bishop of Adelaide in Australia. Maybe these two facts had broadened his mind and made him gentle in approach. He must have been an old man in these post-war years, but bishops like the rest of the clergy went on for ever in those days. He was followed by Martin Linton-Smith, a fierce looking man and reputed to be a martinet, but I cannot recall any break in our Catholic activities. He accepted me for ordination in 1939 and I can only remember a friendly man. His successor, Christopher Chavasse, was different but that is another story!

On one occasion only did we experience the unpleasant Protestant persecution which was still harassing some Catholic churches. One Sunday morning in the late Twenties we had a warning that Mr Kensit with some of his band were on their way from London to break up our High Mass. The rector immediately mobilised our sidesmen and they formed a circle outside the church. The would-be aggressors arrived, but melted away when they saw this phalanx of defenders.

My portrait of a parish is, therefore, an unheroic one for we were never seriously under attack for our Catholic faith. But on one occasion we were able to put our church life into context when a Mr Clifton Kelway, an Anglo Catholic layman, came and gave us a lecture on the Catholic revival. It was illustrated with slides and we were able to see the sad state of religion in the parishes before 1833 and the transformation which followed. It was presented as a powerful drama and we must have been tempted to cheer the goodies and hiss the baddies. We knew, though, that those were the bad old days and that better times had arrived. We did not, however, realise that we were enjoying the zenith of Anglo-Catholicism (but this was certainly true). Evidence for this was all round us because down the road were parishes enjoying the same success, St George's, Bickley, St Mary's, Swanley, St John's, Sevenoaks, and others. This was in one small area of England. Other cities were showing similar success. The secret of this could be found in sound teaching. Famous priests of courage and ability come and go but their only lasting legacy is in the foundation of careful instruction they lay. It is relatively easy to create a lively parish if enough fringe benefits are offered. It is more difficult to give permanence to such success.

Despite the second world war the Catholic tradition continued at St George's, Beckenham and both my father and mother (who lived into her nineties) died fortified by the rites of Holy Church, as the saying goes. Later rectors have differed in their ideas about how to present this faith, but then the suburban picture changed considerably after 1945 and posed new challenges.

Before that, life changed drastically for me when I became the last of the pre-war generation of Cambridge undergraduates and went up to Christ's College in 1935 to read classics. I might well have gone to Keble, Oxford and had a different kind of training but a last minute switch sent me to the other place and this I have never regretted. It may be of interest to note that in those days it was easy to go up to a senior university provided you had the money and could pass a simple exam, called Littlego at Cambridge. I had no interview for a place and the first time I met my senior tutor was after I had gone into residence. In later life I realised how different are the two universities. Oxford men tend to agonise over ideas while a Cambridge man is more down to earth and practical. In an earlier chapter we saw how Cambridge men in the vicarage at Hadleigh tried in vain to plan the future of the Oxford movement. Who knows what would have happened if they had been allowed to organise the heart searchings of the Oxford scholars? They were not and so a Cambridge man who is also a Catholic in the Church of England has to give credit to the other place for success in this field of churchmanship. Oxford became full of landmarks of the Oxford revival, Trinity and Oriel Colleges, the University Church of St Mary's, Littlemore, Pusey House, and Keble College, together with a rich choice of churches, St Mary Mag's, St Barnabas', SS Philip and James', to mention a few.

Anglo-Catholicism had infiltrated Cambridge gently rather than hit it dramatically, and had not hurried on from its Tractarian stage. There were two main Catholic churches, Little St Mary's and St Giles', but church life still centred round the college chapels where attendance was compulsory. Of these latter, King's and Sidney Sussex in my days were known to be sound. It was in these chapels that members of the Catholic society, STC or Sancti Trinitatis Confraternitas, met each term for a Sung Eucharist or Evensong. Sidney Sussex was compact and heavy with wood carving while the glories of King's are known worldwide. Once a year we would go early in the morning to this lovely Tudor building and sing our Eucharist. Eric Milner-White was the Dean and he breathed a Catholic spirituality over us all. Catholicism, then, at Cambridge was restrained and dignified but full of fun. We enjoyed what was on offer. Even the one religious community at the Oratory House near the Madingley road was unobtrusive. Here I served once a week for the resident priests, Fathers Bill Lutyens, Wilfrid Knox and Alec Vidler. There were no Roman extravagances although Fr Wilfrid said Mass so quickly and inaudibly that it might have been in Latin rather than in Prayer Book English. A fringe benefit after early Mass was to watch milk filter through Fr Vidler's beard when he ate his cereal.

The nearest I came to anything more extreme was being president of the Cambridge Reunion Society. This title promises a precocious ecumenism but we were concerned only with closer ties with the Roman Church. Sometimes we were addressed by friendly Romans such as Fr Vincent McNabb and this made us feel we were advancing the Church of England closer to its mother, but there were few defections to the other side. My part in this society earned me the remark of a certain clergyman that 'I was a young pup fouling my own nest'!

All this Catholic activity was very marginal. I soon learnt when I entered this university life that, far from belonging to the mainstream of church life, I was in a minority. Christ's at that time was a very Evangelical college and was full of ordinands of that kind of churchmanship. This was largely due to the former chaplain, Frank Woolnough, who was well known in Low Church circles. He had no opinion at all of High Church undergraduates who found their way to his college. The story was told that he used to invite some of these to breakfast on Fridays and put before them bacon and eggs to test their rule of abstinence! By the time I arrived the huge figure of David Edwards had taken his place. He was Low but not aggressively so. Under him chapel services remained bleak liturgically and the Communion service, celebrated on Sundays at 8 am and on Wednesday and Prayer Book festivals, could well have been untouched by Tractarian reform.

In face of this Evangelical strength the few Catholic members of the college had formed themselves into a small guild of the Holy Name. This met in the rooms of a classics don, Arthur Peck, for prayers and social activities and, as a sort of Catholic missionary enterprise, made it our duty to atttend all celebrations of Holy Communion in the college chapel. A few more words must be said about this Dr Peck whose eccentricities have delighted many through the years. He had a keen theological brain and was a pillar of Little St Mary's, where he acted as a permanent lay subdeacon at the Sunday Sung Mass. No doubt in time a book will be written about his enrichment of the English language and his extraordinary habits. I must admit I was a bit overawed by him, not least because he was my supervisor, but later I recognised that he had been a great influence in my life. As a small token of this I was able to ask him to read the Epistle at the Sung Mass of the 1968 Congress which I organised in the Royal Festival Hall.

Although we were only a short distance from another great war, those Cambridge years were very peaceful and few had any idea of the fate which was about to fall on the world. The only political event which disturbed our peace was Mussolini's invasion of East Africa but this caused little concern except to a few brave souls who hung from the pinnacles of King's Chapel the slogan, Save Abyssinia Now. In case it should be thought that Cambridge was brimming over with religion in those pre-war years it should be said that apart from compulsory college chapel there was little evidence that undergraduates were any more religious than the rest of the country. But they were wonderful years and passed all too quickly. I was, however, steering my way toward the next goal of ordination. For this I had to choose a theological college and after some deliberation went to Chichester where I found myself back again in the Catholic mainstream.

In those years Chichester was the place to be because it was enjoying vintage years under Fr Charles Gillett and a very able staff. This theological college was the first to be founded as a result of the Oxford Movement and, while I was there, we celebrated its centenary in 1939, just before the outbreak of war. Here was sound teaching and a full liturgical programme which included a full High Mass every Sunday, a sung Mass on festivals, a daily Mass preceded by a half hour meditation, and daily offices. We had some notable students including Colin Stephenson who was possibly the last of the great preachers of the Church of England and later became the administrator of the shrine of Our Lady at Walsingham. An entertaining account of our Cicestrian days can be found in his book, *Merrily on High*. This shows the good-humoured way we enjoyed our religion.

War finally overtook us while we were all singing the Sung Eucharist in the cathedral on Sunday, 3rd September and the first siren sounded. Lives everywhere were changed and many parishes which had been enjoying full Catholic privileges were to undergo trial by bombing. This ushered in a new era of their history.

Chapter Nine

The Catholic Social Conscience

The portrait given in the last chapter was of a respectable parish. There were wealthy people living in grand houses and there were the poor, but most lived comfortably. Between the wars a family could be housed, fed and clothed for £300 a year with enough left over for an annual holiday by the sea. I managed Cambridge in my first year for £175, and when I was made deacon in 1939 my stipend was £190, out of which I had to find my board and lodging (£75 a year). We all lived quietly, making our own entertainment, with an occasional visit to the West End for the theatre. So we were cushioned against the harsh living conditions of fellow citizens, even against the rougher types who lived across the border in Penge. Here criminal happenings were expected to take place and they often did, but it was never considered deprived enough for missionary activity from the many Beckenham churches.

For this a journey had to be made to the east end of London where, in the words of a novelist of the time, you found 'a reticent landscape that more nearly suggests hell than any poetic rendering of hell, for it evokes the image of a dead thing with the potentiality of life ... Apathetic streets: tousled gardens, miles of washing; blear windows; squat chimneys; dirt: bugs ... London behind the scenes where life laps at lowest ebb'. The late Victorian conscience had tidied up some of the social problems which the first ritualist priests found, but there were the same disabilities and temptations which poverty brings. Eighty years on and their Catholic successors shared this poverty with the same devotion. Here the body of Christ, the Church, went to work with hands and feet, with voice and brain. At ground level, as it were, parish priests visited and ministered to their flock in the most impoverished conditions. They were like medical men working among the wounded on the field of battle but bowing to the inevitability of war. They could be found on duty by anybody who dared to venture east from the Bank of England, like the journalist who, in 1930, wrote, 'I do not often wander down the Hackney Road of an evening. For one thing, it is too far from my home; for another, the attractions of the neighbourhood are not sufficiently obvious to tempt me there. But Fate, or idle chance took me that way one recent Wednesday. As I sauntered aimlessly, contrasting the grim and forbidding poverty of the surroundings with the spacious prosperity of the City left behind at Liverpool Street, the bell of a church rang out hard by. Church — on Wednesday evening? An idle man's curiosity is easily stimulated; accordingly I passed down a little side street in the direction of the sound and soon found myself in a large church'.[1]

He went on to say that this was clearly an Anglo-Catholic church, the lights; the arrangement of the altars; the images of the Virgin Mary and the Patron Saint made this clear. What surprised him, though, was the congregation, for he could not see any of the dilettante 'spikes' he had expected. On the contrary, many of the pews in the central aisles were filled with ordinary working men and women, drawn from the neighbourhood and weary after a week-day of labour. He had, in fact, stumbled upon St Augustine's, Haggerston and the parish priest, Father Wilson, whom we met earlier in this book, organising the first Anglo-Catholic Congress from Westminster.

The priest had now become part of the hands and feet of Christ's body in London's slum land and has left a record of his life there. The day began with the alarm clock which 'burst into song' at 5.45 am; the kettle was put on for shaving water and then, dressed in cassock, he unlocked the church and said Mass at 6.30. A quick cup of tea and he was off on his rounds of sick communions; then back to church for morning prayers and office, followed by breakfast. The morning was spent in correspondence and other writing. After a lunch of bread and cheese, cake and coffee there was parish visiting to be done until dinner time. The evening was taken up with clubs and similar organisations and the day closed at 10.00 pm with Compline. In all, a working day of seventeen hours. Days off and holidays were rare, yet, despite feeling tired and not over fit, he was completely and utterly happy, unwilling to change places with any other man on earth.

What qualifications were required for a priest in the slums? Fr Wilson answered this in a sermon at All Saints, Margaret Street, in March 1933. He must be a man of prayer, otherwise in the face of many disappointments he will go to pieces, and he must have the discipline of a daily Mass, the daily offices, and meditation. He must be able to pray at any moment where there is an accident or by a sick bed.

Secondly, he must be in love with slums, and, despite a dislike of dirt, bugs, smells and overcrowding, have a respect for those who are compelled to live among them. He must be always available, never superior, and must not cease to be thrilled at his calling to such a life. For who would exchange a way of life where on return from a rare holiday 'a small child drops her Yo-yo, runs down the pavement and shouts, "O farver; where 'ave ye bin? I ain't 'arf missed yer"'. Not this one, writes Fr Wilson.

Elsewhere the hands and feet of Christ were working to create better living conditions. In 1921 a remarkable man, Basil Jellicoe, went first as a layman to the Magdalen College, Oxford mission at the back of Euston and St Pancras Stations. In the next two years he was ordained and joined with Fr Percy Maryon-Wilson in tackling some of the worst slum conditions in Britain. They were heartbroken to see people living in sub-human conditions, in rat-infested, bug-ridden tenements, and set about changing them. With the daily Mass as their inspiration they became the most famous missioners for decent housing which the Church has produced, according to Roger Lloyd's *Church of England 1900–1965*.[2] Fr Jellicoe's Anglo-Catholic faith and wonderful home background drove him to overcome all barriers in his campaign for better living conditions. Although no intellectual, he worked by persuasion and a deep love for his flock. He would wander round the streets, sheltering children under his black cloak. He bombarded people and places everywhere with his housing scheme. In 1925 the St Pancras House Improvement Society was started and began to raise money to purchase slum property so that it could be pulled down and rebuilt. When money was short for this, they organised days of continuous prayer before the Blessed Sacrament. By sheer hard work people, great and not so great, even the Royal Family, gave their support and interest, and by 1926 more extensive improvements were undertaken. Fr Jellicoe became in great demand round the country for talking about slums and giving advice to those who wanted to follow his example. In the end hard work killed him and he died at an early age.

Priests who worked among the poor were often helped by religious communities, especially women's orders. As early as 1845 the Park Village sisterhood was founded with the help of Pusey for work among the poor of London. This order quickly spread to Devonport and Sisters of Mercy began to work from St Dunstan's Abbey in appalling conditions of poverty. In fact the monastic way of life became a great support for those working in the slums of the country. There was an implicit semi-monasticism in the SSC (Society of the Holy Cross) founded by Fr Lowder. It was this background rather than politics which inspired the ritualists, both early and late, and church historians have accused them of sharing in the general obliviousness to the needs of society. In the early Victorian days however the political situation was so sensitively balanced that church people hesitated to interfere. With revolution on the Continent and agitation by Chartists at home, nobody wanted to push the country further into rebellion. Generally, also, these priests had little time to engage in political or sociological justification for their work. As we have seen from Fr Wilson's daily routine, every minute of the day was fully taken up with the immediate needs of his flock. Care for the people whom God loved drove them to the limits of their endurance.

The struggle for social reform came in the first place from two prophets, two Broad Church voices. Despite the poor state of religion in England there was a growing awareness of the need for caring for those who were living below the poverty line. In 1831, Thomas Arnold, who has been called the first real prophet of the Church's social policy in Victorian England wrote in his book, *The Englishman's Register*, that the great need of the age was to open the eyes of the rich to the social misery in the nation. He followed this with a series of letters to the *Sheffield Courant*, where he expressed his social idea: 'the dispersion of a number of well-educated men over the whole kingdom whose sole business is to do good of the highest kind'. Arnold's Broad Church views did not commend themselves to either Evangelicals or Tractarians, but as the century progressed more and more churchmen accepted them, and gradually there came into being that ethic of service which was a hallmark of Victorian life. In his book, *The Idea of the Victorian Church*,[3] Desmond Brown traces the growth of this ethic from a gradual awareness of the duty of the wealthy to the poor, until it reached the bishops who began to recruit the middle classes in the cause of charity. There was a remarkable increase in voluntary charities between 1850 and 1890, and the poor 'welcomes the noble army of men and women who penetrate the vilest haunts, carrying with them the Gospel'. Slum dwellers began to depend upon the welfare provided by missions and Church-inspired charities. All this stopped short at ambulance work and there was a reluctance to help the poor rise above the station to which it was believed God had called them. It should be said that the Church was primarily concerned for the moral welfare of the poor, and there was a concerted effort to fight the social evils of drunkenness, prostitution, and crime.

It was left to another prophet, F.D. Maurice, to raise social reform to a higher plane. He was professor of Theology at King's London in 1848 when he realised through the experience of a friend who had witnessed political troubles in France, that socialism should be christianised. So, in alliance with men like Charles Kingsley, he became a prophet of Christian Socialism. He believed that all class barriers must be broken down and all men brought into the Universal Society of the Church. He might at first sight have seemed a powerful ally of the ritualists who were slaving away in the parishes to bring to their people the spiritual benefits of the Catholic Church, but although he admitted the dedication of these priests, he disagreed with their methods. Being a broad churchman he disliked their concern for men's sins because he took a more optimistic view of man's nature. Rather than a sinful creature in need of regeneration, Maurice saw man as ignorant and in need of education. Nevertheless he was a great influence in Victorian society. He established his Working Men's College in Red Lion Square, London, so that the classes could work together for mutual benefit in education. He also introduced the cooperative movement which was to be continued and developed by later socialist politicians and which was much admired by Charles Gore. His contribution to the Church was to show that it ceased to be Catholic when it devoted itself purely to ecclesiastical affairs, and also that the Spirit was at work in all parts of the created order. It could be said that he prepared a platform for the Anglo-Catholic sociologists who followed.

However, despite these divergencies there was soon a merging of interests between Christian Socialism and ritualism. This came about through the person of Stewart Headlam. Headlam appears to have been a strange mixture, an old Etonian who combined a passion for changing the conditions of the poor with expensive tastes in cigars and ballet. He had sat at the feet of Maurice at Cambridge but he was also very attracted to the ritualists. He was ordained in 1872 and went as curate to St Matthew's, Bethnal Green. The vicar was a Septimus Hansard who chose to live outside the parish in the cleaner air of Kensington, whence he drove to his parish for a few hours each week. Most of the work in the parish, therefore, was left to the curates and this suited the individualistic Headlam very well. Soon he was encouraging the Church to take more interest in social problems, and in 1877 he founded the Guild of St Matthew, which sought to reinterpret the traditional doctrines and rites of the Church and reveal their significance in common life. This guild never attracted great numbers of people, but it had considerable influence upon men like Thomas Mann, Keir Hardy, George Lansbury, the developing Parliamentary Labour Party.

One important convert to this guild was a priest from the nobility, the Revd James Adderley, son of Lord Norton. In 1894 he founded the Society of the Divine Compassion which set up its centre in Plaistow in East London and joined those working among the poor. Headlam himself was dismissed from his parish because of his overfondness for ballet and the music hall, but he devoted the rest of his life to the socialist cause.

Toward the end of the century there was, therefore, considerable activity among the deprived sections of the community, and for this the ritualists must take great credit. Through their battle with the establishment and through their pastoral zeal they had drawn attention to an area of national life which had mostly remained hidden. There was a proliferation of societies anxious to do good, and G.K. Chesterton noted:

> And so they sang a lot of hymns
> To help the unemployed.

More seriously, the Catholic social conscience received an added momentum when two scholar bishops, Wescott and Gore joined the Christian Social Union in 1891. Westcott was perhaps more at home working with two other scholars, Lightfoot and Hort, on New Testament studies, but his scholarship was never an end in itself, and he used it as a basis for sound incarnational theology which stressed the redemptive work of Christ as a very important factor for both personal religion and social development. As Bishop of Durham he worked hard to bring better understanding between the classes and became a firm friend of the miners. Hastings is perhaps a little unkind when he writes, 'Bishop Wescott presided over the Christian Social Union with great enthusiasm but equal vagueness as to what its several thousand members actually hoped to achieve.' There was great sympathy for the poor from the clergy, and Chesterton sums up the speech of one such priest:

> He said he was a Socialist himself
> And so was God.

Charles Gore was also a member of the Christian Social Union. He was, however, a more complex character than Wescott. Early in his career he had thrown in his lot with the Anglo-Catholic party and in 1889 he edited a series of essays, *Lux Mundi, Studies in the Religion of the Incarnation*. These allowed more to modern Biblical scholarship than Catholics of the day liked to admit, but by sheer force of his scholarship and personality he was able to surmount their fears to the extent of founding the Community of the Resurrection. In his recent centenary history of this community, Alan Wilkinson gives a fascinating picture of this bishop who would influence church life into the 1930s.[4] The author describes him as a person who never knew whether he was game-keeper or poacher. This meant that Catholics could never be certain of his support. 'The combination of Gore's personal magnetism and vocational uncertainty had almost paralysed the development of C.R.' Later he was to prove no friend of the Benedictine revival in the Church of England. However as a scholar he was much respected and he applied his thought to the social problems of the day. In his Bampton lectures of 1891 Gore showed that he was attracted by the kenotic theory of the person of Christ which taught that He emptied himself of his divinity in order to become man. He stated that 'It is an act of moral self-denial such as can be an example to us men in our efforts at sympathy and self-sacrifice.' The incarnation brings with it a Christian socialism by the very fact that the law of brotherhood is the law of Christ. Yet he warned that no matter how hard people tried to better social conditions yet the real trouble was within; and here he had a bond with the ritualists, who were trying to deal with this very evil through the sacrament of absolution.

Men like Wescott and Gore, were the brains of Christ's body and they laid a trail which Catholic thinkers could follow in the years ahead. Yet the voices within the Church could still be heard drawing attention to the continuing social ills. Scott Holland spoke out before the First World War, and Studdert Kennedy afterwards. At the 1923 Anglo-Catholic Congress in the Albert Hall, Frank, Bishop of Zanzibar summed up 'our duty' in words which were quoted earlier:

> 'You have got your Mass, you have got your Altar, you
> have begun to get your Tabernacle. Now go out into the
> highways and hedges where not even Bishops will try to
> hinder you. Go out and look for Jesus in the ragged, in
> the naked, in the oppressed and sweated, in those who
> have lost hope, in those who are struggling to make good.
> Look for Jesus. And when you see him, gird yourselves
> with his towel and try to wash their feet.'

It was this Anglo-Catholic inspiration which led Maurice
Reckitt to try to create a Christian sociology through what
came to be called the Christendom Group. More spectacu-
larly, it led to the extremes of a radical priest, Conrad
Noel, to profess a kind of Christian communism. He was
vicar of the beautiful Essex village of Thaxted from 1910 to
1942, and it was a delight to make the short journey from
Cambridge for the Sunday Mass celebrated according to the
Sarum rite. Here amid the plain-song and country dancing,
Catholic socialism was preached. This involved class war
and a united Ireland. On St George's day in this village
three flags could be seen flying from the church tower,
that of St George in the centre, and on either side, the
Red Flag and that of Sinn Fein!

As Hastings has noted of the 1920s, 'Remove the Anglo-
Catholic inspiration and very little indeed would be left of
Christian social endeavour in this period'.[5] Less eccentric,
though, was Maurice Reckitt's Christendom group, which
organised each summer the Anglo-Catholic school of soci-
ology, and attracted both famous writers like T.S. Eliot,
Charles Williams, and Dorothy L. Sayers, and new ones,
P.T. Widdrington, Langmead Casserley, G.B. Bentley,
Patrick McLaughlin, David Peck, Herbert Rees and Eric
Mascall. The last named has left us in his autobiography,
Saraband, an interesting picture of the group of which he
was a member. He himself, early in his career, had accepted
Widdrington's views that Christian sociology ought not to
take its principles from secular sources, but from Christian
dogma and experience. The battle for a Christian social
order must begin in the realm of faith and thought. Fr

Mascall was to become one of the leading Catholic writers in the years after the Second World War, and with great wit and acumen was able to see through the vagaries of modern theology. He has made notable contributions to dogmatic theology, Christology, ecumenism and other subjects. His book, *Theology and the Gospel of Christ* (1977), was an attack on the negative and destructive attitude of many New Testament scholars and the widespread denial of the deity of Christ.

One of his earlier works, *Man: His Origin and Destiny*, written for the Signpost series at the beginning of the second war, showed the developing interests of the Christendom group.[6] The State, under men like Lloyd George, had initiated a welfare state, but now the problem seemed to be the materialism of the age. Mascall argued that there were four orders of being: God, Man, Things, Money, and that each exists for the one before: Man for the glory of God, Things for the good of Man, Money for the production and distribution of Things. However, he argued, with man's modern repudiation of the supremacy of God, the whole scheme had not only lost its first member, but had gone entirely in reverse. Things are for the production of Money; Man is for the production and consumption of Things; and a very hypothetical God is for the convenience of Man. The chart:

GOD	had become	MONEY
MAN		THINGS
THINGS		MAN
MONEY		GOD

Such were the concerns which occupied the minds of this Anglo-Catholic group at the outbreak of the Second World War. In 1941, when the home front was enduring its fiercest trial in the blitz, they published a booklet, *An Introduction to Christian Social Doctrine*, in which subjects such as wealth, finance, labour, government, the family, and education were discussed. Contributors were Ruth Kenyon, Langmead Casserley, W.G. Peck, E.L. Mascall and C.E. Hudson. At the end of each chapter there were questions for discussion, with Service chaplains in mind, no doubt, as well as parish priests. Certainly I remember using it in the Army in Padre's hours, but the religious needs of the average soldier were far more basic.

After the war there was a different social scene as the welfare state came into being, yet the problems of society seemed to increase rather than get fewer. Anglo-Catholics did their best to meet the new challenges, and the minutes of the different Church Union committees and councils record how thoroughly problems such as housing, drugs, marriage and education were discussed. After the second Loughborough Conference in 1983, a committee for social concern was set up and Fr George Nairn-Briggs became its leading light. A more radical approach has been led by Fr Kenneth Leech, with his Jubilee group. So it can be said that from the early beginnings of the Tractarian movement up to the present day, Catholics from the margins of their Church have been active in caring for the bodies as well as the souls of their people. They have provided in full measure the hands and the feet, the voices and the brains of Christ's Body among the underprivileged and needy of our nation.

What have they achieved for the life of this country? It is difficult to say how much influence they had in moulding the British social conscience. As we have seen, there were other churchmen and churchwomen who were at work in this field. Perhaps it is worth saying again that whereas in the early days Evangelicals worked *for* the poor, Catholics worked *with* the poor. As Hastings has shown, it was the Anglo-Catholics who made the running in the years between the wars, and this could quietly have infiltrated into the political parties, especially the growing Labour party. Perhaps their greatest contribution has been to draw attention to the value of each human being in the sight of God. The fact that God has taken our nature so that we might be taken into his, warns that we should never take lightly the worth of even our most deprived fellow citizen. As the Church is a sign to the world that God has visited his world in the person of Jesus Christ, so the Anglo-Catholic sociologists kept alive the responsibilities which this item of faith involved for every human being.

References

1. H.A. Wilson *The Other Half* p.42 (Knott)
2. Lloyd. *Church of England* 1900–65 pp.313 seq
3. Bowen *Ideal of the Victorian Church* pp.261 seq (McGill 1968)
4. Wilkinson: *Community of the Resurrection* pp.19 seq (SCM 1992)
5. Hastings p.174
6. Mascall *Saraband* pp.190 seq (Gracewing 1992) pp190 seq

Chapter Ten

Picking up the Pieces

The enemy has laid waste the whole of the sanctuary.
Your foes have made uproar in your house of prayer
O God, they have set your sanctuary on fire:
they have razed and profaned the place where you dwell.

In these words of the Psalmist is described the state of many churches after six years of a war which ended in 1945. A further Congress had been planned for 1940, but by then the country had been at war for a year and was beginning to fight for its life. London and its suburbs were under attack from the air daily, as indeed were other cities. The enemy had no respect for religion, and congregations had to watch while their parish churches were damaged or totally destroyed. Since the docks of the city of London were especially targeted, churches where ritualist priests had toiled in earlier years suffered badly. St Alban's, Holborn, for example, was destroyed. Hastings quotes from a curate's wife who with her husband had endured endless air raids in a parish near the Elephant and Castle. In 1941 she wrote after their church was hit; 'the beams blazing furiously and then falling one by one, until the Altar caught alight and seemed to fold up and die before our eyes. The church burned with white hot flames. It was a dreadful sight and though we tried hard in the beginning to get the fire under control, we failed hopelessly. The windows had gone, the wind changed its direction and fanned the flames to even greater heights. We could hear the cries of the pigeons in the tower, but we found it impossible

122

to reach them. The Great Bells fell . . .'[1] She speaks for other church people who were forced to witness similar spectacles. Yet the clergy ministered no less devotedly and found all kinds of niches in which to say Mass daily. My parish in south-east London was on the bombers' path, and I shall never forget their first raid when, like huge ugly black birds, they flew in and created havoc to the north of us. Life then became disorganised for all had to take cover when the many alarms sounded. Yet our church routine continued and I can remember walking to my church early in the morning to say Mass and finding a congregation unfailingly present. In the end that church, too, was wiped out by a landmine. In such conditions old feuds of churchmanship were forgotten.

While this bombing was going on in London the comparatively new bishop, Geoffrey Fisher, was trying to bring some order of worship to Anglo-Catholic churches. The much-loved Arthur Winnington-Ingram had been bishop there for thirty-eight years and had mostly allowed Catholics to go their own way in liturgical matters. As a result there was a great variety of interpretation of the Book of Common Prayer, if it was used at all. In his biography of Geoffrey Fisher, Edward Carpenter notes that although the Catholic clergy cooperated well with their new bishop in most matters yet 'in matters relating to doctrine and worship "they were a fortress inside which no Bishop was able to enter'."[2] Liturgical individualism often meant eclectic congregations and these were very difficult to bring to order. Fisher had meetings with High Church clergymen which included Dom Bernard Clements of All Saints', Margaret Street and Father Gage-Brown of St Cuthbert's, Philbeach Gardens in an attempt to get some agreement about deviations from the Prayer Book. Carpenter describes one such contact. 'In 1944 he (Fisher) followed this up by responding to an invitation from Prebendary Merritt to have dinner with a few members of the Federation of Catholic Priests, an extreme Anglo-Catholic group. His account of this meeting, recalled years after and therefore subject to this limitation, is in many ways revealing. He was first introduced, so he relates, into "a vast array of drink" which, being a near-teetotaller, did not initially put him at his ease, particularly since he tended to think of AngloCatholics as rigid in their beliefs but luxurious in their living. However, undeterred, he prepared after dinner to secure a "breakthrough" and to make a working agreement with his hosts. However, just as they were beginning to get down to business, news came through on the radio that the fateful invasion of Europe had begun. All agreed immediately that they could not continue their deliberations, and as the Bishop comments, "at that dramatic moment one hope of mine was extinguished and the great hope of a Nation came to life". This, of course, was no time to put a foot down about obedience to the Prayer Book, for parish priests had enough problems to keep church life going without changing the worshipping habits of the faithful. Not long afterwards Fisher went to Canterbury, leaving a line of successors to deal with such an intractable situation. However, it is interesting to have this cameo of Catholic church life in embattled London.

This war was different from previous ones for both the military and civilians were in the front line. I must admit that sometimes it was safer to be in uniform than out of it. As I said in my introduction, I was quickly removed from my High Church practices in a parish and put down in the thoroughly Protestant army chaplains' department. This had been purged of 'undesirable' Catholic elements by Bishop Taylor Smith, the Chaplain General in the former war, and had been left mostly with a parade service which took the form of what was irreverently called 'mangled Matins'. The Assistant Chaplain General (South Eastern Command) who accepted me in 1941 gave me fatherly advice. He said he had once had Anglo-Catholic learnings but thanked God he had resisted the temptation. 'No place in the Army for things like that', he said. Indeed there was not, as I found out but I did manage to make the most of the celebrations of Holy Communion which occasionally were celebrated, albeit in surplice and stole. So I had to declare a moratorium on my former marginal way of life.

Too late I discovered it was better in the other two Services, and that the Navy could be positively Catholic. However, there was an attempt made to teach soldiers the Christian Faith. At General Montgomery's insistence a weekly instruction period, called the Padre's Hour, was compulsory for every Army unit. This sounded well on paper but in reality soldiers generally were in no mood to have more religion thrust upon them; the Sunday church parade was quite enough. The chaplain had to be both thick-skinned and expert in apologetics to make anything of this opportunity, and I was neither. I still have a nightmare where I am standing in front of a room full of barracking soldiers with whom, strangely enough, I got on well for the rest of the week. I even played rugger for them.

All this I survived, together with being bombed in a parish and shot at on the battle field, and with the rest of my fellow citizens finally emerged into the postwar world.

Looking back I can see that the whole nation went through a sort of recycling experience in the war. If this had been fuelled by Christian faith and practice or by the sound Catholic doctrine set out in the Anglo-Catholic booklets after the 1923 Congress, maybe postwar rebuilding might have been easier, but, as Chesterton said at the 1920 Congress, scepticism had done its worst and made a dreadful mess of the country. By 1939 this scepticism had been further deepened by so-called 'Intellectuals', as Paul Johnson calls them, like Marx, Bertrand Russell, Hemingway, Brecht and others. The British (and others) were in no fit state to fight a Christian war and so they were unable to create a Christian nation afterwards. From the mid-thirties to the late forties there was still a need for religious faith but few could find it in the institutional Church. More insidiously there had been a loss of absolute values as C.S. Lewis shows in his essay, *The Abolition of Man*. 'Certain things, if not seen as lovely or detestable, are not correctly seen at all', he wrote (in a Preface to *Paradise Lost*). All this was not helpful for a Church which tried to teach about holiness and the demands of God. Where was sin if there was no yardstick by which to measure it? All this made the task of a Church in an exhausted country all the harder, and it is true to say that it has never solved the problem of getting to grips with unbelief and apathy. Christianity is revelation, said Newman, and undoubtedly this is the answer, but as we shall see, later scholars did much to weaken the authority of the Gospels which has always been the main instrument of evangelism.

This analysis is all very well in hindsight. In 1945, however, people everywhere were intent to pick up the pieces and try to return to a normal life. Life was made more trying because rationing continued and became even more stringent. Anglo-Catholics were keen to continue where they had left off before the war. They were in a strong position as they could now count on several diocesan bishops to support them, men like Kenneth Kirk of Oxford, Edward Wynn of Ely, William Wand of London, and Noel Hudson of Newcastle. The new Archbishop of Canterbury was Geoffrey Fisher who was to rule his Church like the headmaster he had once been. Nobody could number him among the Catholics, but he did not bear down too heavily upon them, and probably treated them like schoolboys who had tiresome habits.

Chaplains came back from the war having learnt much about human nature, not least that it was not necessarily open on the Godward side. In many parishes curates had been holding the fort while their vicar was away, and now had to adjust to a new situation. There were churches to be rebuilt or repaired and for a time there was some kind of religious revival. The Church of England creaked back into action, trusting in part to a report *Towards the Conversion of England*. An expensive propaganda campaign petered out, however, and as Hastings puts it, 'It could do little about the state of the nation and not much more about itself, being short of both money and men.' The postwar years were far from glorious; winters were cold and wet, food was scarce, clothes were still utility, and petrol was strictly rationed for those lucky enough to own a car.

Some of the younger chaplains, convinced that the Church should make drastic changes and seeing this was not going to happen, went into the different chaplaincies which were increasingly being created. I was one of those, not because I was disillusioned with the status quo, but because this was the only job offered and because I had seen enough of ignorance about religious matters in the Army to realise that sound teaching was a vital requirement for the Church of the future. You might say that the second part of my apprenticeship now started, because I was immediately thrown into the deep end of academic teaching. I found myself not only chaplain of an old public school but senior classics master as well. As in most public schools religion was simple – surplice and stole and a plain Communion service – but it was possible to develop a daily Mass and also teach Confession. All this was far from the full Anglo-Catholic worship in which I had been brought up, but gave me professional experience in the classroom. I had quickly to develop this if my Latin and Greek pupils were to be prepared for further education. Later I was able to apply this professionalism to the teaching of religious studies. I have never thought that this subject should get worse treatment than other departments. In time I came to realise that I was almost alone in this opinion, but Hastings makes this comment:'The unecclesiastical half of the nation was now being educated as never before. The Church's greatest avoidable failure in these years was probably in the field of catechetics, in not pioneering a new style of religious teaching in State schools to make up for the great diminishment in Church schools, and to keep pace with new educational approaches in other subjects. There were plenty of able theologians in the Church in the 1950s but they were mostly too academic to get down to such tasks as this.'[3] I reserve judgment on 'new educational approaches', but when I went took over at the Church Union in 1966 I found there was concern about the gap between the pew and the scholars. Personally I have always felt that my liturgical impoverishment was a price worth paying for professional teaching experience. It certainly paid off in the later stages of my career when people were crying out for sound teaching. A feature of pre-war Anglo-Catholicism had been excellent instruction in the parishes, illustrated by manuals of the time. This was steadily lost after the war and the Catholic movement suffered accordingly. A main requirement for a good teacher is that he should have the right material but, as we shall see later, the authority of the Church's basic documents, the Gospel, was being steadily eroded by the speculations of Biblical scholars.

I said earlier that the war was like a recycling exercise for the country, and this was also true for many church men and women. Within six years of the 1933 Centenary Anglo-Catholic Congress, many of the younger generation who had gathered at the White City were called up into the three services and found that the religious facilities were very different from the weekly Sung Mass of their parish church. On Sunday mornings in the Army, for example, another kind of cermonial took place where immaculate uniform was more de rigeur than the well-starched cotta and clean shoes which Father Jones insisted on at St Mary's. Early Communion might be celebrated but it was a brave man who could leave the barrack room cleaning to others. It also meant that there was less time for the spit and polish which service life required. For there was a Sunday parade and inspection and finally the compulsory church service. The chaplain then at last came into his own and often preached at some length. The sight of so many men in church can easily go to the head of all but the most experienced clergyman and give him a too optimistic idea of his pulpit ability. After one such sermon given by a very senior Army chaplain, I heard one officer say to another that it was like a plane flying in fog and looking for a place to land! All this despite the warning given to us at the chaplains' training school when the cautionary tale was told of a commanding officer who put a pile of half crowns on the ledge of the pew and during the sermon removed one for every five minutes over fifteen.

All this was strange and upsetting for devout churchmen and some took evasive action by declaring themselves Roman Catholics. On one occasion at a training camp I was called in by a puzzled sergeant to deal with a new entry who had registered himself as an Anglo-Catholic. After explaining that I was one myself, I persuaded the recruit that he was basically C of E. I added that I said Mass regularly early in the morning and his support would be a great help. Even in wartime fasting Communion was still expected of Anglo-Catholics and strangely the Army made arrangements for late breakfasts for any who attended the early service. These were not many. I had to perform great fasting feats to preserve my rule, and often celebrated Holy Communion three or four times before my first meal of the day. By the end of Sunday morning I was quite exhausted. The Roman Catholic

Church allowed evening Masses during the war but Catholics in the Church of England found it difficult to take this step. This might seem strange fifty years later but we had all been brought up with a fear of evening Communion and with a commitment to a fast from midnight.

Church life could be far different in the Navy as I was to discover later in my life. Here the wearing of vestments was normal and although there were still parade services to contend with, regular celebrations of Holy Communion by the chaplain were expected. As I read again my old friend Colin Stephenson's hilarious book, *Merrily on High*, I am consumed with envy at what he was able to do in the wartime Navy. He and I had finished our training at Chichester together, and there were already signs then that he would be no ordinary Catholic priest. This came true, for in the 1950s he became Administrator of the Shrine of Our Lady of Walsingham. But during the war he became a naval chaplain and managed to fill all his ships with that warm, humorous Catholicism which was uniquely his. He talks of Sung Mass in the Royal Marine Barracks at Eastney and the chapel of a cruiser fitted out with a proper altar, a Tabernacle and even a shrine of Our Lady of Perpetual Succour. The first two were fully used, even for Benediction! Happy the Anglo-Catholic sailor who found himself in such a ship!

However, generally speaking to be a Catholic Anglican in the armed forces was to be doubly marginal, and some found this an impossible situation. In many cases men were without any ministrations at all, for our forces were far flung; and our chaplains could not be everywhere. I have no doubt that we lost a considerable number of faithful laity during these war years. They discovered they could get on without the Church and never returned to it. It was a pity that more Catholic priests did not go into the forces and make the best of a bad job. After all they had a tradition of working in impossible situations in the slums and no doubt would have found a way round the exigencies of Service life. But these men mostly stayed in their parishes where they were desperately needed, and who can say they faced less danger in blitzed towns and cities than did their colleagues in uniform?

It was a long way from the high noon of Anglo-Catholicism between the wars, and those days never returned. This is not to say that this way of life was finished; it had to be worked out in a fresh style. The writing was on the wall, even while the 1933 Congress was taking place, because new insights about Eucharistic worship were infiltrating into the Roman Church, at least abroad. In Germany priests were beginning to say Mass in the vernacular and to develop a more congregational worship. In addition there was no longer money to build large and elaborate churches and so simplicity became the order of the day. There was a return to the auditory church of Sir Christopher Wren, who had removed rood screens so that everybody could conveniently see and hear what was going on. There was a departure from the mediaeval ideas of worship where the faithful had to be silent spectators of the sacrifice of the Mass. Now the thing was to transform the faithful from 'silent onlookers to active participators in the offering' in the words of Pius XI. Individual worshippers were to join with the priest to form one community united by the sacrifice. Pius XII, the wartime Pope, was to give his support to the use of the vernacular in the liturgy. Later he regularised evening Masses and the relaxation of the fast before Communion. A Liturgical Movement had been steadily gaining momentum on the Continent, and this went further in suggesting that the Mass was as much a communion as a sacrifice. The war slowed down these developments but, with peace restored, they surfaced again, and finally found fruition at the Second Vatican Council in the 1960s. Experience in the war added further power to the changes because the Eucharist often had to be celebrated with informality bringing priest and congregation more closely together.

The Catholic wing of the Church of England was also involved in these changes. Father Hebert of Kelham wrote an influential book, *The Parish Communion*, before the war, and followed it with *Liturgy and Society* later. Yet the greatest work of scholarship on this subject was written by one of our Nashdom Benedictines, Dom Gregory Dix. This was *The Shape of the Liturgy*, published in 1943, which has remained an important reference book until the present day. In view of later liturgical changes inside and outside the Roman Catholic Church it is worth taking a closer look at this contribution made by this Anglo-Catholic scholar. Dom Gregory went behind mediaeval and Reformation ideas of the Eucharist which had been concerned with the idea of sacrifice. He took a look at the Jewish background to the Lord's Supper and the early Christian Eucharist. He showed that there were four actions which form the nucleus of every eucharistic rite known to us from antiquity. These actions are: 1) The offertory: bread and wine are taken and placed on the table together; 2) The prayer: the president gives thanks to God over the bread and wine; 3) The fraction: breaking of the bread; 4) The Communion.

He then looked at the Jewish origins of Christian worship and showed how the synagogue service was eventually taken over by the early Church as the first part of the Eucharist. The thanksgiving ceremonies of the Jews provided the background for the Lord's Supper. Dom Gregory developed his thesis with reference to the early Christian liturgies. For this, the names of Justin Martyr and Hippolytus began to assume importance.

Dom Gregory had enough of the common touch to know that he was treading on very delicate ground in daring to re-examine a form of worship which had been firmly established in the Catholic Church. After mentioning the difficulties of the liturgical situation in Anglicanism of the time, he writes, 'Two years in a parish since war began have left me with an intense sympathy for the lay communicant and his parish priest in facing those difficulties which are not of their making. They have also left me with strong doubts as to whether any of the current proposals, official or otherwise, are based on a sufficiently searching analysis of what those difficulties really are or why they have come to be felt as difficulties.' He was referring to attempts to reform the Anglican Eucharist which had started before the war, and which had failed to gain approval by both High and Low Church wings.

Earlier he had written, 'In England there has been the additional handicap of a great lack of literature on the subject which can be covered by the useful French term *haute vulgarisation* – I mean books which will meet the needs of the thoughtful and educated Christian, cleric or layman, who is not and does not intend to become what he calls a "liturgiologist" but who is aware that ideas are stirring on the subject.'[4] For Anglo-Catholics the Mass which they could now follow in the English Missal, both altar and pocket editions, was like the law of the Medes and Persians and could not be changed. Little attention was given to the history of the liturgy in the training of a priest at theological college. I have kept the notes I was given at Chichester just before the war and see that under the section of Worship there was no mention of the themes developed in Dom Gregory's book. The idea of the Mass as a sacrifice, with Communion attached, governed the Sunday churchgoing of the average Catholic in the Anglican Church and he went to church to offer the great sacrifice of the altar without necessarily receiving Communion. Indeed, at a late morning High Mass, this was almost impossible for all but the celebrant and the sick and aged, because fasting from midnight was de rigeur. If you wanted Communion, you had to go to an early Mass. My family certainly, most Sundays of the year went to 8 am Low Mass and then returned for the 11.30 am High Mass. This was not an unusual practice. Parish Communion at 9.30 am, however, was becoming popular in many quite moderate Anglican parishes but this was often rejected by the more extreme churchmen for lacking theology and sound teaching. Yet, there was an increased interest in Eucharistic worship and this was due in great measure to the success of the marginal Catholics.

Development of thought about the Eucharist had been taking place on the Continent for some years, as we mentioned, but Dom Gregory was the first to carry them on in depth into the Church of England. At the same time a Jesuit, Joseph Jungmann, was working on a book, *Solemnia Missae*, even more thoroughly, as might have been expected of a German scholar. This book was published in 1949 and appeared in England in translation the next year. It was to be a text book for the liturgical reforms of Vatican II in the mid-1960s.[5] I had developed an interest in liturgy and was very excited by both Dix's and Jungmann's books. As

we shall see this interest was to be a great help to me ten
years or more later when I had to explain changes to
Church Union audiences around the country.

Although ideas like these were rumbling on below the
surface of church life, few of the clergy or laity were conscious
of the revolution to come later. Perhaps this was as well,
because they had enough problems to face in trying to get the
Church back to normal. Meanwhile books like *Heavenward
Bound*, a child's manual of Catholic instruction, by Father
Branscombe of St James' Wednesbury, reminded the young
that 'going to Mass is like being at the Cross on Calvary
and that there are four reasons for being there:

To praise and worship God,
To thank him for all his blessings;
To ask forgiveness for all our sins;
To ask blessings on our friends living and dead and on
ourselves.'[6]

It is only fair to say that there is a section on Holy
Communion, but this stands on its own.

The liturgical revolution was still in the future, but there
was another kind of crisis at hand which Anglo-Catholics
had to face. This was a church union scheme which had
begun before the war in South India and was due to be
officially inaugurated in 1947. For the economy of man-
power, it had been proposed that the Anglican Church,
the Methodist Church, together with the South India
United Church (composed largely of Presbyterians and
Congregationalists), should unite and become a Church
of South India. Episcopacy had been accepted as a part of
the scheme but this would come into operation only for
those ordained after the union. This meant that for thirty
years or so there would be an interim period when there
would be anomalies within the Church because there would
be a number of ministers who had not been ordained by a
bishop and yet were accepted as if they had been.

The question was whether the Anglican Communion as
a whole would allow these non-episcopally ordained men
to minister generally in its midst when, for example, these
men came home on leave or retired altogether. The Lambeth

Conference of 1930 had noted that the United Church would
not be a province of the Anglican Communion, and, although
there would be an internal intercommunion, for a time this
would be limited by the rules of those Churches. The signs
were that churchmen in England would not be too bothered
by the problem. India was a long way from their doorstep
and there were more pressing matters at home. The new
Archbishop of Canterbury, Geoffrey Fisher, was known
to be keen for some measures of reunion, and in 1946 in
Cambridge had asked the Non-Conformist Churches to take
episcopacy into their system and grow together, although
slowly. The moment for decision about South India was
now at hand because inauguration was due in 1947. The
next Lambeth Conference which was due to meet in 1948
would undoubtedly debate the matter.

Catholics in the Anglican Church had long been uneasy
about the proposals for unity, and, as the day approached,
began to make firm protests. The spearhead of this action
came from some of the religious communities especially those
who had houses in India, such as the Cowley Fathers and the
Community of the Epiphany. Pressure came also from an
Annunciation Group and soon there was a strong campaign
against the acceptance of these non-episcopally ordained
ministers within the Church of England. Opposition was
the stronger because the diocese of Dornakal with 30,000
Anglicans held out against the union. This formally took
place in Madras in September 1947.

There were other moves for the reunion of churches
afoot and some theologians put the Anglo-Catholic view
in a considerable book of essays, *The Apostolic Ministry*,
published in 1946.[7] It has been the custom of some later
scholars to dismiss lightly the ideas expressed here, but
with men involved like Kenneth Kirk, Bishop of Oxford,
Austin Farrer, Gregory Dix, Lionel Thornton, it was clearly
a symposium of some importance. It sets out the conditions
for the reunion of churches, based on a sound doctrine of
episcopacy.

The foreword of this book anticipates criticism from
'a school of thought which denies that the traditional
doctrine (of the ministry) has any genuine warrant in

apostolic teaching and practice'. The first essay sets out
to investigate the problem. The Editor, Kenneth Kirk,
writes that schemes for Christian reunion over twenty-
five years had mostly agreed that a United Church should
normally be organised or administered on an episcopal basis
because episcopacy was the oldest or most widespread form
of ecclesiastical organisation. He warned that such a premise
led to the idea that the episcopate must be merely consti-
tutional, that there must be no hint of prelacy, and the
bishop must always be within the machine. His next words can
be seen today as prophetic: 'Indeed he may be so limited in
function that he will end up as a very unimportant cog indeed.
Everything which in modern Anglicanism for example is left
to his discretion may be put into commission and he may
degenerate into a mere executive drudge, carrying out the
decisions of innumerable committees.' He complained that
this rubber stamp theory of the bishop's office had already
gone far enough.

The task, then, for his fellow writers was to state
the view that 'the episcopate is the divinely ordained
ministerial instrument for securing to the Church of God
its continuous and organic unity, not a club of like-minded
worshippers or aspirants to holiness, but as a God-given city
of salvation'.

All this was in the Tractarian tradition coupled with a
balanced view of recent Bible scholarship. Austin Farrer
handled this subject and said that the great myth of
nineteenth century liberalism had been overthrown. 'The
religion of Jesus was not, on any evidence we possess,
a simple ethical piety in absolute degree.'[8] So with confidence in the authority of Holy Scripture, ministry in the
New Testament and in the early Church was traced, the
latter by Gregory Dix, whose knowledge of that period had
been also employed, as we have seen, in liturgical studies.
The later history of the episcopate was dealt with by experts,
and the book rounded off by Canon F.W. Green of Norwich
Cathedral. He applied the findings of the writers to current
schemes for reunion and warned that although union was
good, it does not necessarily result in unity. This he illustrated
with reference to the Church of England itself.

He continued that it would be a bad day for Christianity if valuable traditions in other churches were to become merely anglicanised by an acceptance of formal episcopacy. Indeed some of 'agreed syllabuses of reunion bore a family likeness not only to the present constitution of the Church of England but even to that of the British Commonwealth of Nations. This was unfortunate especially in India where that part of the Commonwealth was in process of division. Non-Conformists were afraid of a legalistic view of the ministry. He quoted one as saying that there was indeed an apostolic succession in the fellowship and in its ministry but it was a succession guaranteed by the Word and sacraments, not guaranteeing them. The purpose of these essays, *The Apostolic Ministry*, was to try to clear the air and show the better side of episcopacy. A question of that time was, Is episcopacy of the esse or bene esse of the Church? Was it an essential part of the Church or did merely help to its well-being? There is no doubt that these essayists backed the former view. Almost the final words of the book summed up that moment of truth which all reunion schemes with Non-Conformists would have to answer. Is the Church regarded merely, geographically, as a province or, politically, as a voluntary society, an association based on a Scriptural and historical model, or is it a wonderful and sacred mystery, a life carrying its own law of development with it?

Confidence in the reliability of the Scriptures underlay the high doctrine of episcopacy which is the main theme of these essays. Although Austin Farrer could say that the liberalism of the nineteenth century had been overthrown, a new kind of radical Biblical criticism was at hand which threatened traditional ideas of the ministry and indeed the whole Christian kerugma or proclamation. It is therefore not surprising that a later generation has relegated these essays to a remote library shelf.

Since we are now returning to sanity in our understanding of the New Testament, this work of Anglo-Catholic scholars could bear a re-reading.

I have spent time on this book because I have no doubt that it spoke so strongly that the Lambeth Conference of 1948 had to take its views seriously, especially since they were pointed firmly in the direction of the South India scheme. It says much for the power of Anglo-Catholicism of the time, as Hastings indicates, that Lambeth did not dare commit itself to full recognition of this newly united Church but 'weathered the storm by sticking pretty closely to its tradition of episcopal ordination'.[9] Fisher, who had wished to go further, contented himself by firing a broadside against the Roman Catholic Church, denouncing it as perhaps the greatest hindrance to the advance of the Kingdom of God among men. This upset some Anglicans like Hugh Ross Williamson and Walton Hannah who joined this denounced Church.

However, Catholics in the Anglican Church were able to hold their first Congress after the war with heads held high. This was held in the early summer of 1948 and, despite the fact that congregations were struggling to return to normal life, clergy were overworked, and some famous shrines had been destroyed, it was a great success and 13,000 members enrolled. The Royal Albert Hall was not available but Methodists overcame their principles by allowing the Central Hall Westminster to be used. The Church Union had now taken over the organisation and its secretary, Father Harold Riley, was in charge. The subject was, What do we mean by the Church? The substance of the talks owed much to the book, *The Apostolic Ministry*. The editor of that work, the Bishop of Oxford, was President of the Congress and he was joined by other diocesans, among them Ely and Newcastle. The Bishop of London, William Wand, was a good Catholic and was a power behind the Congress. Gregory Dix spoke on the ministry and, a new face, Eric Mascall, spoke on the Church. There was no shortage of great teachers in those days, T.S. Eliot, Dorothy Sayers and C.S. Lewis, to mention a few, and there was much to encourage the Catholics in the margins. It might be thought that they had put the bad times behind them, yet more battles were awaiting them.

References

1. Hastings p.384
2. Carpenter: *Geoffrey Fisher* p.118 (Canterbury press 1991)
3. Hastings p.438

4. Dacre Press p.xvii
5. Mass of Roman Rite (New York 1951 655)
6. Pax House 1941
7. Hodder and Stoughton
8. Op. cit. p.116
9. Hastings p.467.

Chapter Eleven

The Last of the
Good Old Days

Despite subterranean liturgical rumblings, it was business as usual in the Roman Catholic Church, notes Hastings in his survey of the Churches in England from 1920 to the present day. The partial lowering of the barriers between Rome and Canterbury in this country by Cardinal Hinsley, with his Sword of the Spirit movement in the war years, came to an end with his death in 1943. After that it was back to the old routine. Roman Catholics lapsed into splendid isolation under Archbishops of Westminster like Griffin and Godfrey who virtually ignored the Church of England as a 'well-meaning old dodderer'. We sometimes talk about Anglican bishops having the same old school or university tie but this was also true of Roman Catholic authority in England in the postwar years. Godfrey had been Rector of the English College in Rome, the Venerabile, and he gathered round him men like Griffin, Masterson, Heenan, Grimshaw, and Dwyer, and other bishops who made certain that nobody rocked the ultramontane boat in Britain. This elite, Hastings notes, had existed in a world of their own in the middle of Rome, and had fenced themselves in with a penchant for Christmas theatricals and cricket in the summer, a dislike for Continental theology, a disdain for Anglicans, and a failure to learn the Italian language. Such insularity they transported in time to this country. Godfrey's time at Westminster has been labelled as the 'safe period', and certainly Roman Catholicism marked time while he was in command.[1]

139

This lack of movement suited those Anglo-Catholics who from time to time looked respectfully over the fence to make certain they were doing the right things at the altar. Some were members of the Catholic League, for instance, founded in 1913 and for many years ruled somewhat autocratically by Father Fynes-Clinton until his death in 1958. To see 'old Fynes' as he was affectionately called, herding the faithful with his handbell round the grounds of Otford Court in Kent during the annual Corpus Christi procession of the Blessed Sacrament, was a sight not easily forgotten. I can remember seeing it as early as the mid-1920s. The Catholic League came into being as a pressure group for unity with Rome and pressed as closely as possible round the barriers which kept non-Romans out. In 1958 the League sent warm messages of support to the Holy Father, John XXIII, when he announced his Ecumenical Council, but later found the spirit and teachings of Vatican II difficult to digest, as a short history of the League notes.[2]

The Catholic League was typical of organisations which breathed down the neck of the more respectable Church Union when they thought it was not going fast enough. Later we shall see this repeated in the affair of the Anglican/Methodist Reunion scheme. It is easy to criticise the so-called papalists in the Anglican Church. I was once called a 'pup fouling my own nest' when I was President of the Cambridge Reunion Society before the war because we were only concerned with reunion with Rome. Some however were desperate, and still are, for some kind of authority in our church life. Looking to one's own diocesan can be a very uncertain business because, although he might be sound — Truro and London have been very fortunate in Graham Leonard in recent years and there have been similar bishops in the past — yet he might be plucked away and replaced with somebody not so good. Even good Catholic bishops can be disappointing when elevated to the purple. Rome, therefore, has provided a focal point of authority for those it would by no means acknowledge as Catholics. With all their faults and illogicalities, Anglo-Catholics have always been uneasy with unsupported individualism.

I spent all the Fifties very much in the margins not only of the Church but of the world, because I became a naval chaplain. As I shall show, this gave me a glimpse of the Church beyond our shores, but it also showed me what was going on in Britain, for I served in shore establishments in Chatham, Scotland, East Anglia, Yorkshire, and finally Cornwall. It seemed to me that churches had returned to normal and were ticking on as they had done before Hitler struck. This view is confirmed in Paul Welsby's, *A History of the Church of England 1945–1980*. I can do no better than quote from his summing up of the Fifties. 'By 1959 the Church of England had changed comparatively little since the end of the war. It is true that moderate alterations had been made in the parochial system and that heroic efforts had been made to cope with the needs of new housing areas, the repair of war damage, the demands of the Education Act and the financial problems of the clergy, but in many ways it was a Church sailing on an even keel, content with the old tried ways and the conventional orthodoxies. There was an atmosphere of complacency and an apparent unawareness of trends already present which were to burst to the surface in the sixties. For the majority of churchmen Christian theology was an assured package of unalterable truth and Christian ethics unchallengeable. Services in most parish churches were much as they had been for a century. Bishops, deans and archdeacons dressed, as they had done for centuries, in apron and gaiters — an apt symbol of an old order which was soon to change as the Church in the sixties was to encounter challenges from all sides.'[3] In this state of affairs Catholics went forward and were confident enough to plan another Congress in 1958, the time of another Lambeth Conference.

This year, in fact, was the centenary of the Church Union and suitably enough members returned to the Royal Albert Hall for all the functions except the opening Evensong on 1 July. This was sung in Westminster Abbey and was attended by Princess Margaret. William Wand was no longer Bishop of London but had been succeeded by another friend of the Catholic Movement, Henry Montgomery Campbell, a noted wit. He and the President of the Church Union, the

Master of Lauderdale, the Hon Patrick Maitland MP, called Catholics to support enthusiastically the programme whose bold theme was The World for God. The sermon in the Abbey was preached by Father Hugh Bishop, CR who had been in a prisoner of war camp in Italy. He insisted that man has to have a faith to live by. As in former Congresses there was a galaxy of speakers including the Archbishop of York, Michael Ramsey, Austin Farrer, Eric Abbott, the Bishop of Llandaff, Tom Driberg and others. The Congress was organised by Father Fr F.P. (Percy) Coleman, the Secretary of the Church Union who eight years later was to become my colleague.

Each day, words from the action of the Eucharist were used as titles, He took, He blessed, He gave. Dom Gregory Dix would have been very much at home with these subjects but he had died at an early age in 1952. However, another liturgical expert, Father E.C. Ratcliff spoke about principles governing liturgical reform.[4]

As I read through Professor Ratcliff's lecture (for it was that) I realise what a good preparation he gave to Catholics for the changes which were necessary to bring the Church back to something like primitive practice. He brought before his audience names like Dix and Jungmann whom we met in the last chapter. Few would have heard of the latter, and few would have known the implications of the work of the former, for he tried to tread delicately in suggesting reforms. Michael Ramsey in the first address had spoken about the Parish Communion movement and had warned about its dangers. He saw that it could easily become man-centred and not God-directed, if the doctrine of the offering of the one sacrifice of Christ was not emphasised. Ratcliff took up this point of the Parish Communion and said that the liturgy provided by the Prayer Book Communion Service was unsatisfactory. He showed that the framework or shape of this Eucharist was wrong because it was not based on the two distinct services of the early Church, the synagogue worship and the Thanksgiving meal of the Lord's Supper. For example, the Prayer for the Church Militant or intercession had been wrongly placed after the offertory. The first part of the service should be instruction and prayer and the second part thanksgiving and homage offered to God for his mighty acts recorded in the Scriptures. For this latter the Deuteronomic command, Thou shalt not appear before the Lord they God empty, was all-important. The Christian should come before God with the sacrifice of the Lord.

Professor Ratcliff then made suggestions for the reform of the liturgy, but one wonders what impact it made on an audience for whom the Mass was untouchable. Photos of the Congress High Mass in the Albert Hall show a vast congregation taking part in a traditional High Mass centred on a traditional altar, and few would have wanted it different.

The Congress ended with a pageant, the World for God, and photos suitably show actors and actresses of many nations taking part. The verse for the four choruses of this pageant were written by my old Classics tutor, Arthur Peck, who employed that poetic talent which so far he had saved for his Christmas greetings. 'I have seen the fossilised relics of organised religion' he put into the mouths of the Second Chorus. This was a critical spirit which surprised his friends but seemed to fit in with Father Ratcliff's recommendations. The future looked promising for those who wanted the world for God but practical suggestions about how this could be achieved were few. They could well have taken a look at a movement within the Roman Catholic Church which was gaining strength. This was the post-war expansion of the lay apostolate movement which included Joseph Cardijn's Young Christian Workers and, also, Young Christian Students. The strategy used in this was to train keen laymen and send them back into their daily work to convert their fellows. This was done at the expense of suspicion from the official Church but as we shall see it was given a great boost at the Second Vatican Council.

Yet another Congress therefore, ended with fine sentiments but with few ideas. No doubt many would have gone from there on pilgrimage to Walsingham where the Shrine of Our Lady was attracting more and more tourists, sacred and profane. Here at least they had an advantage over their Roman pilgrims who had only the old Slipper Chapel as their destination. Anglicans between the wars had staked out their claim on the original site and well. This was due to Father

Hope Patten who patiently had rebuilt the old ruins. On this foundation Colin Stephenson established the Shrine as a popular place of pilgrimage.

As Geoffrey Rowell has shown in his admirable book on the Catholic Revival in Anglicanism, *The Vision Glorious*, issues which were being fought over at home were transported into the mission field, especially the ministry.[5] The Church of England had followed the flag into the far corners of the earth. It had been in India since the seventeenth century under the auspices of the East India Company and, as the British Empire expanded, so did Anglican foreign missions. By 1837 there were eight bishops in British overseas territories: Calcutta, Bombay, Jamaica, and Barbardos in the West Indies, and Australia. Soon there would be an increase in Africa, New Zealand, the Western Pacific and elsewhere. This posed two main problems. Were bishops essential to the life of the Church in those parts or were they just useful for the administration of Christian activity? We have seen that in the nineteenth century neither State nor Church seemed to have a high idea of their spiritual value and that it was a task of the Tractarians to raise episcopal morale. Even in 1842 when bishops had reacted badly to Tract XC, Newman could urge obedience to the bishops as standing in the apostolic succession, 'like de facto rulers being of the blood royal'. This however was not the line taken by the Church of England generally. A second problem was involved, Who was to control these missionary bishops? Would the long arm of the Crown reach out and keep them under its authority? This clearly was not possible in days when the line of communication was stretched to its very limit. There was the prospect of bishops and priests being able to operate outside the Establishment and this must have been attractive to those brought up under Tractarian influence. We have seen how at least two of the revived religious orders started with priests who had intended to work overseas.

Once the principle that bishops were of the esse of the Church was established, then that had to be the form of government wherever the Anglican Church was planted. Even Bishop Wilberforce could state bluntly: 'The great object, I am sure, which we ought now to aim at in our missionary exertions is to give them a much more distinct Church character than we have done – to send out the Church and not merely instructions about religion. This is the way in which in primitive times the world was converted, and if episcopacy, a native clergy, a visible communion, the due administration of the sacraments, Confirmation etc, etc – if these things be really important, then how can we expect full success until we send out missionary bishops, i.e. bishops and a visible Church?' To these sentiments the Tractarian Fathers would have said Amen. A missionary bishop was one sent out by the Church, not one to complete an organisation. He was a leader and not a follower.

This could be said to be another result of Anglo-Catholic activity and it paved the way for flourishing Anglican dioceses abroad. These quickly organised themselves into their own forms of church government, something not possible in England. Churchmanship, of course, played a part because there were Low Church and High Church missionary societies. The CMS, or Church Missionary Society, was Evangelical, and the SPG, Society for Propagation of the Gospel, was Catholic, to be joined later by the UMCA, or Universities' Mission to Central Africa. These Catholic missionary dioceses and provinces provided bishops in plenty for the different Congresses when diocesans at home were shy at attending, but few in the audiences, I imagine, would have understood fully how this too was a triumph for marginal Catholics at home.

To my shame I knew nothing about this background when in 1936 I went on a college mission to Portsmouth with other ordinands. The object was to give us a first experience in preaching and for this we were given the subject of foreign missions. I chose the UMCA as being a safe Catholic missionary society, although I had scarcely left home shores in my young life. With help from books and from notes sent by UMCA I was able to make a contribution. In 1949 I found myself destined for the Indian Ocean in what we in the Navy call the grey funnel line. This was my first sea commission since I joined the Navy, and I joined HMS *Mauritius* with some trepidation because I was not a good sailor. I could write much about the trials of living on board while the ship was still in dockyard hands, but will merely mention the joy of finding my own small chapel up for'ard near the bridge. It was all beautifully fitted out and even had an aumbry for Reservation. The first task was to fill this chapel. This is somewhat of a lottery in Service life for it depends on how many keen churchmen are caught up in a particular draft. As I looked over the side on commissioning day and saw 800 sailors waiting to swarm on board I wondered how many would find their way to the chapel. I was lucky and had enough men and officers to keep a daily Mass going through most of the commission. On the hottest days my congregation would leave a patch of sweat on the floor where they had knelt. We had no air-conditioning in those days!

So I took my own small part of Holy Church out on to the high seas to distant parts which had been well-served by missionaries in the past. We had time to note the well-appointed cathedral in Gibraltar and the pro-cathedral in Malta before arriving at our base in Ceylon, as it was then called.

We were to be there, off and on, for two years. Much later I returned to give a series of lectures on education round the island. The island had first been colonised by the Portuguese, then by the Dutch and, finally, by the British in 1798. The Church followed in two waves, first Low then High, and this is an interesting fact, because it occurs in other areas. The Tamils who had emigrated south from India and settled round Jaffna were a hard-working, thrifty race rather like the Scots in character and were better suited to Evangelical ways. The Sinhalese, natives of the island, are a happy go lucky, volatile race who easily took to Anglo-Catholicism. Colombo not only had churches with a full Mass ceremonial, but the convent of St Margaret (East Grinstead sisters) whose founder was Fr John Mason Neale. Much later I was to find myself in the beautiful hill-country with a youth conference and when this was over we had a pontifical High Mass followed by a procession of the Blessed Sacrament through exotic gardens. It was a lengthy business, I remember, because the bishop's sermon was given three times, in English, in Tamil and in Sinhalese, but time does not matter much to the last named. A good time was had by all and I shall never forget it. Talk about marginal

Catholics – you could not be more on the periphery of the Church and the world than that! It was all possible because of what had taken place in Oxford many years before.

It is I suppose a case of cuius regio, eius religio which would apply to parts of Britain as well. My ship had to patrol a considerable area of the world, from Aden to Singapore and Iran (Persia in those days) down to Central Africa. We had the coasts of India and Pakistan on our beat and this put us in a delicate situation. Only a short time before, independence and partition had been negotiated by Lord Mountbatten, and there was still considerable unrest. Our ageing cruiser, however, seemed to command respect and even affection.

This gave me some experience of church matters ashore. For instance, on a visit to Madras I was able to meet some of the local people and obtain first hand information about the newly formed Church of South India which was causing uneasiness at home. I gathered it had not changed the religious orientation very much because congregations were not mixing, but preferred their old ways and buildings. When I returned to Jaffna some thirty years later I found the situation had not changed overmuch and that the CSI Church had not joined the others. In Bombay and Calcutta the situation was different. The Tractarian influence showed in the Anglican churches and cathedrals. The Oxford and Cambridge missions, together with the SPG, generally radiated Catholic faith and practice. In Calcutta there were Anglican monks and nuns of the Community of the Epiphany, and I was able to take some of my naval candidates to be confirmed in a mud hut church at Behala. The building was simple but the ceremonial was not! The same could be said for our Church in Central Africa where the UMCA had been at work for nearly a century. I preached at High Mass in the cathedral in Zanzibar which stood on the site of a former slave market. I also took some of our younger sailors to play football in an isolated mission school. Afterwards in the evening we attended Benediction in their chapel. I still have a photo of a young coloured thurifer heating his thurible.

All this is a diversion from my study of Anglo-Catholicism. I learned however some important facts of life from that commission. Not the least of these was that in a ship's company there were those to whom church life came more easily than to the rest. Therefore you should not try to talk the latter into church when they are not ready for it. The chaplain had to be readily available for inquirers and also had to make certain that the quality of worship was the best. These two lessons have guided me through the rest of my priesthood. They have not been generally learnt by our clergy who are often happy to raise a congregation by any means, and then present it with a slipshod liturgy. As we shall see the experience of travelling round the world in a warship which could level its guns at any danger spots gave me an illustration for developments at the Second Vatican Council. By the time this was in full swing I had returned to civilian life. Later I took over the reins of the Church Union, which had played a notable part in the history of the Catholic movement within the Anglican Church.

References

1. Hastings p.479
2. Catholic League 1913 – 1988 Farmer
3. Welsby: p. 94 Oxford 1984
4. World For God 1958 p.64 (Church Union)
5. Oxford Chapter 8

PLATE 1   *Benedictine Mass — Elmore Abbey 1989*

PLATE 2   The concelebrants at the Church Union Congress, 1968, (from left to right) Fr K. N. Ross, the Bishops of Willesden, Peterborough, Crediton, Bishop Victor Shearburn, CR, the Bishop of Sherwood, Canon C. D. Smith

PLATE 3 *The session on the Renewal of Faith at the Church Union Congress, 1968, (from left to right) Fr F. P. Coleman, Mr P. Winckworth, Fr J. Andrew, the Archbishop of Canterbury, the Bishop of Crediton, Bishop C. Butler, OSB, Archbishop Cardinale, Bishop Butler's Chaplain, Fr H. I. Clutterbuck*

PLATE 4 *Hursley Church, vicarage in background*

PLATE 5 *St. George's Church, Beckenham, June 1925*

PLATE 6 *Fellows' Drawing Room (Oriel)*

PLATE 7 *Fellows' Common Room (Oriel). Newman's portrait in the centre*

PLATE 8   Oriel College – Library (above). Fellows' Drawing and Common Rooms (below)

PLATE 9 Oriel College. Newman's rooms and Oratory (right corner)

PLATE 10 *Festival of Faith, Wembley 1992. Photographs by courtesy of Rev'd K. W. Church*

PLATE 11 *Festival of Faith, Wembley 1992. Photographs by courtesy of Rev'd K. W. Church*

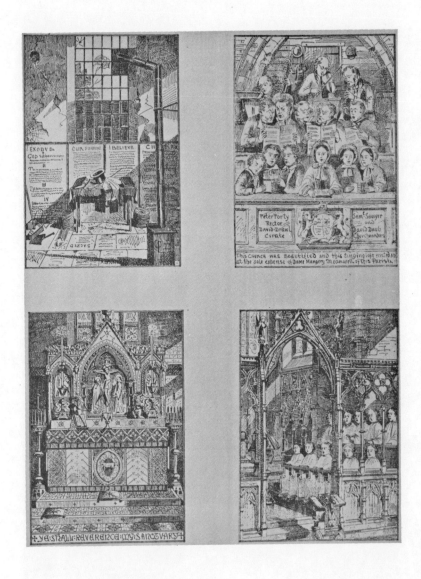

PLATE 12 *In these four cartoons, reproduced from* The Reformation and the Deformation, *published by Mr. Mowbray of Oxford in 1868, we see what the Ecclesiologists found in many English parishes churches, and how they strove to make them both 'correct' and devotional*

PLATE 13   *St. Barnabas', Pimlico (1850)*
*'The most complete and, with completeness, the most sumptuous
church which had been dedicated to the use of the Anglican
Communion since the Reformation' (T. Francis Bumpus,* London
Churches Ancient & Modern, *p. 185)*

PLATE 14   *St. Mary's, Primrose Hill, London (The Lenten Array, 1908) Typical 'English' altar. Frontal and curtains of brown holland; the frontal ornamented with red linen* appliqué. *Cross veiled, and doors of triptych-reredos closed*

PLATE 15   *'Back to Baroque' 'Correct' S.S.P.P. Altar (c. 1920)*

PLATE 16   *The Hall and Chapel, Oriel College*

Chapter Twelve

Aggiornamento or Nervous Breakdown?

It is not given to many men to change the face of history on the verge of his eightieth birthday but this happened to Cardinal Roncalli, the Patriarch of Venice. After his seventy-sixth birthday he was elected to succeed Pope Pius XII. It was one of those rare moments of inspiration which have punctuated church history through the ages. One thinks of the unbaptised Ambrose being elected bishop of Milan nearly sixteen centuries before and how quickly he brought order out of chaos in that troubled diocese. Pope John XXIII was also faced with a mounting unrest within the Church but might have well marked time until a more obvious candidate for the papacy could be found. His predecessor during a long reign of nearly thirty years had made some tentative reforming moves, but the occasion demanded more, especially in the face of spiritual and intellectual change in northern Europe. It could be said that, unlike Ambrose, John added to religious ferment. Yet, as the saying goes, you cannot make omelettes without breaking eggs, and the Church at large desperately needed a new diet to meet the modern age.

Undoubtedly, conservative cardinals had elected John as a makeshift Pope, and even when he made the surprising decision to call another Vatican Council they were not unduly worried, for they had inherited an age-old talent for containing enthusiasm. There was no need to call another council because the defining of papal infallibility had made that unnecessary. As Hastings says, the Catholic Church might well have sat out the storms of the 1960s with hardly a change anywhere, as it had sat out many another storm. This, no doubt, was in the minds of the periti, or experts, who prepared the agenda for the Council. It was to be the mixture as before. There were scholars, however, like Congar and Rahner, waiting in the wings with suggestions for aggiornamento, for bringing the faith and practice of the Church up to date. The new Pope, too, although he was no theological innovator, knew what he wanted and that was the reunion of Christians. There had to be a melting of the ice between the monolithic Church of Rome and other Christian bodies, and this could not happen if Catholics continued in their triumphalist, clergy-ridden and legalistic way. So when the curial old guard presented their draft texts for the Council, they were sent away to do better and, as a result, a most exciting programme of revolutionary change took over. The Church is still trying to come to terms with it.

Many books have been written about this extraordinary episode in modern church history and my object is to suggest how it affected the Catholic movement within the Anglican Church. It will be enough, therefore, if I outline the main business of the Council.

Overall, the Church of Rome apologised for past mistakes and promised to do better. In the first place it acknowledged that other churches might not be entirely wrong. No longer were they to be regarded as heretics, but separated brethren who can possess 'significant elements which together build up and give life to the Church'. Although 'deficient in some respects yet they have been by no means deprived of significance and importance in the mystery of salvation'. The Anglican Church was singled out for special mention because 'of churches separated from Rome in the sixteenth century the Anglican Communion occupies a special place'. Here was something to give Anglo-Catholics encouragement, although they might have said that they knew this all the time. Certainly it was the foundation upon which the Tractarian Fathers had taken their stand.

As a token of the new attitude toward other Christians, observers from other churches were invited to the Council, and the Church of England sent a strong delegation including the Bishop of Ripon, John Moorman. These observers, under the editorship of Canon Bernard Pawley, gave their impressions of the Council when it was over, and these make interesting reading.[1] As Pawley says, the Second Vatican Council was primarily a domestic affair. Pope John himself said that 'the Council was to be celebrated for these special purposes; that the Catholic Faith may increase, that people may be brought to a new and higher standard of Christian morality and that Church law and discipline may be brought up to date according to the needs and conditions of the times'. Indeed, unless there was a move toward a less rigid and monarchical government, other churches might say, Count us out. So there was an attempt at power-sharing from top to bottom. Measures to introduce synods were accepted. Yet the doctrine of the infallibility of the Pope remained and this meant that in the last resort any democratic action could be defeated. Pope John might want to share his power, and his successor Paul VI might do the same, but, once a more conservative pope took over, the process could be reversed and this, of course, has happened today. Roman Catholics, anyway, were not used to being consulted, but rather were happy to be told what to do. Generally the old ecclesiastical bureaucracy has re-asserted itself today. Although fulsome words drawn from Scripture itself were spoken about the importance of bishops as colleagues of the Pope these were balanced by the judgment that 'the College or Body of Bishops has no authority unless understood together with the Roman Pontiff. The Pope's power of Primacy over all remains whole and intact. In virtue of his office the Roman Pontiff has full, supreme and universal power over the Church which he is always free to exercise'. In other words no matter what the Church's Parliament might decide, the sovereign could overrule it. That was a situation which British people certainly could not understand. Nevertheless there was an attempt to soften down the officialdom which kept Roman Catholics everywhere imprisoned within a rigid legal and administrative system.

More positively, the Council discovered Holy Scripture again. This had been thought the distinguishing preserve of

Protestants and therefore to be used with the utmost care. Now in a Dogmatic Constitution on Divine Revelation, it was stated that 'Like the Christian religion itself, all the preaching of the Church must be nourished and regulated by sacred scripture.' It went on to say that easy access to scripture should be provided for all the Christian faithful and that all clergy, catechists, and other teachers must study scripture. Readings from the Bible were also to have a prominent place in the liturgy and this was to be done 'as soon as possible'. If tradition had been the guiding principle of the Church in the past, now it was to be balanced by Scripture. This introduction of the Biblical Trojan horse into the Church's life was to have considerable influence in its spiritual reflowering but it also sowed seeds of religious radicalism in parts of the Church like Holland and Belgium. It was unfortunate that the rediscovery of the Bible, and especially the Gospels, came just at the time when scholars outside the Roman Catholic Church were reducing its reliability by extreme speculation. The 1960s saw the nadir of orthodox scholarship. As Hastings writes, 'A good deal of the more publicized theological writing in the sixties gives the impression of a sheer surge of feeling that in the modern world God, religion, the transcendent, any reliability in the gospels, anything which had formed part of the old "supernaturalist" system had suddenly become absurd'.[2]

It was then a bad time to be born again into a scriptural way of life. The tide was beginning to turn, however. The radical critics had overstretched themselves and a more conservative school was establishing itself. This enabled Catholic scholars to take the best out of both worlds. This they did, as Raymond Brown's commentary, *The Gospel According to John* (1966 and 1970), shows. Teaching programmes both inside and outside school became Bible-based and have provided a healthy example to other Christian churches. Throughout the three years of the Council (1962–1965) documents and decrees flowed out into the world. The change of Pope after the first session made little difference because Paul VI was also keen on aggiornamento. There were statements on Divine Revelation, the Church, Communications, Ecumenism, Eastern Churches, Non-Christians, the

Clergy, Missions, Priestly Formation, Christian Education, Religious Freedom, Liturgy and the Laity. All this was too much for the ordinary Mass-goer who would have been happy if things had gone on as before, and who had not been expected to do anything about it. The last two subjects, however, were to touch him deeply and make him reconsider his personal commitment to Holy Church. For instance, the lay apostolate movement, which had started in the First World War, had steadily grown, especially on the Continent, despite little official encouragement. This now found a place in the Council although it was still heavily hedged round by clerical supervision. There was, however, a call to all lay Catholics who so far had just sat in their pews and quietly heard Mass, to move up into the front line of mission. There was still uncertainty about how they could be used without getting above themselves, but a sentence was uttered which was full of promise for the future: 'Many people can only hear the Gospel through the laity who live near them.' There were all sorts of exciting possibilities if this were to be taken seriously, but the Council trod delicately when it came to making definite recommendations. For this it was criticised as being too tied to the clergy, yet a priest-ridden body would always find difficulty in sharing power with a people who for a very long time had been treated as second class citizens. I was to meet this kind of difficulty when a few years later I tried to harness lay people to a missionary strategy. I will deal with this in another chapter.

There was one area, however, where lay Catholics could not ignore the Council, and that was in the field of worship. For much of history, Catholics had attended a Mass which changed very little. Even the reading of the Epistle and Gospel had been in Latin; public participation had been minimal even in the intercession; the celebrant murmured the most sacred parts of the Mass to himself and the congregation had to be warned of these by a sanctus bell. People were content just to hear Mass. Fasting regulations meant that Communion was received only a few times a year. However, as was shown in the last chapter, a liturgical movement had been in progress for some years and this was changing the pattern of Catholic living. The Council now gave its blessing to this and ordered that changes should be made as soon as possible. The new direction was signalled in words of the Constitution on the Sacred Liturgy: 'The rite of the Mass was to be revised in such a way that the intrinsic nature and purpose of its several parts, as also the connection between them, could be more clearly manifested and that devout and active participation by the faithful could be more easily accomplished'. This was further supported by a statement on the Liturgical year: 'Holy Mother Church every week keeps the memory of His resurrection. In the supreme solemnity of Easter she also makes an annual commemoration of the resurrection, along with the Lord's blessed passion. Within the cycle of the year, moreover, she unfolds the whole mystery of Christ'. This cycle of the Lord's mysteries was to be preferred to the feasts of the saints. In other words, the Church's year was to be simplified so that the Lord's mighty works should have central place.

Very quickly, Roman Catholics changed from being Good Friday people to becoming Easter people. This meant a drastic change from gathering merit through sharing the Lord's suffering to being lifted by thanksgiving into the Lord's risen presence in His Church. Later I shall work out the implications of this because they affected everybody and had to be understood by Anglo-Catholics if they were to keep in step with the main Catholic family. There was a sudden change from Counter-Reformation religion to the simplicity of the early Church. This meant a reordering of churches so that altars were moved forward in order that the celebrant might face the people; the shape of vestments changed flowingly, holy pictures and decorations of medieval piety began to disappear, and new churches were built with Protestant austerity. This had been happening on the Continent and even in some places in Britain before the war. Peter Anson shows in the last chapter of his book, *Fashions in Church Furnishings 1840–1940*, the Church of the First Martyrs, Bradford (1935) with a central altar, and notes this 'Roman Catholic return to early Christian austerity'.[3] He also shows a Mass facing the people with a plain stone altar with two candlesticks. He says further that the supper room at Jerusalem became the pattern for the perfect Christian church and there was an urge to return to a primitive type of holy table free from all unnecessary accretions. Since Anson ends his survey in 1940, we can learn that the wind of liturgical change had been blowing for some time before the Council.

When you add to these structural changes, a new order of Mass in the vernacular, evening Masses, frequent Communion without a long fast, a joyful participation assisted by 'pop' hymns with guitar accompaniment, and a more relaxed clergy, it is clear that the unsuspecting Roman Catholic was in for a shock. It could not fail to affect Catholics within the Anglican Church who had ordered their churches and their worship according to Rome. It was the more confusing because their own Church was also revising its liturgy along the same liturgical principles. It is no exaggeration to say that consternation reigned in some quarters and there was the feeling that the Roman Church had gone out of its mind.

This thought had also occurred to some Roman Catholics in this country. At the beginning of 1968 the Catholic monthly, *New Blackfriars*, greeted its readers with the words, 'The Church has had a breakdown', and Rosemary Haughton in her dialogue with Cardinal Heenan of Westminster said, 'the Church is troubled', and went on to give the cause, 'the trouble started with the Council'. The straitjacket which for most of history had contained Catholic thinking and practice within a competent and rigid system had been loosened, and, with its loosening, a chaos of new thinking had begun. It is uncertain whether this process started with the Church's acknowledgement of past mistakes, or with the statement that through baptism all men belong to Christ's family, or with the encouragement given to modern biblical scholarship. A further statement in the *New Blackfriars* mentioned above summed up the root cause. This said that we were moving from a situation which says, 'This is so', to one which is now saying, 'This is so, isn't it?' It went to say that this does not mean that all truths are for haggling but it is difficult to know when the questioning has to stop. Sufficient to say that the old method of salvation, which started with God in glory in heaven and built a fixed ladder of merit, sacraments and discipline by which all men could ascend to His eternal happiness, seems to have been replaced by a way which started with man in his present state and then opens a number of roads which he can take to reach a God who cannot be so clearly described as mediaeval thinkers and artists thought.

The position in the Anglican Church was slightly different because it had known great freedom of thought and practice. Nevertheless that Church too had been deeply troubled and thrown into confusion by too much and too thoughtless speculation. I quoted Hastings earlier as saying the 1960s were a bad time for orthodox belief. He notes that there were plenty of new insights, but too little stringent analysis of the new positions. A New Reformation was announced by some scholars like the Bishop of Woolwich, but it was clear that it was not going to come quickly if at all.

Generally this relaxation of religious thought had been started off by Christian scholars who were trying to find a solution to modern unbelief. A struggle developed between new and old ways of thought, often in terms incomprehensible to the ordinary layman and, just as in a military campaign, it is not only the opposing armies who become casualties, but also the poor civilians caught between the two fronts, so in the present conflict of ideas, the poor layman and even the word of God was injured while the professional theologians, fighting from prepared positions in their studies were relatively unscathed. The trouble was that scholars were destroying in simple words what ordinary people had been content to believe and trying to rebuild in more difficult language what men should be thinking.

The Anglo-Catholic might well have supported attempts to make an inroad into modern unbelief and apathy, because the tone of his Congresses since 1920 had been one of going out and seeking what had been lost. He had, however, often clung closely to what had been established in his local church. When this began to be changed he was very puzzled. He could not retreat into a ghetto because he never knew when that might be invaded by new ideas. According to James Bond, there is a Japanese proverb which says that a reasonable number of fleas are good for a dog otherwise it forgets it is a dog. On the same analogy we might say

that it is a good thing for human beings to have a reasonable number of problems otherwise we might forget we
are humans, but sometimes it seems as if the difficulties are
overwhelming and we become discouraged, rather like an
over-infested animal. Some Christians were beginning to feel
like that. It was made worse by the fact that there were few
to teach people in this situation. The 1967 Crockford preface
said, 'many of the clergy are not intellectually or morally
strong enough to retain their mission in a world of flux'. If
the clergy were like that, heaven help the laity!

So was it aggiornamento or nervous breakdown? This was
the question I had to try to answer, because in 1966 I became
a secretary of the Church Union and had to travel round the
country, speaking to all kinds of Catholic gatherings. In eight
years I covered a quarter of a million miles and was in a good
position to know what Anglo-Catholics were suffering. It
was then that I started writing small books to try to explain
what was happening in the Church. The matter was urgent
because I had to prepare my people for the 1968 Congress
which was suitably entitled, All Things New.

Before describing that, it might be helpful to reproduce
what another Anglo-Catholic priest was thinking about the
situation. In my first months at the Church Union I helped
at All Saints', Margaret Street where Father Kenneth Ross
was vicar. He had already had published a number of helpful
books, so I asked him to write something for my new series.
He wrote several small books, but one, *What Is Happening
to Our Church* seems to sum up what I have been saying in
this chapter.

References

1. Pawley Second Vatican Council Oxford
2. Hastings p.545
3. Anson p.362

Chapter Thirteen

What's Happening to the Church?

As I said in the last chapter, when I became a secretary of the Church Union in 1966 I was faced with the problem of explaining to the ordinary member what was going on in his Church. I gave a series of talks on this subject and these were published by The Church Literature Association, the Church Union's publishing firm, in booklets. I also sought the help of others whom I knew were good communicators. Kenneth Ross was certainly one. I am reproducing the substance of what he wrote about the Church in 1968.[1] His little book has long gone out of print, but can still be read with profit today. It is a fact that, more than twenty-five years after Vatican II, Catholics in and out of the Anglican Church are still trying to come to terms with its changes, and many would prefer to have the old ways back. How often one hears the cry, 'I wish we could go back to the old Prayer Book', or, 'I miss the old Latin Mass!'.

Kenneth Ross imagines himself as an ordinary churchgoer who has returned to his home parish after several years absence. He goes into the church where he was brought up, made his first confession, and was married. He prepares to kneel down and say his prayers when he looks round and gets a shock. Has the place been bought up by a Protestant trust or is spring cleaning going on? The high altar, which used to look so dignified with its cross and six candlesticks and flower vases, at the east end, has disappeared and stands under the central tower, with no cross, no candlestick, no flower vases – just a plain table. He is heartbroken, and more so when he sees most of the little shrines under the windows in the nave have gone as well – and the Stations of the Cross.

As he sits there dumbfounded he hears somebody enter and looking round sees the old verger, Tom, who also recognises him. The following conversation follows:

Hullo, Tom, it's good to see you again, but who on earth is the ghastly Protestant you have got as Rector now?

Protestant? What do you mean? Father Hippolytus is the leading Catholic of the diocese.

But what about all this? It's so different from what it used to be. There used to be such an air of mystery about the church; it was like being in the Middle Ages with all the twinkling lamps – I see they've disappeared too.

Yes, said Tom, I'm a bit biased because there is a bit less work for me than there used to be! But seriously, from an artistic point of view, isn't the building more dignified now than it used to be, with all that clutter? You can see the lines of it far better now.

Maybe, but since when were you so keen on architecture? In the old days you were keen to have everything as Catholic as possible – I remember how you schemed and schemed to get rid of the lectern until you finally succeeded during an interregnum. And now there it is again, and in a more prominent position than before.

I was a terrible spike in those days, I must admit. But I've got to like the new way of doing things, though I was violently against it at first. I'd always thought that what Rome had been doing for hundreds of years must be the best and so the right thing for us was to come into line.

And now because Rome is making some changes, you think we ought to make changes?

Not exactly. But we are left out on a limb if we make our ways as Roman Catholic as possible and then they make radical changes! No, what I've learnt, rather painfully sometimes, is to think what the Mass really is, and what is the most *sensible* way of doing things.

In the old days, what we were concerned with was what was *correct*.

Yes, and it's surprising what a difference it makes when you stop thinking along those lines. Take the lectern for example. Having explained that the first half of the Mass was really a Bible-class, Father asked me where would be the best place for hearing the Bible read from. I couldn't say, up at the east end, facing north into the organ loft, *correct* as I had always thought those places to be. If the object of the exercise is to let people hear what is read, then we've got to have the lectern back and to put it *there*. So I pocketed my pride, gave the thing a clean and hauled it back. Of course, Father uses the new translation.

Tom, I can see what you mean about that; but you can't approve of making the altar so mean and bare as it is now. It used to look marvellous with those masses of candles — you couldn't help worshipping.

It didn't help you to remember that you were taking part in a meal, did it? The altar looked like anything but a table and, unless you were very attentive indeed, you couldn't see the bread and wine placed upon it or the Bread being broken or the Bread and Wine being received. The only thing you were aware of was the consecration.

I'd have thought that that was very important.

Granted. But so are the other three ways in which what our Lord did at the Last Supper are repeated. It's a lot clearer now. You can see all those things taking place.

I'd rather not *see* them. It is distracting, if you want to say your prayers.

But the purpose of the Mass is not first and foremost to give *me* an opportunity to say *my* prayers. It's the gathering together of God's Family to say the Family prayers and still more to partake of the Family Meal. You have no right to isolate yourself from those around you, when the purpose of the Mass is Holy Communion — Holy Fellowship.

But what's happened to the Stations? It used to mean a lot to me, doing the Stations during Lent.

Oh, we still have the service on Tuesday evenings in Lent but the fourteen pictures have come down — they weren't exactly works of art, were they? Now that they have come down, there's a certain dignity about the church and you can appreciate the statues and pictures which remain.

Is this sort of thing going to be the rule everywhere now, Tom? Surely there are some places where you can't just pull the altar out from the wall and where there isn't space to do things as you apparently do them here.

No, plenty of places will remain much as they have always been. We are fortunate here, as you say, in having plenty of space. But other churches will be doing the best they can, within their limitations, to get the same view of the Mass across, even if they can't move the furniture about as we can.

Tom, you are sold on these newfangled ways — tell me, if they are all so good, why has everyone been such a long time getting round to them?

Tom thought for a moment and then he said: I think we have grown up. Until recently the Catholics — both Roman and Anglo — felt obliged to spend their time being non-Protestants. — And the Protestants spent their time being non-Catholics. It was quite absurd. You remember the old days here; anything the Protestants did, we kept clear of; anything the Bishop ordered, we disobeyed. If he said, preach sermons on the Bible, the sermons were preached on anything but the Bible — perhaps they weren't preached at all. And it was the same the other way round; if we wanted to make the cemetery chapel into a decent place of worship, that was enough reason for our friends down the road to oppose it. At last we are trying to discover two things, what is in accordance with Scripture and what is sensible and likely to work well. So now when we find a thing is scriptural and sensible, we don't worry whether it lands us in the arms of Rome or the arms of the Methodists, we just go ahead and do it.

I don't know any Methodist chapels but I'd guess this place resembles one now.

It doesn't, you know. But some of the Methodists are dead keen on our Parish Mass — it makes sense to them. In the old days they would run a mile rather than darken the door of the church. And their minister preaches some good Catholic doctrine in his sermons.

How do you know? Have you been taking part in schismatic worship?

I plead guilty. A party of us went along to their evening service last Lent. What do you think? Their minister wears a cassock!

Do they do everything back to front too? If you don't take care, you and they will never meet. You'll be getting so low and they'll be getting so high, that you will pass one another without noticing.

It's time for me to go and ring the Angelus. Come and have a drink with me afterwards.

I'm glad there's *one* thing anyhow that hasn't changed!

Reference

1.   C.L.A. 1968 Ross

Chapter Fourteen

Easter Every Day

As an introduction to the *What's Happening* series which covered most areas of the Christian life, worship, prayer, Bible, discipline, morals and even God, the last also by Kenneth Ross, I wrote an essay called *Easter Every Day*.[1] This sought to go more deeply into the lessons of Vatican II. Since this is also long out of print, I reproduce most of it here to give further proof that we in the Church Union were still very active in the teaching business.

'Change and decay in all around I see' could well express the feelings of many church people as they watch the pattern of their religious life changing today. And what changes! Some of us no more than middle-aged can remember several jolts to our faith when some new theory of biblical criticism was published before the war, but never have we had such a hammering as now. When we go to church we find the services are changing and we are told we have to think differently about God and the Church and that we do not have to observe the old disciplines. We ask 'Why all this change?' and are told, 'The Church must keep up with the modern world. Can't you see how mature it has become with its advances in science and technology? It has really come of age and the Church must speak in a grown-up language to it'.

We are puzzled. We were quite happy thinking about God on his throne of glory, we were perfectly at home with the old Sung Eucharist and we never found the fast from midnight difficult to keep. The great thing is that we should not lose our heads amid this change nor think that

163

nothing is worthwhile any more. We should try to understand what is happening and remember that in its long history the Church has seen many changes and survived them all. The basic Christian truths cannot change but, as the world changes direction, so they have to be presented in a different way. If you look hard you will see there is a change of direction now — whether for better or worse is a matter of opinion — and it is important that the Church should be equipped to deal with the situation.

In whatever way we view our world, one thing is clear about the Christian Church. It has become a small body in a large, unbelieving world. For the first time in over a thousand years the Church as an institution is no longer in the driving seat of our country. True, great national occasions will start or end in church, and most people are baptised, married and buried by our clergy, but this would appear on the whole a matter of convention rather than conviction. The Church has lost its hold upon our people and shows no signs of regaining it. The number of practising Christians is small, the number of unbelievers is large.

This fact can provoke two reactions from the Church. First, it can see itself as a faithful remnant who must hold on to the full faith to the last ditch, hoping that God in his own good time will use it to save the world. It is strengthened in this idea by history, which shows that the Church has several times suffered great loss of power only to burst into life again and lead a religious revival. These people view change with suspicion, compromise as treachery. This outlook should not be despised, because it has a fine heroic quality about it. At the same time men should ask themselves if their Church is adequately equipped to show unbelievers the message of joy and hope which they need to hear today. They should take note that other Churches, including the Roman Catholic Church, think considerable change necessary. To refuse any change could well put them out on a limb, supported neither by their own Church nor by any of the great denominations.

The other reaction could well be panic, sending Christians to extreme self-criticism and unsuitable experiment. It is not easy to accept the verdict that the world on the whole does not want our religion and we might conclude that they are right and we are wrong. Such self-examination is praiseworthy and yet it must not drive us to make such compromise that we abandon valuable Christian beliefs and practices. Extreme measures have been proposed. It has even been suggested that if you want to worship God, you must keep away from church at all costs. Much dust has been raised and, before it is settled, more has been stirred up, so that the faithful are worried and confused — you cannot carry on your spiritual life in a perpetual sandstorm!

No doubt we have several generations of change and experiment ahead, but do well to pause now and see in what direction we should go. If we decide change is necessary we shall not imply that we have outgrown the old Catholic faith. Each age no doubt sees salvation in its own way, according to knowledge and circumstances and it is no good thinking that the particular view of the last generation will necessarily satisfy the needs of a later one.

A Guide from the Past

Has the situation Christians find themselves in today happened before? Yes, to a certain extent in the first three hundred years of Christian history. For this period the Church went forward as a small body of believers surrounded by a hostile, cynical and even dangerous world. It was a world which had seen mighty empires rise and fall, had known great learning and tried many religions. It resisted for a long time this new faith which centred on a Jew who was born of a virgin, suffered on the Cross and rose from the dead — and yet it was won over. How did this happen? Not because the Church had all the answers, but because it offered a sure message from God and an attractive community experience. A simple description of this experience would be Easter Christianity. The early Christians kept Easter all the year round. To them our Lord was not merely in the past nor yet in the future, but very much a present companion, alive in their midst, giving joy and strength to those who had been baptised into his family. To understand the full meaning of this you have to think of the most wonderful Easter you have ever had. Spring was beginning to break out in its full glory, the hardships of Lent and Passiontide were over and you went to the first Mass of Easter. Everything – the Spring bringing new life from death, the release from the tension of Holy Week and the Gospel message of the day – seemed to create an atmosphere where the risen Lord was really near and all was happiness. Now it was easy to speak to our Lord as one who was very near, to be really thankful with the Church at the Eucharist and to return to one's daily work with renewed confidence and joy. Alas! The glorious period of Easter was finished all too soon and on Trinity Sunday you were back to a less exciting practice of the Christian life where you watched almost in tableaux form, the other events of the Lord's life pass before you. It will be a year before you can hope to experience such happiness again. But the early Church knew no such seasons of the year. For them Easter was not only *the* festival of the year, it was the only one. Every Sunday was a celebration of the Lord's resurrection. On this day of the week Christians stood for prayer, because through baptism they had risen with Christ and therefore stood up with him. They also faced the rising sun, remembering the true son who had risen.

This was the message which swept the heathen world. Jesus had died only to rise triumphantly. Moreover he had established a new family not only for earthly fellowship but for present membership of the Lord's victorious kingdom. You did not have to wait for death before entering this kingdom but entered it by baptism. The first Christians in every way displayed this joyful fact. They set the risen one at the centre of their life. This Easter-every-day faith was clearly shown in the decorations and mosaics of the first places of worship. These do not give us a mere narrative of great events of the past but show plainly an experience which is always taking place. The central figure is always Christ, the bringer of salvation, the living Lord of all. Always it is the completed work of redemption which is shown – the Easter theme – and you know as soon as you enter such a place of worship that Easter is being celebrated all the year round. This Easter theme is shown in the catacombs, the underground burial places of Christians. No drooping, mourning angels here, but only pictures which represent the new life which Christ has won for his family through his resurrection.

The whole atmosphere of the early Christians was one of invincible happiness. They did not just look back to our Lord's life in the past, but saw him as the living Lord in their midst. By baptism a Christian began to live his life side by side with his Lord. It sent him out to do his daily work with what a modern toothpaste advertisement on TV calls a 'ring of confidence'. He started with the glory, then went out into the world to put it into practice by obedience and discipline. This did not mean that he was already assured of salvation, because, as long as he was in this life, he could always fall away by sin, but provided he avoided this, he could be joyful because he belonged to a community which had the risen Lord at its centre.

The time has come to consider this Easter-every-day way of life as our own objective today. It involves drastic rethinking of our spiritual life, yet we are not moving toward an unknown goal but one which Christians once had and enjoyed.

Instead of using abstract words such as grace, virtue and merit we will think in terms of a person helping us to do great things. In everyday experience we know what a difference it makes to have a person with the power to command or of leadership among us. We are able to do things we never thought possible. This infusion of new strength is hard to define, yet it is accomplished. On a higher plane our Lord inspires us in the same way and gives us the power we need. The sacraments are the visible ways in which we encounter the Lord, the giver of life and strength. No long pipeline from heaven is needed but a communication of strength from closer quarters.

The way in which our moral life will be affected can be seen from an illustration of how children are taught in our schools today. Watch them at work and you will see they learn their lessons by playing games with fasinating apparatus. While they are enjoying themselves they are unconsciously being taught lessons which earlier generations learnt by discipline and sweat of brow. So if we concentrate on the joyful fact of the risen Lord among us, we shall find we are steadily advancing in the spiritual life, taking care to avoid wrong, and generously taking on all the Church demands. Our Christian faith will flow naturally into everything we do. This does not mean discipline will be unnecessary. Without it we cannot remain faithfully in the Lord's company.

Our prayers will certainly receive a new stimulus. No longer will we think of them as a series of petitions but as entrances into the presence of one who was dead and is alive for evermore. So we shall be able to share his concern for other people. We shall no longer be mere onlookers sending up a long chain of requests, but real partners with him in the salvation of the world. This is true prayer. The Bible, too, will be judged today not so much for its historical and scientific accuracy, but for assuring us that the Lord of the Church really did live and for filling in details about one who is the centre of our life.

The Eucharist from being just a weekly duty which we may or may not carry out will become the joyful meeting place of Christians who both offer thankful praise to God and also renew their union with the risen Christ. Here the faithful bathe in the splendour of the Lord's glorified life and remember that, as St Paul says, 'we are received into the kingdom of God's beloved Son'. The unbelieving world might well be impressed with such a display of confident joy. But to help us present such a message there will have to be changes in the Eucharist which at present says little about the joys of the resurrection and much about the Cross. Our Church is in fact at work upon a new order of service which will bring us nearer to what the Church at its best once used.

As for the clergy, such a return to the full mature faith of the first Christians can bring nothing but new confidence and encouragement. They will see themselves no more as officers keeping a local unwilling organisation going with difficulty, but rather as leaders of victory celebrations which last not just for a few weeks but all the year found. The outward show of these celebrations will be the Sunday Eucharist. So, as St Thomas Aquinas says, all pastoral care ought to prepare people for this service. 'This means', says the famous liturgiologist, Josef Jungmann, 'that all instruction, preaching, child welfare, youth work, all charity and all care of particular classes and conditions of people, all work for Catholic education and all religious journalism, can be seen as a preparation which will lead the faithful to that outlook on life, that disposition of faith, hope and love, that attitude of thankfulness to the revealing and redeeming God which breaks forth on Sunday like a mighty stream in the corporate celebration and presents to God all honour and glory.' This is surely a noble programme for every priest. With such faith the priest, with his people, will not shrink from their duties in the world, but will approach every occasion with confidence knowing they have a contribution to make. For we have been called to work for Christ, and prayer and the sacraments are not merely for personal security, but preparation of tools for service. The major occupation for all Christians will not be to avoid hell and gain heaven, for through membership of the Church we are already in the heavenly life.

This return to the Easter-every-day outlook can make a positive contribution to the reunion of the Churches. So much of our time is being spent unravelling the misunderstandings and mistakes of Western Christendom that to return to the life of early Christians must take the pressure off local controversies. In the past new denominations have declared their intention of returning to the simple Gospel but somehow have failed to reproduce the church life of the primitive Church, possibly because they have approached it with certain prejudices. Thus they have overlooked the triumphant joy of that age, or neglected the Eucharist which was the early Christian way of celebrating that joy in community. It should even be a requirement of unity today that each Church should have within it the ability and equipment necessary for producing an Easter-every-day religion.

No doubt a series of books will be needed to work out the full implications of Easter Christianity on our religious life, but the potential of such a system is tremendous. It will lift us up above a mere individual seeking after salvation and make us fellow workers with a living Lord. It could enable us to be well ahead of all modern thought instead of having to make constant alterations to meet the challenges of our age. Change is certainly necessary but if it is in the direction of the glorious early Christian Church then there will be no decay.

References

1.   Ivan Clutterbuck C.L.A. 1968

Chapter Fifteen

All Things New

Polruan-by-Fowey could be said to stand at an end of the earth, because you arrive there along a narrow Cornish lane and can go no further, unless you take a passenger ferry across the harbour. It was here I came as vicar after my travels in the Navy, and I was just settling down in this very beautiful parish when I received a phone call inviting me to organise the Church Union in London. Once again I uprooted myself and my family and returned to my suburban home country. I do not know why I was chosen for this job because I had been out of circulation for many years. I had, however, begun to play a part in Truro Church Union activities and had made some forthright criticisms to the General Council in London. I felt the Union had gone to sleep at a time when it was needed to deal with the current Anglican/Methodist reunion scheme which Anglicans in Cornwall felt would not work — and neither did the Methodists. Perhaps it was thought that my naval experience would bring a bit of efficiency to the organisation.

Anyway in the early summer of 1966 I left the still waters of Polruan and for eight years spent much of my time on the road, penetrating to every nook and cranny of Anglican parish life. When I came to add up my journeyings I found they amounted to almost a quarter of a million miles. There was much work to be done because I discovered few church people knew what the Church Union was. The Anglican/Methodist debate was nearing its climax and we were due to have another Congress in two years time. The former was such a crisis for Anglo-Catholics that it needs a chapter to

171

itself. Meanwhile my first task was to go round to the Royal Festival Hall on Southbank and sign the contract for a three days hiring in the spring of 1968. I felt very much as Father Wilson must have felt when he was told in the summer of 1919 that he was to organise the first Anglo-Catholic Congress. In fact, my experience was similar to his because, although I had a high-powered committee behind me, they decided only on the theme and the speakers. The rest was left to me and my admirable secretary, Kate Rogers.

I next started to go exploring round the country, to discover the state of the Union. The fact that our offices had been gradually moved out from Central London to a rather run-down house in Shepherd's Bush illustrates how we had fallen from favour. Complacency had overtaken Catholics because they thought there was nothing left to fight for and so membership had fallen. This meant that our income had dropped and we were mostly living from the grave: from bequests. A new generation had arisen which did not know the Church Union and its glorious past. I had to redress this ignorance and apathy and also to revive morale by speaking and writing about what was happening in the Church. The last two chapters indicate how this was done. I see from my diary of 1966 that my first engagement was the Church Union festival at Tewkesbury followed by another in Norwich, but later engagements were not so respectable and I wandered in many down town areas. I spoke in many places from a beer cellar to cathedrals and I slept in many beds. Fortunately I had used some of my time in the still waters of Cornwall to read hard about the religious issues of the day and was not too badly prepared to deal with the many questions fired at me.

Meanwhile planning for the Congress continued. I must first confess that I had attended none of the former Congresses, so I was able to approach the coming one with an open mind. The theme was, All Things New, and since it was to be held just after Easter I established with the help of an artist relation the logo or symbol of a Paschal candle. Our speakers for the renewal of faith, spiritual life, and parish life easily fell into line. It seemed that few now had scruples about appearing on such a platform. The speakers were drawn from different Churches, Archbishop Michael Ramsey, Bishop Butler (Roman Catholic), Archbishop Athenagoras (Orthodox) the Abbot of Nashdom, Brother Bernard SSF (Anglican) and a monk from Taizé. There would also be a Saturday evening rally in the Kingsway Hall for the younger people. A prize was offered for the best religious pop group which would perform at this rally.

The matter which occupied our committee most was what liturgy should be used for the opening Mass. To understand the problem, something must be said about the debate on the liturgy which was taking place at the time. It was clear that the older generation of Catholics mostly clung on to the old Mass and were not ready for change, whereas by 1967 the Church of England had authorised two new liturgies, Series 1 and 2. These had much in common with the new Roman rites and had gained considerable (though not universal) approval. Catholic proctors had entered wholeheartedly into the debates in the Church Assembly and their expertise produced new rites which, despite Evangelical opposition, said most of the things which Catholics wanted to say at the most important parts of the Mass. It will be remembered that at the Congress of 1958 Professor Ratcliff had shown the direction in which the debate ought to go. Generally this meant showing clearly the division of the Mass into a service of the word of God with sermon and prayers (corresponding to the Jewish synagogue service) and the Eucharistic meal with a prayer of thanksgiving which stretched from the offertory through the words and action of the Last Supper to an act of offering and communion. Some Catholics wanted more explicit words of offering the bread and cup after the consecration, but had to be content with something a little less. Nevertheless it was a great advance on anything the Church of England had had in the past, and most Catholics were able to use it, if they had not fallen in already with the Roman Catholic changes. In fact the Series 2 service was only authorised first for use in certain churches where congregations had been carefully prepared. In the event there was a general rush to use it and much damage was done from which we are still recovering. An experience I had in the Channel Islands might illustrate the chaos which followed. I took a locum in Jersey at that time and found myself singing the Corpus Christi Mass on arrival. The vicar had quickly departed having imparted the information that it would be the Series 2 rite. By now I was well-used to this and plunged boldly in, only to find they had never had it before and had not even been instructed in it. The organist (who had not been briefed) and I were soon at such cross purposes that it was clear something was wrong, and all I can say is that we at least finished together!

This sort of thing was happening elsewhere and it was clear that congregations were resentful. I found that part of my work was going round talking about the changes. From one of these talks my first small book, *What's Happening To Our Service*, was produced just before the Congress. I have personally always felt that we should have continued with Series 1 for much longer because this was the old Prayer Book words in a new framework. Series 2 changed both order and words and this was too much for some Catholics.

So we had an important decision to make. Should we play safe and opt for the old-fashioned High Mass or should we go for liturgical progress? Gordon Phillips, Dean elect of Llandaff, put his finger on the problem when he preached at the Mass and asked whether Catholics would be coelocanths, a living fossil brought up from the sea which had failed to adapt to change, or an axolotl which started life as an unprepossessing mudfish and then marvellously changed into a gorgeous little creature in a new environment. This summed up the substance of most that was said during the Congress; faith, spiritual and parish life all had to look forward, yet without losing valuable insights from the past. In the event, we decided to use Fr Kenneth Ross's version of Series 1 which was called the Red Book and was in use at All Saints', Margaret Street. This combined all manner of rites, including the Swahili liturgy, and managed to be both traditional and progressive at the same time. It had that liturgical licence for which Anglo-Catholics had been well-known! In fact, the Festival Hall had a modern austerity which would not have suited the Martin Travers décor.

As at the first Congress of 1920 we did not know how many would come. The sale of tickers was slow, but many were bought at the last minute. When I stood in front of the microphone at 7.30 pm on Friday, 26 April to give out notices before Mass started, I could see that the hall was full. Four thousand people made their Communion. This was a change from the past when both evening Mass and non-fasting Communion would not have been acceptable. There were no complaints and all were full of praise for the dignified ceremonial which commended the new liturgy even to the doubters. If the Congress did nothing else, I believe it took Anglo-Catholics responsibly and carefully into the new age of aggiornamento.

When it was all over I had to write an introduction to the book of speeches and the sermon.[1] I can do no better here than reproduce some of the things I said. I began by saying that for several reasons it was remarkable that the Congress was held at all. At a time when most of the battles for Catholic faith and practice appeared to be won and the very word 'Anglo-Catholic' outdated, it might have seemed nostalgic or an attempt to revive issues no longer live to continue the line of congresses which started after the First World War. It had also been noticeable that Church Union members lately had been reluctant to come together in great numbers when events had been arranged for them. Yet the 1968 Congress had been held and was a great success.

This success was due to several factors. First, there was little attempt to reproduce the atmosphere of the old congresses. The Royal Festival Hall, splendid in its modern functional austerity, not only reflected the church of the 1960s compared with the Royal Albert Hall which was associated with the past, but also proved to be a much more convenient centre. People could sit about in the different lounges and restaurants and meet friends from all over the country. The high quality of the speeches given by members of different churches sent people away with real help in the renewal of their faith, spiritual and parish life. Not least, the Solemn Eucharist on the first night was an experience few will forget.

The setting for this Eucharist, although bare by former standards, was more than balanced by the number of bishops who concelebrated, by the dignity of movement of the assistants and the hearty singing of the whole congregation. If the sermon was challenging, it certainly whetted people's appetites for the answers which were to come from the different speakers. The concelebrants were the bishops of Crediton (Wilfred Westall), Peterborough, Willesden (Graham Leonard), Graham, Sherwood and Bishop Victor Shearburn CR, assistant bishop of Wakefield, together with Canon Charles Smith and Fr Kenneth Ross. After the Eucharist there was a reception and Princess Margaret's visit to this, where she met many people, gave the Congress a further importance.

On Saturday morning the first session on renewal was held. The Bishop of Crediton, president of the Church Union, was chairman and introduced the Archbishop of Canterbury and Bishop Christopher Butler OSB who both spoke on the renewal of faith. A surprise visitor to this session was the Apostolic Delegate, Archbishop Cardinale, who brought the Pope's blessing and spoke about how much we both had in common. This delighted the older generation, who remembered that the 1923 Congress had sent a message to Rome which was not returned.

On Saturday afternoon Bishop Victor Shearburn was chairman of the session which dealt with the renewal of spiritual life. Archbishop Athenagoras, Metropolitan of Thyateira and Great Britain, and Dom Augustine Morris, Abbot of Nashdom spoke on this. His Excellency the Greek Ambassador was in the audience.

In the evening a rally was held in the Kingsway Hall. This was in more light-hearted mood with an amusing opening address from the Bishop of Montana and some excellent music, both new and old, from choirs and pop groups. During the evening two generations of Catholics were interviewed about the difficulties of practising their faith in the modern age and neither seemed unduly depressed. The evening came to a rousing climax with fifty girls from the school of St Agnes and St Michael, East Grinstead, assisted by boys from Ardingly College, performing a jazz cantata, *Jonah-man Jazz* by Michael Hurd. As a journalist wrote afterwards 'everybody had a whale of a time'! This display of youth was no artificial intrusion into the Congress for the number of young people who attended the different sessions was considerable.

There remained the final session on Sunday afternoon when, under the chairmanship of the Bishop of Willesden, Brother Bernard SSF and Brother Thomas from the Protestant community at Taizé spoke about the renewal of parish life. Bernard said he believed that many priests had lost their hold on the Gospel and were trying to justify themselves by other means and here he put his finger on a problem which has refused to go away. A young layman, later to become a prominent politician, John Selwyn Gummer, concisely summed up the Congress for us and sent people back to their parishes with the slogan, taken from Homer and used by Newman and Froude when they returned to England to start the Oxford Movement, 'They shall know now we have returned'.

I have written at some length about this and former congresses because they have been underrated in modern Anglican history. Pickering thought the 1968 Congress was greeted with indifference, but this was not my experience.[2] There were those who had been anxious to write a requiem for Anglo-Catholicism since the centenary celebrations of 1933. Yet if, as the years went by, people came less readily to London, or any other city, for great events, social reasons might be sought. Cities became places to escape from rather than to travel to, especially after a hard day's work. As one who was commuting from the suburbs to a London office, I can vouch for that. It should be remembered, however, that within two years of this last Congress, Catholics filled both Canterbury Cathedral and Westminster Abbey for the St Thomas Becket celebrations.

Anglo-Catholic congresses were never meant to be mere demonstrations of enthusiasm, but have had two practical purposes. The first was to instruct the faithful and the second to send them out into the world to minister to others. One has only to read the addresses to realise what a torrent of sound teaching flowed from the different platforms. The Congress of 1923 was followed by a series of booklets by great teachers which laid a firm foundation of faith and practice; the 1958 Congress gave guidance on the liturgical changes which were imminent and in 1968 the *What's Happening* tracts accompanied speeches on renewal. Anglo-Catholics had less reason than other Christians to be thrown off course by the changes of Vatican II. That many of them were puzzled and even hurt by these was not surprising, but so were Roman Catholics, as the radical literature of the time shows. The change from 'This is so', to, 'This is so isn't it?' was bound to provoke revolutionary thinking. In Rome, this was done on the back of a continuing authority. Anglo-Catholics were not on such solid ground and it is said that their compasses went crazy at Vatican II. The Festival Hall Congress however showed that their steering equipment was intact. The first leaders of the Oxford Movement had wisely taken their stand on Scripture and the early Fathers and, so long as these were followed, the Church could weather any change of course. It was the rest of the Church of England which was in peril for, as Hastings has shown, this was trying to keep afloat without leadership, Scripture or orthodox principles. 'At times it looked as if the authority of the Bible, the Church, scholastic theology, and Christian spiritual experience were all alike' being rejected as 'irrelevant' and outdated, to leave as the new sources of enlightenment little more than sociology, linguistic analysis, modern Marxism or the study of other religions.'

On such a shaky foundation this Church was now preparing to embark on all sorts of experiments, ecumenical and otherwise. Already the Anglican/Methodist reunion scheme was coming up to the moment of decision and Anglo-Catholics were quickly diverted from digesting all things new to very divisive debate.

References

1.   C.L.A. 1968
2.   Pickering Anglo-Catholicism p.250

Chapter Sixteen

The Anglican/Methodist Affair

According to Adrian Hastings, the Anglo-Catholic party lay devastated in the 1960s.[1] This was not my experience when I re-entered it after several years travelling round the world. In the face of the revolutionary changes in Rome, it adjusted very well. Responsible Catholics now accept that Vatican II tried to do too much too soon and then left the faithful struggling to keep up the same breathless pace. This was largely due to a lack of teaching. But in the field of worship, at least, Anglo-Catholics had been in the vanguard of scholarship. Dom Gregory Dix's book, *The Shape of the Liturgy* had set out the pattern of future change. This had been clearly described by another Catholic, Professor E.C. Ratcliff, at the 1958 Congress. In the field of liturgical education Anglo-Catholics, therefore, were not found wanting. It was true that they no longer came so readily to Church Union meetings and did not join other Catholic societies, but they could be excused for thinking that these organisations had achieved their objectives. As they looked round they saw more and more churches, even cathedrals, adopting worship which was not far different from their own. In the past meetings had been both social gatherings and even entertainment as well as informative. Now people were coming less and less out of their houses at night and were enjoying TV at the end of a busy day. During my time organising the Church Union I had an excellent view of Catholic parish life and certainly would not have described it as 'devastated'.

179

This is not to say that church life was flourishing. It was not. People were learning everywhere in this and other countries to manage without the ministrations of the clergy.

Toward the end of the Sixties, Catholics in the Church of England were called upon to make yet another stand for the faith. Over the years their traditional conscience and practical common sense had stopped their Church from making a number of unwise moves. Now it was necessary to apply these to an unity plan called the Anglican/Methodist Reunion scheme. This was a great crisis for marginal Catholics, because there was some disagreement within their ranks about the worth of this project. I saw the later stages of the debate unfold round the country, and so was in a good position to understand the confusion and the unpleasantness which threatened to divide dioceses, deaneries and even parishes. It is my belief that this did more harm to the Anglo-Catholic movement than the changes of Vatican II. It certainly spread a distrust of the Church Union which continued for a long time.

This reunion scheme is now old history and the fact that it quickly faded away is perhaps proof that neither side was really enthusiastic about it at ground level. Since Anglo-Catholics emerged as the villains of the piece with little said in their defence, I have devoted a whole chapter to this episode of modern church history. Fortunately I have kept my diaries of the years from 1966–70 and these show I travelled to almost every corner of the Church of England, speaking about the scheme and listening to the views of congregations of every kind of churchmanship. In the end, I was the person who had to stand up before a Church Union meeting in London and call for a rejection of the project. This did not endear me to church authority. Since memories are short I will outline the course of this affair.

Even in the best of years, November is a raw month in Cambridge. Mists curl in from the Fens and filter under the ancient doors of the city. Town and gown draw closer to their fires and the great buildings of the past need massive infusions of twentieth century heat. There can have been little of this in the university church of Great St Mary's on Sunday, 3 November 1946 when the short and stocky figure of Geoffrey Fisher, Archbishop of Canterbury, delivered his University sermon. The war had been won but shortages of food and fuel seemed greater than ever and the large church must have been very cold, to say the least. Over the centuries many great preachers had addressed themselves not only to the University, but to the nation and even the world from this pulpit. Few I imagine sensed that any kind of history was about to be made when the archbishop gave his text, 'I am the Door; by me if any man enter in, he shall be saved and go in and out, and find pasture. The thief cometh not but to steal and to kill and to destroy; I am come that they might have life and that they may have it more abundantly.' The sermon then dealt with a 'step forward in Church relations', in the course of which came the suggestion that 'the Free Churches might consider taking episcopacy into their own systems'.[2] After all, the archbishop said, it was generally agreed that episcopacy must exist in a reunited Church and so why should they not try it out on their own ground first. The archbishop meant no more and no less and left the pulpit having launched his cause of reunion.

We might ask in retrospect why the archbishop should have chosen that subject for his sermon. It would have been extraordinary if he had not dealt at some time with the subject of reunion with the Churches of the Reformation. Before the war, as we have seen, there had been an attempt to grasp this nettle when the Church of South India was being formed. It had been agreed that episcopacy should be accepted for this united church. Geoffrey Fisher, therefore, had merely returned to a subject which had been disturbed by the war. It was also clear that in the rebuilding of the ruins of post-war Britain, unity in all parts of the nation was essential. Fisher himself said, 'I became Archbishop just as the war ended and I wanted to do what I could to bring about a renewal of the inter-church discussions which had been everywhere halted by the war and if possible a renewal on more promising lines.' As Roger Lloyd writes, 'it did take the inter-church movement out of the deep freeze and get discussions started again'.

Since Fisher has been strongly criticised for rejecting, in his retirement, the Anglican/Methodist scheme, it is important to look at what he actually said and meant. He said that disunity weakens the Church and imperfections cause disunity. He then said that the theology of ministry causes most problems but he also noted that there were other barriers, among them, 'domestic habits'. By this phrase one would understand differing forms of worship, the use of unfermented wine, the remarrying of divorced persons and others. He noted that the Church of England was an established Church – a character the Free Churches would not want to take on. There were also unresolved tensions within it, by which he meant High and Low churchmanship. In the face of these seemingly incompatible 'habits' the churches were not ready for organic union. However, the process of growing alike ought to begin.

Fisher saw that one hopeful sign of agreement was in the kind of ministry the churches should have. The Lausanne Conference of 1927 – the first Faith and Order conference, attended by all major denominations except Roman Catholics and the Orthodox Church – had moved toward accepting episcopacy as a necessary form of church government. Therefore – and here he made his own striking point – why should not the Free Churches take episcopacy into their system? They could begin to grow together without being thrown together, warts and all. He saw reunion like two lines *slowly* converging and not suddenly joining. In the event the Anglican/Methodist scheme speeded things up or planned to do so, just as a cinema or TV film might slip into a quicker gear and cause distortion and confusion. Fisher was aware of the pastoral problems which such haste could cause and thought there should be no close communion until the 'domestic habits' had been re-examined and, if necessary, reformed. This was to be the theme which the Bishop of Willesden pressed while the actual scheme was being debated twenty years later. Fisher was thought to be a distant and severe figure, yet in the matter of reunion he showed a surprising pastoral awareness. If the Free Churches and especially the Methodists had acted quickly upon the Archbishop's sermon of 1946, the whole matter of reunion might have not been so complicated and fraught with division twenty years on. As we shall see, the idea was taken up only after much hesitation and then by one denomination. The solution was not so easy as some people thought.

Eric Kemp, at that time Fellow and Chaplain of Exeter College, Oxford, who became a chief protagonist of the scheme, tells us in a booklet, *The Anglican Methodist Conversations; a Comment from Within* (Oxford 1964) that Fisher's sermon caused great interest and led to a meeting between the archbishop and representatives of the Free Churches in January 1947. Discussions began and resulted in a book, *Church Relations in England*, published in 1950. Much common ground was discovered and the prospect of episcopacy for all was discussed. Safeguards were written into the report by which the Church of England would officially recognise a Free Church which had adopted episcopacy into its system. Each would entertain the other's communicants. Confirmation would probably be accepted by the Free Church, but significantly the Free Church contingent demanded that it should be allowed to maintain an open-ended relationship with other non-episcopal bodies. It was finally stated that the transitional period, when there were these two episcopal churches, should be regarded as temporary and the aim was organic unity as soon as possible.

At this stage, Eric Kemp tells us, there was a period of quiet consideration during which all the Free Churches dropped out except the Methodists. Maybe there had been a testing of temperature at ground level. Anglicans and Methodists, however, persevered and by 1956 official conversations had begun. A report of these, published in 1963, tells us the names of those who took part. Some had either died or withdrawn for other reasons, and the final line-up was as follows:

For the Church of England
The Bishop of Oxford (Right Revd. H.J. Carpenter) Chairman
The Bishop of Liverpool (Right Revd. C.A. Martin)
The Bishop of Winchester (Right Revd. S.F. Allison)
The Bishop of Sheffield (Right Revd. F.J. Taylor)
Very Revd. Lionel du Toit (Dean of Carlisle)
Canon S.L. Greenslade (Regius Prof. of Ecclesiastical History, Oxford)
Professor H.A. Hodges of Reading University
Mrs Mark Hodson BD
Canon E.W. Kemp, Fellow and Chaplain, Exeter College, Oxford
J.V. Loach, Registrar, University of Leeds
Revd. Harold Riley, Vicar, St Augustine's, Kilburn, formerly Gen. Sec. Church Union
For the Methodist Church
Revd. Dr Harold Roberts, Principal Richmond College, President of Methodist Conference 1957
Revd. Dr E.W. Baker, Secretary of Methodist Conference, President 1959
Revd. Dr C.K. Barrett, Professor of Divinity, Durham University
Revd. L. Davison, Secretary of the Home Mission, Conference President 1962
Dr Dorothy Farrar, lately Vice Principal Wesley Deaconess College, Ilkley.
Dr T.E. Jessop, Emeritus Prof. of Philosophy, Hull, Conference Vice President 1955
Revd. W. Walker Lee, Chairman of Bolton and Rochdale District
Revd. T.D. Meadley, Principal Cliff College, Calver, Sheffield
Philip Race, Conference Vice President 1957
Revd. Dr Gordon Rupp, Prof. Ecclesiastical History, Manchester University
Revd. Dr Norman Snaith, Principal of Wesley College, Headingley
Revd. Dr Marcus Ward, Tutor Richmond College, Surrey

It is worth looking at this list of representatives because it might give us an idea why the scheme did not commend itself finally to the ground level of their churches. The first thing to notice is that there is an embarras de richesse of talent in several fields. Dr Kemp and Professor Hodges on the Anglican side and Dr Barrett and Dr Rupp on the other enjoyed world-wide respect in academic circles. Many of the others would have been used to the corridors of ecclesiastical power either at Church House, Westminster or at the Methodist Conference. Mrs Hodson was the wife of a bishop and even Father Riley had spent many years away from parish life. This leaves Revd. Walker Lee who almost alone seems close to local chapel life. There would, therefore, have been an initial respect for each other and a lack of abrasiveness which would easily lead to a camaraderie. An innocent glass of sherry for the more broad-minded Methodists leading to a more sinister Chateau Neuf du Pape with the roast beef could form a very clubbable group. We are told that in secular politics, members of Parliament who rant and rage at each other in public, are wont to mellow at more intimate select committees. The authorities of both churches who set up this negotiating committee might well have been persuaded that if these eminent church people could agree, then there was no reason why Anglicans and Methodists at parish level should not fall into each other's arms. Certainly some of the dignitaries who later supported the scheme with the full weight of their office did not think it worthwhile to enquire into local church faith and practice.

Meanwhile, priests and ministers at parish level were being fully stretched to maintain any kind of active Christian life. If Anglican vicars worked very much in watertight compartments, Methodist ministers also remained mostly behind their denominational walls, although the latter were open-ended to all other Protestant bodies. What went on in parish churches and local chapels was normally kept from the other's eyes at that stage of proceedings. Barriers began to come down subsequently, but there was seldom a whole-hearted sharing of the other's distinctive services. Remember, this first stage of talks was still in the 1950s.

Meanwhile this inner circle produced in 1963 its first detailed report for consideration. This book of sixty three pages has a long preamble about the different traditions which were being brought together. On the one hand there was the Anglican Church with its framework of the Lambeth Quadrilateral (Bible, Creeds, Sacraments of Baptism and Holy Communion, and the historic episcopate). Clearly there would be little difficulty over the Bible although there was concern from the Methodist side that tradition should not distort its authority in any way. The Creeds, Baptism and Communion were found in the Methodist Church, but not universally. Here it should be noted that although some Methodists were clergy-organised and had not departed too far from their Anglican origins, there were others like the Bible Christians who were mainly lay-orientated and these might not insist even on baptism as part of church membership. Lay celebration of Communion was also found in some parts of the country, notably Devon and Cornwall where the Bible Christians had been founded in 1815. As Hastings says, Methodist unity had been broken time and again over who should govern their Church, the clergy or the laity. Protestant-minded members had hived off to found smaller churches. Although in 1932 these had become united in one Methodist Church, yet this was mainly for economic reasons, and hard and fast divisions remained. There were High Church Methodists and Low Church ones. The latter were very Low indeed.

The real obstacle was the historic episcopate and here all the ingenuity of the scholars was required. The Methodists were anxious that they should not be seen as poor relations begging for the favours of episcopacy. They wanted to be regarded as members of the Body of Christ (this was before Vatican II) and not as schismatics; they wanted the same liberty of interpretation with regard to episcopacy and priesthood as Anglicans − here they referred to the Evangelicals' 'low' attitude to the laying on of hands. Finally and significantly they insisted that no proposals should rupture their communicant relationship with non-episcopal churches.

After looking at these limitations the committee put forward the following proposals:

Overall there would be union in two stages. Stage One would be intercommunion, followed by a period of increasing co-operation between two distinct churches. Then in Stage Two union into one church would be effected. The whole scheme would be achieved by 1) a Service of Reconciliation to inaugurate Stage One, to reconcile the two churches, and to unify their ministries, as each prayed that God would give to the other the distinctive characteristics which it believed it had received from him; 2) the acceptance by the Methodist church of the ministry of bishops in continuity with the historic episcopate and of the invariable future practice of episcopal ordination of its ministers; 3) the provision of means for growing together during Stage One.

So the Service of Reconciliation now appeared on the stage and remained there until the final curtain.

The product of the final report apparently was too great a strain on the bonhomie I have mentioned earlier. Four Methodist ministers – were they the tomato juice drinkers? – dissented from the report because 1) they felt the report did not sufficiently subordinate tradition to Holy Scripture, 2) far too much, they said, was claimed for the historic epis-copate and insistence upon it was unwarrantable, 3) the use of the laying on of hands in the Service of Recon-ciliation looked suspiciously like ordination, 4) the term 'priest' was used with what they regarded as its unhappy and unevangelical associations, 5) they were opposed to the denial of lay administration of Holy Communion in the united Church – they meant 'celebration' by this – 6) they feared the absorption of Methodists by the Church of England. This dissentient view was signed by C.K. Barrett, T.E. Jessop, T.D. Meadley, Norman H. Snaith. These were no light criticisms.

Indeed, on looking at this report again after many years, one is led to ask why, at the other and of the scale, there was no dissension from Father Harold Riley. He had been Gen-eral Secretary of the great and respectable Catholic society, the Church Union, and must have seen the insuperable diffi-culty of being in communion with a church which insisted on being open-ended to other Free Churches who had no desire to be part of the scheme. Anglicans could find themselves

but they realised that on both sides there were those who had reservations. A new commission was appointed to revise the Service of Reconciliation and also to prepare a new ordinal for use in both Churches after the beginning of Stage One.

I have given a full account of the negotiations because I think Anglo-Catholics have been unjustly condemned for defeating this move for unity. There were warning signals flashing from early on and these were not heeded by our Church authorities. Not for the last time they pressed on regardless of considerable difficulties, and this was to cause anxiety and hardship for those who followed their own principles and common sense.

There was now a lull in the proceedings and this gave different parties in the Church time for reflection. The Church Union called a large general council reminiscent of the meetings in the middle of the last century. This was held on a Saturday at Mary Sumner House and was my first introduction to the world of ecclesiastical politics. I had been elected to this council from the Truro diocese and went up to London like other parish priests with little idea of the state of play. However, I did know that, in my Cornish parish of Lanteglos-by-Fowey, Anglicans and Methodists lived happily side by side, but in their own religious compartments. At this council under the chairmanship of Bishop Newnham Davies we studied the report on Conversations between the Church of England and the Methodist Church. As I read it now I realise how gently we debated it. We commended the unity move and then quietly drew attention to problems which had already emerged elsewhere, of Creeds, ministry, status of bishops, sacraments, the service of Reconciliation, marriage discipline and, not least, relations with other Free Church bodies. Yet the statement issued after the council encouraged further progress. The fact that it was not more stringent was probably due to the guidance of the General Secretary who, as we have seen, favoured the scheme, anomalies and all. So we went away, hoping that we had made some positive contribution to continuing debate. Little did I know that within a year I should be back in London organising the Church Union, and being swept up in a controversy which was steadily becoming more bitter.

As I said earlier, my first task in this appointment was to spell out to Catholics round the country what the Church Union was, and for this I used the story of an Israeli kibbutz which I told in my Introduction. I quickly discovered that people generally knew little about the Anglican/Methodist debate, that they knew even less about what Methodists believed and more seriously were very short of teaching about their own faith. Later, after speaking to mixed gatherings, I found that Methodists were in the same boat. I also had a continuing contact with Methodists in what has been called 'the gin and jag' belt of south London, because the parish in which I lived and worked as an honorary curate shared the Sunday evening service with them. One week we went to the Methodist chapel, the next week they came to the old parish church. There was no movement in our worship: the Methodists kept what was irreverently called their hymn sandwich and we had our Prayer Book evensong. For the first time I began to understand the fear which Methodists had of being completely merged and losing their own beloved chapel.

As I went round the country talking to all kinds of gatherings I found a variety of views and opinions ranging from indifference and ignorance to strong opposition. One vicar saw the scheme as 'an insult to our Queen' because Methodists were against her supremacy in religion. Another welcomed it because it brought change and 'change must always be good'. But a moment of truth came when I addressed a rural deanery conference in Canterbury. I was one of four speakers. The rural dean spoke first followed by his Methodist counterpart. They had already formed a close partnership and would have implemented the scheme on the spot. I regretted having to stand up and indicate why this beautiful friendship was not possible on the present terms. Finally a speaker from the Voice of Methodism movement, which had been formed to oppose the reunion scheme, spoke so vehemently that the meeting which had started in a friendly spirit ended almost in violence. I left quickly, leapt into my car and was glad to get away with my life! But this did make me realise that instead of ending with one united Church we could easily end up with three, since there might be continuing

on for a vote in their top elected assemblies in July 1969. As the day approached Catholic action was increased, and I found myself in a Chiselhurst vicarage with the Bishop of Willesden, sending out last minute exhortations to the members of the Convocations to vote against this divisive measure. The Bishop of Carlisle had seen the warning signs in his own diocese and had made an agonising decision to vote against the motion. He was not generally supported by his fellow bishops. It had been decided that a majority of 75 per cent would be required in the Convocations and the Methodist Conference accepted this figure, too. On the day, 8 July, Methodists scraped home with 76 per cent but, although the House of Bishops of both Canterbury and York gave overwhelming approval to the Scheme, it was defeated clearly in the Lower Houses (67 per cent for in Canterbury and 68 per cent in York). Somebody started to clap in the gallery of Church House, but was reduced to silence by a wave of righteous good taste which the Church of England can muster on occasions when it is embarrassed.

So ended a thoroughly unhappy episode which did few people credit except, I believe, those Catholics and Evangelicals who, despite considerable unpleasantness and recrimination, followed their conscience and good sense and prevented their Church from embarking on a disastrous course. It has been held against both parties that one opposed the Service of Reconciliation because it was not a proper ordination of Methodist ministers and the other because it was. But there was far more to it than that.

Not unusually the Anglo-Catholic party took the blame for the defeat of the project which many saw as being a substantial step forward in ecumenical relations. It has been said that their opposition was illogical because what they had insisted upon for the Church of South India was not now sufficient for Anglican/Methodist reunion. However, India was a long distance away with a situation not understood by people at home. It should be pointed out that in the CSI scheme there was concern about agreement on doctrine and this was achieved in the North India scheme. The Church of South India, despite this, went on to be a new Church in its own right, and began to proselytise in Sri Lanka. In Jaffna in 1979 I found Anglicans, Methodists and the CSI with their own bishop, a subject of complaint to me by the Anglican archdeacon. It was clear as I travelled round this country before 1969 that this would have happened here: three churches instead of one, as I indicated earlier.

It must also be said that Anglo-Catholics, especially the Church Union, did not rush into immediate opposition to the scheme, but looked at it positively. It was only when its ambiguities and anomalies began to appear and the fact emerged that there were considerable numbers of Anglicans and Methodists who were not prepared for the merger, that it seemed practical common sense to call a halt. It was clear that if episcopacy could be accepted by Methodists, it would be an administrative convenience rather than being of the *esse* of the Church. Tractarians had fought this battle a long time before and did not want to go down the same road again. It was clear that from the start Anglicans would be brought into contact with practices which were contrary to Catholic practice; invalid Eucharists since Methodists were open-ended to all other Free Churches, unfermented wine, remarriage of divorcees, and other distinctive usages which had been accepted during two hundred years of separation from their parent body. The ordination of women which was to become a controversial issue in the Anglican Church would have entered in by the back door because the Free Churches found less difficulty with this kind of ministry. Indeed locally both sides, especially Methodist, viewed the proposals for unity in a different light from that of their negotiators. In a considerable essay, *Non-Theology: Or the Unasked Question*, written for the Church Union, Valerie Pitt, a university lecturer, wrote: 'It would be very surprising indeed if the expectation of cultural change implicit in the scheme for Church Unity did not create tensions and conflicts in Church members and no doubt that is tiresome for ecumenical enthusiasts.... What is, however, even odder and of a profounder importance, is the unstated assumption, painfully evident in the Anglican/Methodist debate, that a Church's doctrines have no context.' Experience of Catholics in more than a century's struggle to restore their Church

Chapter Seventeen

The Gospel to our Neighbour

Newman was delighted that one of the *Tracts For The Times* was written by a layman, Bowden, in 1833,[1] for he believed that laymen had an important part to play in the Church. This confidence was all very well while he was an Anglican, but it earned him disapproval when he became a Roman Catholic. He clashed several times with the Roman hierarchy when he tried to involve laymen in church affairs. When he was engaged in founding a Catholic university in Ireland he was in trouble with Archbishop Cullen because of his 'desire ... to make the laity a substantive power in the University'. Later his article, *On Consulting the Faithful in Matters of Doctrine*, earned him more suspicion from his church authorities even though he advocated only a mild participation by the laity. This intensified when he drew attention to the fact that in the Arian controversy in the fourth century, it was the laity who remained more faithful than the episcopate. The ecclesia docta set an example to the ecclesia docens. This was not a popular idea in nineteenth century Roman Catholicism.[2] The laity had few rights in their Church. Their position was later described as kneeling before the altar, sitting below the pulpit, and putting their hand in their pocket!

Newman's interest in the laity, therefore, was doomed to failure. It was a Roman Catholic priest in Belgium, however, who tried to bring lay people into the mission of the Church. Joseph Cardijn (later a Cardinal) experimented by sending lay teachers into atheist factory life during the First World War. He had to endure the suspicion of the Vatican, but sheer determination won the day. Not only was the Jocist movement established in France and Belgium, but Rome finally recognised the achievement. Jocism – the name comes from the words, Jeunesse Ouvriere Chrétienne (Young Christian Workers) – fathered other movements where lay people were involved in mission to their fellow countrymen. Later I shall describe my encounter with these lay apostolate pioneers at a conference in Madrid. Progress was slow between the wars chiefly because the gap between priest and layman was wide. The 1939–45 war helped to break down this barrier. Priests and laity on the Continent found themselves living closely together in resistance activity and in prison camps during Nazi occupation. Here a dialogue began. As a result, lay apostolate activity began to blossom on the Continent, leading to such movements as Action Catholique, Mission de France and the Catechuménat. The last is particularly interesting for there is a natural partnership between priest and layman for bringing inquirers – those in search of faith – through a set strategy to baptism and church membership. Lay members, both singly and in groups, assist in the instruction of those in search of belief.

Such missionary strategy meant that priests had to operate outside the traditional Catholic Church on the Continent, if they wished to get a hearing from the outsider. This was frowned upon by the Catholic hierarchy. It meant that groups mostly had to operate from houses rather than church buildings, thus creating a double-banked church life in some countries. In France such activity found its theologian in Yves Congar whose work, *Laymen in the Church*, published in 1957, spelt out the implications for lay ministry. He listed three duties of the layman: priestly, kingly, and prophetic. The first two were no more than would be expected from a committed Christian who should always be offering his life as a living sacrifice and should be prepared to help with the organisation of God's kingdom on earth. He says it is the prophetic or teaching office which assumes a new importance in a world which has parted company with religion. Congar was writing in the fifties and there is still

So a person receives the gift of faith, which is equivalent to the moment of conception in the womb. He brings this gift to the Christian community, which now has to make certain that the conditions for growth are right, just as a mother-to-be relies on medical services and experts during pregnancy. All the faithful, priests and laymen, were involved in this service. Even if all are not involved in the teaching process, everybody must make certain that the welcoming and worshipping atmospheres are entirely right. In other words, conditions in the local congregation must be helpful for the birth of new Christians. After a period of growth, the candidate is baptised and this is similar to the birth of a baby. The first letter of St Peter abounds in this kind of imagery — 'as new-born babes, long for the spiritual milk which is without guile, that ye may grow thereby unto salvation'.

This idea of a catechumenate, therefore, was not new, and has been revived in many parts of the Church. In 1969, however, it was certainly revolutionary to the Catholics in the Church of England and was not easily understood. I was excited by its possibilities and organised a young people's summer school at Seaford where Cranswick could unfold his ideas with the help of charts.

My next stage of education followed when I received an invitation to the Catechuménat European Conference in Madrid in May 1970. This meant little to me at the time but I was assured I could learn some useful lessons from it and my expenses would be paid. Late one night, therefore, I found myself wandering in the suburbs of Madrid looking for the conference centre, the Hostel Mater Ecclesiae. When at last I found it, all was in darkness. I knocked repeatedly on its huge doors which were finally opened by a young man dressed in slacks and sweater, who turned out to be a Swiss priest. When he learned I was a member of the conference, he greeted me like a brother. Soon others appeared, priests and lay people, bottles of beer were produced and a party quickly got under way. This companionship was to last throughout the conference despite the fact that I was the only non-Roman Catholic and did not speak French (the common language of the delegates), very fluently.

This was my introduction to a different form of church life. Here was a new type of priest, working on the fringe of the Church and assisted by a professional laity. This formed a parallel community which operated outside the walls of the traditional Roman Catholic Church. A certain insecurity showed during the conference but this was understandable because they had dared to challenge an age-old rigid conformity. Members came from seven countries, France, Belgium, Germany, Switzerland, Spain, Portugal, and Holland. All had one purpose – to break down the barriers which had grown up between the Church and the general public. One who was a marginal Catholic in the Anglican Church met marginal Roman Catholics! It was not strange that we had much in common.

It was fitting that this conference was held in Madrid because the not-so-distant Spanish war had thrown up the same problems of evangelism as those which Belgium and France had been facing for many years. Church and State found themselves in a sharp confrontation. The subject of the conference was: How does the new lay apostolate movement fit into the traditional structures of the Church? This was clearly a burning question in Roman Catholic countries where new communities of faith had been raised up outside regular parish boundaries. It was not such a burning question for me, as an Anglican, yet there were lessons to learn. Not the least was the danger of sweeping converts too quickly into the Establishment. As I write, over twenty years after Madrid, when the Anglican Church is in danger of splintering apart over the ordination of women, I can see there are lessons for a separated church in what was discussed at our conference.

Can you join new and old? It seemed like a case of new wine and old skins. Yet there was no desire to change the structures of the Church and certainly not the sacraments. This, despite the fact that the word of God in the Gospels had a prominent place in the daily life of the catechumenate. As the conference unfolded, it seemed no country was without its difficulties. How do you start new communities of faith? Still more vitally, how do you keep them going once they have been formed? This posed the question of group eucharists

friends and their company sought. People will do almost anything for them – except go to church! The message they preach is somehow thought irrelevant, because a continuing optimism about the human condition makes the Englishman feel he is capable of saving himself. If a Frenchman finds himself at some distance from his Church, perhaps the Englishman is too close to it. He has grown up side by side with the Church of England and takes it for granted. To be honest, our national church has not done much to turn affection into deep commitment. We, therefore, have a missionary situation as desperate as that on the Continent. The Church has become a diminishing religious community with little influence on the general public. This, then, was the situation for which I had to organise a lay apostolate.

The Madrid conference had discussed a return to the life of the early Christian Church. This had been the thesis of the two essays I had written. Since I used this material for a first year study programme, I will give an outline of my ideas. In the first essay I showed that, although a Christian in the early church lived a lonely and often dangerous life because the Faith was being persecuted, nevertheless he was inspired by the message that the Lord of the Church had not only lived, suffered and died, but had also risen from the dead. He was the living head of the family of baptised members. He was the true shepherd who would lead them through life to heaven. He was the teacher, the true Wisdom, the fisherman and king. The Eucharist provided the main school of instruction as well as being the focal point of worship and inspiration. Here was to be found the presence of the risen Christ, in the assembly of the faithful, in the reading of the Scriptures, and in the Prayer of Thanksgiving which included the narrative of the Last Supper. The Eucharist was celebrated with great joy and everybody took part in it. So the joyful explosion of Jesus' resurrection was kept alive in the hearts of Christians who would then go away and resume their daily life among unbelievers.

It was a great time for those in search of God, because not only would they be met with the apostolic witness to the saving work of Christ, but they were recreated through baptism as children of God. In this way they could share his glory and therefore his holiness. So the words of St Peter's first letter, 'But you are a chosen race, a royal priesthood, a dedicated nation', could be applied to all believers.

In a later book on the lay apostolate I wrote that the early Church thought it natural that all Christians should be engaged in mission.[4] I quoted from Michael Green's book, *Evangelism in the Early Church* that 'enthusiasm to evangelise which marked the early Christians is one of the most remarkable things in the history of religion. Men and women in every walk of life were so sure they had the answer to their religious problems that they let nothing stand in the way of passing the good news on to others'.[5] I added that if they wanted Gospel support for this, they could find it in the story of the man cured among the Gadarene swine. The man wanted to stay in Jesus' following but our Lord sent him away. 'Go back to your people', he ordered, 'and tell them all the Lord in his mercy has done for you'. St John Chrysostom urges this duty on all Christians, 'Nothing is colder than a Christian who does not care for the salvation of others ... you cannot plead lowliness of birth for the apostles were also lowly men and of humble parents. You cannot plead want of education for they too were unlearned men. You cannot plead infirmity, for Timothy was of delicate health and was frequently ill. Everybody can be of profit to his neighbour, if he will fulfil his role.' What was this role? I asked, and suggested that the hospitality, which both Peter and Paul mention in their letters, refers not only to material entertainment, but to spiritual refreshment which could be found in the houses of church members. There was a need for a place where inquirers after faith could come and discuss the new Jesus movement and the joy which followed the acceptance of it.

In my second essay, *Yesterday and Today*, I showed how the happy partnership between clergy and laity began to be dissolved. With the conversion of the Emperor Constantine a new element of compulsion entered the Church. He tried to solve religious controversy by force. This was done with the best of intentions, but although he did not succeed, he set a precedent for bishops who were not slow in following

wars but the clergy of the sixties and seventies were suffering from poor theological training, as I shall show in my next chapter on sound teaching. For a successful lay apostolate, the priests's teaching office had to be rediscovered. In some areas a team of tutors could be formed from experienced teachers. Fortunately there were still a number of older priests who had received a sounder training. This problem remains. The Church's teaching duty remains paramount for the formation of a new generation of Christians.

The lay apostolate movement is based upon the principle of lay people being trained to train others. A priest may undertake the first steps but then must give responsibility to his laity. There are several difficulties and dangers here. After lecturing to a large crowd of priests in London on the subject, I heard one of them say, 'I am not going to allow my congregation to do my job.' As long as this attitude remains there can be no lay apostolate movement. The object of the exercise after all is summed up in those words of Vatican II, 'many people can only hear the Gospel through the laity who live near them'. If the laity cannot be entrusted with this duty, the Gospel remains unheard.

Lay people in the past have been happy to sit under their parish priest and leave the evangelising to him. They will not find it easy to step up into the front line. This was a big obstacle in the seventies. In recent years, however, lay people have had to take on more responsibility so that parishes might survive. To them the idea of an apostolate will not be so revolutionary. Yet the right kind of layperson has to be found and given a sure foundation of faith.

This is a major challenge for a lay apostolate. As will have appeared from this book, much has happened since the high noon of Anglo-Catholicism between the wars, to shake the faith, if not destroy it, of the most faithful churchman. There is much secular competition for those engaged in a search for holiness. The Christian finds himself daily in company where he is the odd man out. In a book, *Invitation to Sociology*,[6] Peter Berger shows how slim are the chances of survival for 'deviants'. 'It has been discovered that in group discussions going on over a period of time, individuals modify their originally held opinions to conform to the group norm....

What lies at the bottom of this apparently inevitable pressure towards consensus is probably a profound human desire to be accepted, presumably by whatever group is around to do the accepting.' Since most groups in everyday life are anything but Christian, the pressures for the layman to opt out of his religious beliefs are enormous. This, then, is the place to give an illustration from an incident I witnessed in Ceylon, or Sri Lanka, some years ago. I had taken several hundred sailors from our naval ship into the cooler air up country. It was Easter and we needed a church for our services. Helped by local information we found one which had been used during the war. Since then it had been neglected and was covered with jungle growth. This was cleared away and the church revealed to the world. In the vestry there was a vestment chest but the drawers had been taken over by a colony of huge cockroaches. We removed these by flipping them out of the door on to a sandy compound which surrounded the church. The creatures fell stunned on their backs and lay with legs twitching. After a while we went to finish them off but found this was unnecessary. Thousands of ants from the edge of the compound had efficiently dismembered the helpless cockroaches and nothing was left. We were just in time to see the rearguard of the army of ants disappearing with little bits of body in their feelers. I suppose the cockroaches were so stunned they did not know what was happening to them.

This seems to me an illustration of what happens to many Christian believers who do not understand how their faith can be eroded quietly by the demands and ideas of a non-believing world around them. If a biblical parallel is sought, it can be found in the parable of the Sower, where the seed either springs up too quickly without sufficient root or is strangled and choked by weeds. Much of the blame for this must lie with the Church which has been sending its people out, ill-prepared, to meet daily challenges.

Any programme for the training of the laity must include first the consolidation of personal faith. Just as a teacher taking over a new class of pupils discovers first how much they already know, so a priest will do the same with his lay apostolate. When this has been done, the real instruction can

the positive plan of salvation God has realised "in Christ and in the Church" '. The text from St John's Gospel must always be uppermost, 'I came that they may have life and have it more abundantly'.[6]

We are looking for a special person for our lay ministry. My own father would have been ideal. He was a consultant engineer on a small salary and very limited means. Circumstances did not allow him to train for the priesthood and so he settled for being a faithful layman. As a young man he had learned his faith from a series of excellent parish priests and this faith he kept embedded inside him, to be brought out when occasion demanded. He enjoyed life, his great pleasure being to talk and laugh with others — anybody from a bishop to a street cleaner. People liked to meet him, just to enjoy his company. In a very small field of life he became an influence, listening to people's problems, advising the young, and generally stabilising a parish which was undergoing change. Of such men are lay apostles made!

As I write this twenty or more years later, I understand how much I was expecting of parishes. Yet I had seen what had been accomplished on the Continent and knew that nothing less would do. I warned at that time that it would take years to build up such an apostolate, but that a beginning had to be made. If my words had been seriously heeded, by now we would have established this missionary strategy and created a generation of well-instructed church people — and priests. The problem twenty years ago was that there was a general shortage of sound teaching. Study programmes abounded but lacked a cutting edge. Most were verbose and destined for the vicarage waste paper basket.

Always there was the danger of assuming too much knowledge. As I was trying to develop my lay apostolate, an Institute of Christian Studies was being formed at All Saints', Margaret Street. I thought at one time that this would be a good training place for my laity but realised it was too advanced. As one member of the Institute said, 'We cannot understand the titles of the lectures, let alone what is said.' I was not present at the first Loughborough Conference in 1978 because by then I was engaged in the classroom. As I read an account of the lectures, however, I recognise they also were too advanced for my movement. I looked in at the second conference at Loughborough and sensed that everybody was more intent on being 'renewed' than on being educated. For me 'being renewed' has meant a serious return to Gospel study, but this I cannot see happening.

By 1974 we had lay apostolate cells throughout the country. I still have a list of ninety parishes which were experimenting with the material the Church Union provided. A thousand other parishes had asked for information. The movement needed consolidation and for this I was not available. I had already been a Church Union secretary for eight years and it was suggested I should move to another post. I had never been able to convince my executive committee that what I was doing was either desirable or safe. Like Newman I suffered from too great a confidence in the layman's office.

I have written at length on this subject because I believe it is important for the future. I am not alone in this. In a recent essay, *What Future for the Church of England?*, Alan Warren, Provost of Vanbrugh College, York, concludes that the laity will be required to play a more and more important part in the Christian community.[9] My venture into the lay apostolate field has been followed by similar ventures, but so far this new strategy has not been soundly established. I suspect there has been too much theorising and philosophising about the layman's ministry and too little action. Once one has agreed with Vatican's II's conclusion that many people can only hear the Gospel through the laity who live near them, a partnership between priest and people can begin. In essence the plan is simple; the priest teaches his people to teach others. Joseph Cardijn did this in Belgium earlier in the century and the movement grew. As I have said, however, it is not so easy in the closing years of this century. The keen parish priest, the right teaching material, and dedicated pupils must be found. A parish will not find it easy to change to this missionary life-style. Yet it must be done if the Church is to grow.

This is a strategy for Catholics because sound teaching and eucharistic worship are essential ingredients. The only

joined with the aggiornamento of Vatican II, it created a period of spiritual ferment from which the churches are still suffering in the 1990s. We are living in an age of unsound teaching. A few voices have been raised in protest but are mostly unheard at the popular level. All forms of churchmanship are being affected, among them Anglo-Catholicism. In this chapter, therefore, I will try to give my thoughts on the situation in the teaching world. It will have become apparent from my text so far that I have spent much time in different fields of education.

I take for my starting point some words from the autobiography of Father Eric Mascall, an Anglo-Catholic scholar who for over fifty years tried to bring common sense into the world of theology. He took a brilliant degree in Mathematics at Cambridge, was ordained and spent the rest of his life lecturing in theology in Lincoln, Oxford, and London. As he finally summed up his life, he said 'while I am only too conscious of the handicap which I have suffered through a complete lack of the training which it had come to be assumed as proper and necessary for a future theologian to receive, I also discovered that the intellectual discipline in which I had been trained as a mathematician gave me an approach and an instrument of which theology was badly in need and which the accepted means of theological education not only did little to supply, but, where some traces of it existed, could even do something to destroy'.[2]

This 'instrument' he employed over many years to stem the flow of unsound teaching. His contribution to Christian sociology was mentioned in an earlier chapter. In addition he has written on many other areas of Christian concern (by 1977 his books numbered seventeen). The invitations he received to lecture round the world, inside and outside his Church, show the stature of this Anglo-Catholic scholar.

In the last chapter of his autobiography he sums up the present situation in thse words:

'For the question which faces every Christian body today and which underlies all individual practical issues in this: is the Christian religion something revealed by God in Christ, which demands our grateful obedience, or is it something to be made up by ourselves to our own specification, according to our own immediate desires?'[3]

This was also the question which faced the first Tractarians as they set out on a search for holiness based on sound teaching. Their task was to bring the nation back to its religious duties by their teaching, and for this they turned to the Bible, which was the source of God's revelation to his people. They then studied the early Fathers. It is said that the more Newman studied these Fathers, the more he saw that Scripture was used by them to prove the doctrines they had received from the Church's tradition. This latter he regarded as no more than the interpretation of Scripture. It became a matter of the Church to teach and the Bible to prove. In his *Grammer of Assent*, Newman wrote that Christianity is a revelation, 'a definite message from God to man, distinctly conveyed by his chosen instruments and to be received as a message; and therefore to be positively acknowledged, embraced and maintained as true, but as absolutely certain knowledge, certain in the sense in which nothing else can be certain because it comes from Him who neither can deceive nor be deceived.'

Newman, therefore, was prepared to defend this revelation from rationalism which he believed 'was to make our reason the standard and measure of the doctrines received; to stipulate that those doctrines should be such as to carry with them their own justification; to reject them, if they come into collision with our own existing opinions or habits of thought, or are with difficulty harmonized with our own existing stock of knowledge'. He continued by saying that rationalism is 'to accept the Revelation and then explain it away; to speak of it as the word of God and treat it as the word of man'.[4] For Newman the great danger of rationalism was that it made man the centre — not his Maker.

Pusey knew how dangerous was the challenge of rationalism because he had studied in Germany and for a time had been impressed by biblical theology there. Under the influence of his friend Newman at Oriel, no doubt, he rejected it and retracted any writings in which those German studies had been commended. Like Keble, he even adopted an obscurantist view of Scripture and defended every aspect of it, even in the face of reasonable scholarship. For them both, the doctrine of hell and eternal punishment must not be jettisoned. This led them to fight strongly ideas expressed in a book, *Essays and Reviews*, published in 1860, which called in question both a belief in the literal interpretation of the Bible and a belief in everlasting punishment. The language of those essays was moderate and few churchmen today would want to quarrel with it. In those days, however, Darwin's theories of evolution were in their infancy, and the Tractarians believed such writings were a challenge to the reliability of the Bible and thus to the very foundations of Church authority. Incidentally, this clinging to the literal interpretation of the whole Bible explains why, from 1860 to 1894, the Church Union fought a bill in Parliament to legalise marriage with a deceased wife's sister, on the ground that it was against Divine Law found in the Old Testament.

The Tractarians, therefore, based their search for holiness on the revelation of God in Christ. While they were teaching this, however, liberal criticism of the Bible was advancing relentlessly and sometimes making unwarranted claims. The Old Testament first and then the New Testament, including the Gospels, came under close scrutiny. Once miracles and the divinity of Our Lord had been denied because they did not fit into developing scientific discoveries, the barriers were down, and almost everything, including the authorship of the Gospels, was called in question. The progress of this scholarship can be seen in an essay from a recent book, *Jesus and the Politics of His Day*.[5] This chapter, headed 'The Revolution Theory from Reimarus to Brandon', shows the theories held about Jesus over the last two centuries. He was variously described as a messiah, politician, worldly leader, revolutionary, social reformer, Zealot and, even, a mere social myth. A book, *Ecce Homo*, written by Sir John Seeley in 1865, showed Jesus only as a moral reformer and further undermined his authority as God's son.

When I was studying theology at Cambridge just before the war, the authorship of the Gospels was receiving attention. St John's Gospel had been accepted as having been written very late in the first century and for this reason as more a work of devotion than as serious history. There was much speculation about how the Synoptic Gospels came to be composed. Their date became later and later until the theory was advanced that they were more the work of the next generation of believers than of eye-witnesses of the Lord's life. In the words of a post-war biblical scholar, John Robinson, 'the history of Jesus was thus reduced to the history of the Church's understanding of him'.[6]

This speculation became even more radical in the sixties in the hands of scholars like Nineham and Houlden. We were told that the authentic words of Jesus could be reduced to a few sentences. J. Houlden contended that since scripture and tradition have lost their authority, all decisions in Church matters must be made in the light of 'appropriateness' and 'expediency'. Nineham proposed that, philosophy having ceased to function as a partner for theology, a new partner, a senior partner, should be found in the guise of sociology and, in particular, of the sociology of knowledge.[7] Eric Kemp, the Bishop of Chichester, protested in a debate in the General Synod in July 1975 that there was a strong sceptical school which taught that we can have little certainty about what Our Lord said, did, or intended. The historicity of the Gospels was being called in question, and this doubt remains in the minds of many churchmen today. I suspect that most bishops and clergy continue to be dazzled by the continuing speculation and theorising of Bible scholars for these are still taught in our theological colleges. In a recent book, *The Bible Without Illusions*, the authors, R.P.C. and A.T. Hanson, suggest that a common attitude among clergy today is: 'Let us accept a moderate dose of biblical criticism. We are not fundamentalists. But we will drop it when it begins to hurt.'[8] With such a philosophy it is not surprising that the Church's prophetic office has been emasculated. it has led one Indian convert to Christianity to say; 'You English are a very strange people: you teach Christianity critically; but every other religion sympathetically.'

The truth of this comment can be seen in the way we handle religious education today. I visited a leading teachers' training college recently to find out how our future teachers of religious education were being instructed. I was courteously received by the head of that department and given a copy of the Main Course in Religious Studies, which lasted for two years. There were courses in myth, ritual and symbolism; the secular alternative to religion; religion and morality; science and religion; religious language; philosophy of religion; the nature and destiny of man. In the middle, five weeks were given to the Christian Scriptures with a further optional course. Since I knew that many students went to college with a scant knowledge of the Bible, I realised that such a training would not make them competent communicators of the Christian basic documents. This conclusion was supported when I was asked to lecture to the teachers of religious education of a Midlands county. I pressed my views strongly on the importance of teaching the Gospels to children. In the discussion which followed, one of my audience said that in all the conferences she had attended, this was the first time it had been suggested that teaching the Christian faith was part of religious studies. This brought assent from the rest of the teachers.

I am still in contact with teachers in State schools and am consulted about material for the daily or weekly assembly. When I suggest a Christian subject I am told that this could not be used because it might offend some of the pupils. A director of education told me that she wanted to put gospel study into the county's agreed syllabus but the diocesan education committee vetoed it! This fitted into my own experience when I finally left the classroom. I made it known that I was available for education work in the Church at large, and was invited by a diocesan bishop to be master of a medieval foundation and to help with diocesan education. After my installation I waited for information about the education work, only to be met with silence, and, later, by evasion. I had by then given a talk to a deanery about the poor state of religious education in schools and pressed the teaching of the Gospels. This sealed my fate and I heard no more from the diocesan education adviser. I learned from another source that the teaching of the Bible in schools was considered to be indoctrination. I also learned that priests who had actual classroom experience were not asked to be on the diocesan education committee. When I learned that my services were not required by my Church, I accepted an invitation to lecture in Latin and St John's Gospel in the local college of further education.

In my early teaching days after the war the Bible was still within my school's syllabus. It was taught chiefly by the headmaster because my time was mostly employed teaching classics and English to examination standard. As I have noted elsewhere, this was an important part of my training as a professional teacher. I found this experience invaluable when later I found myself in the Royal Naval training service. This has been acknowledged as the best educating system in the country. The reason for this excellence is the urgency to teach young sailors the skills of keeping a ship safely at sea. There is no doubt about what has to be learned, nor about the necessity for keeping a boy at school until he has learned it. Everything was taught with a purpose. I applied this principle when for three years I taught two thousand boy seamen (fourteen to sixteen years) at HMS *Ganges*. Going to church was part of their weekly routine and since few had ever had this experience, it was necessary to explain Christian worship to them. Since every boy took a Bible to sea with him, it made sense that he should be taught how to read it intelligently. Later, when teaching toward the end of the 1950s in a comprehensive school for Service children, I employed the same course, and taught the Gospels to examination standard. By accident (I had not been trained as a teacher) I had discovered a cardinal principle of teaching — the material had to be substantial enough to command the respect of both teacher and pupil. The Bible is such a massive piece of literature that it poses challenges for both teacher and taught.

My first indication of changes in the religious education world came when I started work as a Church Union secretary. At an executive committee the future of our education work was discussed. We were told that there were such exciting developments in their field that we would do well to leave it to the experts. We therefore decided to suspend our education committee. I learned the extent of those 'exciting' changes when I returned to the classroom in the seventies. RE teachers had become lost in the various theories and speculations which surrounded their subject. I did not understand this at first when I was appointed director of religious studies at an important school. On my arrival, I found little evidence that there was a department at all. My office was empty; there was no syllabus; no notebooks, progress reports on pupils, no Bibles. The only textbooks I found were beautifully illustrated softbacks which contained a profusion of subjects: mosques, Indian dancing-girls, old parish churches, animals, Bible characters, religious leaders among whom I found Jesus Christ. Every page contained material and questions which seemed too advanced for younger pupils and too simple for the older. In vain, I tried to discover what my predecessor had taught.

The first teaching period approached and I went empty-handed to the classroom. The first weeks were taken up with getting to know the pupils, talking about my experiences at home and abroad and discussing subjects like exorcism, satanism, Moonies (they had a college not far away and were a source of fascination) and the like. Then my repertoire ran out. I consulted my classes about what they had been taught in the past. 'We used to look at topical events and discuss them'. 'It was boring', one voice interjected. 'We were told about other religions, but he did not know much about them'. 'Sir, why don't we get Christian studies?' The last teacher clearly employed what can be called a DIY Religious Education technique. A series of events or topics is discussed and principles deduced from them. Such programmes are often dull and confusing even though they may be relieved with visual or audio aids. Comparative religion was part of the 'exciting' new developments. The picture builds up of a teacher who was the product of the 1960s. As Hastings wrote, the Bible and supernaturalist Christian theology had been ousted in favour of sociology and the study of other religions.

My solution to my classroom situation was instinctive. I employed a set-book technique which had served me well when I was teaching English and classics. Instead of Shakespeare, Livy and Homer, I used books of the Bible, especially the Gospels. The local SPCK gladly sold hundreds of the New English Bible and we were in business.

In time, every girl took the O level examination in the first three Gospels. Comparative religion and moral matters were not neglected. These came at the beginning and end of the syllabus when the pupils had learned their basic Christian faith. My experience was not an isolated one. At public school chaplains' conferences I found confusion about the teaching of religious education. The lectures given on those occasions gave no encouragement or help for specifically Christian material. In retirement I gave temporary help at another school and found only text books on Hinduism in the senior classrooms.

Such, then, is the state of religious education today after a prolonged period of unsound teaching. It is found in schools, colleges and even ordination courses. Religious studies have become a fringe subject, children leave school without learning the Christian faith and the preacher has nothing distinctive to offer his congregation. If we return to Eric Mascall's words, we learn that 'the Christian religion as something revealed by God in Christ has become something made up by ourselves, to our specification'.

The root of the problem is historicity. I began to understand what had been happening to our scriptures when I read Fr Mascall's book, *Theology and the Gospel of Christ*, published in 1977, after my return to the classroom. On the first page he boldly states, 'we have taken for granted the desupernaturalisation of Jesus and substituted the study of early Christian psychology for the study of divine revelation'.[9] He then produces evidence from scholars who were notable in different fields, to show that the modern pessimism about the reliability of our Gospels for understanding God's revelation is unfounded. Mascall's book marked the beginning of the end of radical biblical criticism, and a new generation of scholars showed a more balanced trend. John Robinson's *Redating the New Testament* showed that late dates for the writing of the Gospels might not be accurate. His *Priority of John* showed that this Gospel was very early, rather than late, and could be a prime source for the life of Jesus. His thesis, first put forward tentatively, has been taken up by other scholars and developed. Robinson's confidence in the historicity of John's Gospel has been shared recently by a classical scholar, Robin Lane-Fox. This author wrote in a searching book: *The Unauthorised Version: Truth and Fiction in the Bible*: 'Nameless or not, a primary source was still the author: marvellous vistas open for those who accept this.'[10] These are interesting words from an author who professes to be an atheist! The theory that the Synoptic Gospels were the work of a later Christian community is being challenged by the alternative view that they owe much to the catechesis or instruction given in a Jerusalem 'school' soon after the Lord's ascension. It would have been natural for the early converts to demand more information about the Lord who had changed their lives.

The very methods used by the former radical biblical critics are also coming under fire. I quote at length from Bishop Neil's book, *The Interpretation of the New Testament 1861–1986* (brought up to date by Tom Wright) which is a realistic analysis of bible scholars' work over a century:

'The theologian might consider to his advantage the methods employed by scholars who are engaged in other fields of knowledge, and particularly by the physical scientists. He would observe that physical scientists are strong in two points at which theologians tend to be weak. The first is the ruthless spirit of self-criticism in which a scientist tests his own work; he asks himself again and again whether the hypothesis he is putting forward is really related to the phenomena which it purports to explain or whether some other explanation is equally possible. In all scientific progress there is an element of inspired intuition, one may call it adventurous guess-work; but this is followed by a long process of experimental verification before results are put forward with any confidence that they are reliable. The second strength of a scientist is in the rejection of hypotheses which have failed to stand up to tests to which they were subjected. The elimination of the impossible and the highly improbable clears the way for the emergence of the highly probable or the certainly established truth. In theology certain proof or disproof is much less often possible than in the physical or biological sciences. But what hinders progress is the persistence in currency of hypotheses in favour of which solid and satisfactory evidence has never been adduced. Because some view has an eminent name attached to it, because it has often been repeated with authority without adequate experimental testing, it comes to be assumed by those who have not the opportunity to test the evidence on which it was originally based that it has a far greater measure of certainty than can legitimately be ascribed to it.'[11]

A study of biblical theology of this century in this country shows how true are the strictures of Bishop Neil.

It appears that we are emerging into a period when sound teaching may once more be restored to the religious teacher in and out of school. We might ask what we mean by 'sound teaching'. We use the word 'soundness' in different walks of life. In cricket we look at a batsman who is making runs and ask if he is sound. We want to know if he has had good basic coaching, for, if he trust only to his natural ability, a bowler will surely topple him in time. We hear a member of Parliament making rousing speeches and attracting a following and ask, Is he sound? Is he just speaking as the spirit moves him or has he got a sound political philosophy? In the end a professional must have patiently laid a solid foundation for his trade so that he may inspire confidence in others. In this sense we call an apple 'sound' if it is good through and through and comes from a good tree. As Jesus said, 'Every good tree bringeth forth good fruit', and this slogan holds good in most walks of life. Make the foundation sure and you will have soundness. A Latin word for 'sound', 'integer', takes us further. Horace begins one of his odes, 'Integer vitae'. This can be translated feebly 'a good-living man'. It means more, and this is shown in our English word 'integrated'. Not only has a good foundation been laid but this has been carefully built upon and the end product is entirely reliable. A person's life must be similarly constructed with perhaps a few flashes of inspiration. Sound teaching in any subject must be soundly based. After many years of experimental education, we are now returning to more traditional methods.

Religious education needs to review theories which have made it innocuous. Despite the compulsory period of religious studies in every school, pupils are leaving without knowledge of the Christian faith. In vain parents protest. British RE has become a kind of religious philosophy which leaves pupils bored. It is time to return to traditional methods which have served the Church well throughout Christian history.

Eric Mascall asks: is the Christian religion something revealed by God in Christ or is something else? The Catholic Church has always taught that Christianity is rooted in history. The Incarnation was an unique historic event and Jesus is an unique historic person. At a certain time God sent his son, born of a woman, to teach us the way of holiness, how we might be like him. A new family of believers was created with a special pattern of life focused on the risen Christ. Eye-witnesses passed on their experience of God-come-to-earth by word of mouth and written documents, the Gospels. These writings together with Christian family life have been passed down through every generation for two thousand years. They are reliable guides for understanding God's revealed will and must be interpreted according to the needs of each age. They must be accepted with gratitude and obedience.

In the course of two centuries, these Gospels have become unreliable witnesses in the hands of speculating scholars, some of whom started from the canon 'if miraculous, therefore unhistorical' as C.S. Lewis wrote.[12] As a result few people today have a balanced picture of Jesus. A caricature of him has been presented in books, on TV and on the stage. It is time the eye-witnesses to his life were read again. For this, new, simple commentaries will be needed for the classroom and parish study group. With this in mind, I produced a small book, *Another Look at St John's Gospel*.[13] Similar treatment is required for the Synoptic Gospels. It is important that each Gospel should be read and studied from beginning to end. The study of a Gospel should stand at the centre of every syllabus. This will still give time and opportunity for studying other matters of religious interest.

Sound teaching in any subject depends on its being taught according to its own discipline. Science and mathematics have their own methods based on experiments in the past and present. English and other languages bring pupils to study great authors; the study of evidence of past events and people belongs to History. If Christian RE is focused on the person of Christ who in history revealed God his Father to us, then it must be true to its own discipline and help pupils to see him as he really was and not as the product of modern imagination. The elimination of false conceptions is an important function of history. This is being done at present in the field of English mediaeval church history. We have long thought this was a period of superstition, decadence and decay. Dr Duffy's book, *The Stripping of the Altars*, which I have mentioned elsewhere, produces abundant evidence to present the opposite It seems that there was a rich church life and that ordinary people were carefully instructed to make the most of it. It has led me to the conclusion that this might have been a high noon of popular piety and religious instruction which we have never regained. It is far more urgent that we should see in a true light the Lord from whom the later Church took its origin.

Anglo-Catholics must be the first to return to sound teaching, for it is part of their tradition. Without it the Christian teacher has no distinctive message and ends with giving moral and social advice without theological support. Eric Mascall sums up his inspiration as a theologian in the words; Theologizandum est in Fide, which means that all theology must be done from within the Faith. He adds that the theologian's motto should not be 'It all depends on me'. He is not committed to beginning all over again; rather he is in a very great tradition.[14] Bible scholars made the mistake two hundred or so years ago when they started to argue away from God's revelation in history and to work outwards from man as the centre. While this philosophy prevails, the Church will have no unique and distinctive message.

I have found unexpected support from a lecture given in a London club by Cardinal Godfried Danneels of Belgium. The subject was, The Future of the Church in a Secularised World. After first delineating the problems of modern Europe with its 'spiritual torpor' and practical atheism, he made a suggestion as to what the Christian Church should do about it. He said that: 'evangelisation in Europe today seems to be suffering from a lack of balance between two different yet corresponding methods of proclaiming the Gospel, the kerygmatic and the didactic'. He defines kerygma as the direct, abrupt proclamation of the saving work of Christ. St Peter, he said, was the inventor of this method when he left the Upper Room and started immediately to preach the good news, without the preparation of his listeners. Life could never be the same again because the Christian faith was different, new, refreshing. On the other hand, he illustrates Christian teaching, or didache, from St Paul's sermon at the Areopagus where he made a more gradual approach and started from a situation his hearers knew, the human situation. (It should be noted that this was the one occasion when St Paul failed to carry his audience with him.) The Cardinal pointed out that in recent years there had been a fantastic effort in the catechetics (didache or didactic) field, supported by a wealth of new techniques, programmes, audio and visual resources. Despite this, pupils leave religious instruction at church or school with little real faith, if any. Their first contact with the living faith still has to come. Too often, it may come only from peripheral religious sects. The Cardinal appealed for more kerygmatic preaching and by this he meant proclaiming the paschal mystery of Jesus together with a profound knowledge of his person, his message and that of the Church. The listener should be led to make a decision for or against the Christian message. When this note has been sounded, the slower processes of catechesis and didache will be needed.

The Cardinal's insight into the future duty of the Christian Church demands our further attention. The word *kerugma* must be understood. A kerux or herald was a very important person in the ancient world, for his duty was to pass on special announcements. He would descend into the market place and proclaim, War has been declared, the enemy has invaded us, peace has been made. At once people would change their life styles to meet the new circumstances. Life would not be the same again. In our modern age we have learnt what a declaration of war can mean, blackouts, rationing, call-ups, sacrifice. The Christian kerygma or proclamation should have the same effect: changed lives. Just as an indefinite message from the herald could be ignored, so the Christian teacher or preacher deserves to be disregarded if his proclamation has no cutting edge.

In this chapter I have mentioned life in the classroom. Here a teacher may be able, charming, good with children. Without the right material, however, he will be merely an entertainer. He will have nothing of importance to communicate to his pupils, a herald without a message. This is the situation of a Christian teacher who has not been trained in the use of the greatest text book of all, the Bible. This is a work of literature which demands a reverent approach from both teacher and pupil. It is the book which is still found in most homes when the rest of the bookshelf is empty. It is like the score of a great piece of music which awaits translation into beautiful sounds, into a symphony for the delight and edification of an audience.

The Catholic teacher, priestly or lay, must be like that under-estimated person, the conductor of an orchestra. To the untutored eye, he has the easy job of waving his hands about in front of skilled players. In fact, the conductor has the most difficult job because he must understand the composer and his work from beginning to end so that the right music may be reproduced. Further, he must understand both the abilities of his musicians and the limitations of their instruments. He will seek to draw out the best possible performance. This, too, is the task of the Christian teacher. He must understand the immense demands of the Gospel writings and accept that they cannot be perfectly rendered. He will, however, do his best with the available performers. He will teach with sensitivity, with the empathy which is essential for a good teacher of any subject. A priest may think that private tuition in the form of spiritual direction is necessary. Here the confessional will be used. Catholics in the modern world have often accepted lower standards or even thought themselves above spiritual advice with the result that the greatest symphony of all the Christian community, has been given a mediocre performance. The priest can easily forget how great a piece of music he has to communicate.

In the last chapter we learned that Père Congar listed the three duties of a layman as priestly, kingly, and prophetic. The priest has the same duties to a greater degree. These offices need to be exercised according to the state of the Church in the world. When it is in a triumphalist situation, in other words when there are captive congregations over large areas, the kingly and priestly offices are mostly required. It is important that Christians should be well-organised and have regular celebrations of the Holy Eucharist. When the Church faces massive unbelief, apathy and ignorance, however, the prophetic or teaching office must be employed. People must be brought back into the Church by teaching, otherwise there will be no congregations to assist at the Eucharist. It would not be right to say that under those circumstances the teacher becomes more important than the celebrant, but his office should not be thought inferior.

The Oxford Movement inherited a situation where the clergy had mostly been concerned with the kingly office. In the first chapter they were described as being respected, even feared, local administrators. Dean Church was quoted as saying that the vicar could be 'the patriarch of the parish, its ruler, its doctor, its lawyer, magistrate, as well as its teacher'. This clearly did not help forward the spiritual life of a parish. For this, the vicar had to be seen as one who derived his powers, not from secular authority, but from the apostles, the early Church, and so from Christ himself.

The Tractarians, therefore, with their concern for holiness, gave priority to teaching this doctrine.

Today Britain again needs to be taught back into the Christian faith. The church which first produces a programme of sound teaching will take the lead in evangelism. Anglo-Catholics can look back on a long tradition of good teaching, and should put it in the forefront of their local church life. It will not be enough that they have taken the orthodox line on ecumenism or the ministry. They must base their liturgy and preaching on the revelation of God in Christ which is found in the Scriptures, and which, when understood, demands their grateful obedience, as Mascall counsels.

'Who was your master in theology:' the Curé D'Ars was asked. 'I had the same master as St Peter', was the reply. The parish priest today could profitably take that as his starting point.

References

1. Hastings p.545
2. Mascall: *Saraband* p.378 (Gracewing 1992)
3. Op. cit. p.380
4. Ker *John Henry Newman* p.121 − Ker
5. Ed. Bammel and Moule 1984
6. *Priority of John* p.30 (SCM 1984)
7. Quoted in *Theology and the Gospel of Christ* (Mascall) p.4 SPCK 1977
8. SCM p.5 1989
9. *Theology and Gospel of Christ* p.1
10. Lane-Fox: *The Unauthorised Version* p.208 (Viking 1991)
11. Oxford p.447
12. *Fernseed and Elephants* p.43 (Fount 1975)
13. The Church Literature Association 1990
14. Mascall: *Saraband* p.383

Chapter Nineteen

Ending in Controversy

Paul Welsby's *History of the Church of England 1945 – 1980* notes that the failure of the Anglican Methodist Scheme for Union in 1972 caused much disappointment. It may well have done to the upper levels of both churches but, as I have shown earlier, it raised little interest at ground level. Indeed as I continued to travel round the country afterwards, there was almost a relief that there would be no more changes to the local religious situation. Anglicans and Methodists had enjoyed meeting each other more than in the past and even sharing the occasional service, but once the debate was over, both sides sprang back gratefully to their own ways of worship. There was always the fear, anyway, that in the event of a merger one side would lose its beloved church or chapel. As I noted near the beginning of this book, the requirements of the ordinary man are much more simple than some of us would like to think and a change of place, worship, or even relationships, can alienate for ever.

Ecumenical Anglicans were loath to give up, and began to search for other approaches which in due course resulted in a scheme for covenanting between a number of churches. This search for unity was fired by different compulsions. The Free Churches probably had the least need for organic union because they had an 'open table' for anybody who wanted to join them at the Lord's Supper. A façade of unity could be produced at any time without the complication of episcopacy and a firm package of doctrines. They had, however, a financial problem because it was becoming increasingly difficult to maintain the many chapels which could be found round the country. So they began to unite among themselves, starting with the United Reform Church of Congregationalists and Presbyterians and if others did not join them, soon they were sharing buildings.

The Roman Catholic Church took an increasing interest in ecumenism in this country, possibly because they wanted to shake off the image of a religious fifth column within the national life. This interest was made easier because Vatican II had taken up a less exclusive stand toward other religions, and had even indicated that there could be more ways to salvation than via Rome, although they might be less safe. A growing relationship between the Pope and Archbishop of Canterbury had led to the setting up of a commission to study differences betwen their two churches with a view to closer union. This Anglican-Roman Catholic International Commission began optimistically in 1967 in Malta and proceeded apace with agreement on many issues including the Eucharist. In 1976 in Venice it showed some consensus on the matter of truth and authority. All this, no doubt, wetted the appetites of many Anglo-Catholics who felt that soon they might be able to share a common Catholic altar. Progress was not maintained, however, when Pope John Paul found his feet in the Vatican, and the Anglican Church found an excuse for not going further by becoming involved with the ordination of women.

The Church of England pressed on with their efforts for unity because Archbishops of Canterbury, starting with Geoffrey Fisher had seen it was in the national and Christian interest, and had set up an ecumenical bureaucracy to work out viable arrangements. Such quangos in the corridors of ecclesiastical power are not easily dissolved! In fairness, however, it must be said that the vision of an united Church was one which any true Christian was bound to follow. Anglicans had been involved in a search for unity since before the first world war.

From the margins of the Church, however, I have formed the opinion that the Church of England found it easier to follow unity and other projects than to put its own theological house in order. Hastings notes that 'no church can continue for long without a theology possessing a fair

measure of internal coherence, one related organically both
to the actual religious practice of believers and to certain
basic requirements of credibility or utility posited by contemporary society,' and goes on to say that by the 1970s
Anglican theology as taught at Oxford and Cambridge was
not fulfilling these needs.[1] At one of my first Church Union
committee meetings as secretary, I found the chief topic was
the gap between academic theology and the theology of the
pew. Hastings says that men like Gore, Temple, Ramsey,
and Farrer were able to bridge that gap, but later scholars
like Nineham, Hick, and Cupitt could not. As I have indicated in the last chapter, radical biblical theology was very
damaging to the teaching of religious education.

When Nineham remarks, 'Is it any longer worthwhile to
attempt to trace the Christian's everchanging understanding
of his relationship with God directly back to some identi-
fiable element in the life, character and activity of Jesus
of Nazareth?'[2] he is striking at the very heart of the
belief and practice of the ordinary Christian, priest and
layman alike. Similar views expressed in a report, *Christian
Believing*, produced by the Doctrine Commission of the
Church of England, undermined historic Christianity as
being unacceptable to the modern mind. When one considers
that this radical school of thought had been responsible for
the training of most of our present bishops and clergy, it is
easy to see how the heart has disappeared out of Anglican
parish life. Read the monthly newsletter of any diocese and
parish, and you will be lucky to find any sound teaching or
even mention of the author of our salvation. Other religions,
social activities, and charitable giving are there in plenty, but
little mention of the Gospel. Meanwhile we have a new generation of scholars who are trying to reveal the reliability
of the New Testament, but are not receiving a mention in
church training. The Church of England blunders on in a
fog, entering new fields of belief and practice which are not
based on the teaching of Jesus and the apostles. We might
display the notice, Danger, Keep out, to any church which
seeks to unite with us at present.

The Church of Rome understands all this and may well
be glad that it has the excuse of the ordination of women

to back away from closer contact with Anglicans. Yet this Church, too, has its problems. It took some time for the decrees of Vatican II to work their way through the Catholic system but when they did they left two opposing parties. First, there were those who did not want change and were happy to give their obedience to a strict ecclesiastical system. This became centred on the Catholic Priests Association which was set up to combat the neo-modernism which was threatening the very vitals of the Church, and also on Archbishop Lefebvre and his Fraternity of Pius X. These supported the old Latin Mass and the traditional disciplines of the Catholic Faith. They found an echo in a lay movement in Britain called Pro Fide. To the left were the Dutch Catholics who followed some of the aggiornamento decrees to their logical conclusions and ended up with a very open-ended Catholicism which embraced very liberal ideas of the Church, the ministry and liturgy. These infiltrated into other countries and among other things produced a casualness in worship which contrasted with the old rubrical Mass. I remember attending a Mass in Northern Italy a few years ago where the priest was dressed untidily, entered informally with a pile of service books under his arm, and proceeded to say Mass with a minimum of ceremonial. The assisting priest was dressed in T shirt and jeans, and this brought home to me a remark made by a friend, that the Romans were using their liturgy like a man knocking his pipe out on the Elgin marbles! On the theology side, Hans Kung, a German Catholic professor, was presenting this liberal approach in books such as, *On being a Christian*, and, *Does God Exist*?

While Pope Paul VI was alive, such variety was allowed to continue and when Dom Basil Hume became Archbishop of Westminster all sorts of ecumenical advances seemed possible. The saying 'Vatican II raised the temperature and the snow melted at the bottom' could well have been extended to include a total thaw. When Pope Paul died, therefore, it was not only Catholics who waited anxiously for the election of his successor. When John Paul II was elected, the first non-Italian pope since the sixteenth century, there was hope that the themes of renewal sounded at Vatican II would be further developed. This did not happen. If it was not back to the bad old days, the temperature of aggiornamento certainly became chilly and an air of uncertainty took over and has remained. Although the new Pope's pastoral concern included a real desire for reunion with other Christians, his enclosed life in Poland prevented him from understanding them. When he returned his Church to more traditional ways, it became impossible to reunite with anybody. Hastings makes the remark that John Paul showed 'an absolutism just a little reminiscent of the Stalinism he had fought so hard against. . . . For Christians in general who had put such large hopes in the unfolding of aggiornamento there could now be only the expectation of a long winter'.[3]

This situation has remained, yet there is much good will and even love. All Christians started to love each other as never before, inside and outside church. At the Eucharist it became the custom to make a break in the liturgy so that there could be handshaking, hugging and even kissing, and it became a mark of a real Anglo-Catholic that he was not less affectionate in giving the Peace. Outside, the Romans joined the local council of churches and even took office there. Lent was given up in many areas to joint courses of study, and again Catholics were to the fore. All enjoyed being entertained in each other's homes and churches. If there was not an open table for all, nevertheless everybody worshipped together. Who knows where all this would have ended under another kind of pope? The snow has continued to melt at the bottom, even though it has frozen again at the top. It would be true to say that never has there been in this country such a breaking down of religious barriers. Maybe we should not attempt more at this stage.

This has not satisfied those in the ecclesiastical corridors of power and there have been renewed efforts to achieve more organised unity. With the churches in some disarray, as I have shown, this could be negotiating from weakness, ending up with a least common multiple rather than the highest common factor. This was the danger of a new move, Covenanting for Unity, by which the main churches would agree to seek visible unity and meanwhile 'recognise' each other's members as true members of the Body of Christ. There would be intercommunion without conditions and a recognition of each other's ministries provided that episcopacy was accepted by non-episcopal Churches. Strangely, the doctrine of 'recognition' was put forward by a broad-minded Jesuit, Father John Coventry, who in turn had received it from a Dutch Catholic, Father Schillebeeckx. Starting from the idea that the Church itself is the basic sacrament, an historically visible and effective sign of the presence and action of the risen Lord in the world, he taught that if all the Churches act formally and precisely as Churches, in an act of mutual acceptance and reconciliation, they thereby effect all that could be brought about by any particular actions of a sacramental nature, such as ordination. If the Church of Rome or of England accepted a non-episcopal Church in the covenanting action envisaged, it would thereby incorporate its ministry into the historic episcopate, and 'validate' or supply anything that might be needed, without further and lesser acts of ordaining. Coventry was a man out on his own in the Roman Catholic Church and admitted it, but his ideas found some acceptance with a few Anglo-Catholics who a few years before had supported the unity scheme with the Methodists. Later, Eric Kemp pointed out that if this idea of Schillebeeckx was extended to baptism, it would mean that in a reconciliation with the Society of Friends, Quakers would effectively become baptised — 'and that would be a very strange doctrine'.

In the event, the mention of 'bishop' scared some of the Free Churches. Shamed, however, or challenged by a motion at the Nottingham conference of the British Council of Churches in 1964 that all should covenant to work and pray for union by Easter Day 1980, fresh attempts were made to get a workable solution. When these were put before the General Synod in 1980, they received a mixed reception and the Catholic group voted against them. In 1981 the Church Union's Theological Committee met and produced a report, *Proposals for Covenanting, Some Considerations*.[4] This committee was a high-powered one with such names as Eric Kemp (Bishop of Chichester), Rowan

Williams, Roger Greenacre, Brian Horne, Cheslyn Jones, Roy Porter. It noted that there seemed to be no agreement about theological matters such as the doctine of the Church and the ministry, especially the episcopate. No doubt they had in mind the disagreement which surfaced with the Church of South India and Anglican/Methodist reunion schemes. Was a bishop of the esse of the Church or only the bene esse, was he essential or merely a convenience? They were also worried about the clause which said that covenanting discussions should 'in no way pre-judge the admissibility and acceptability of women to the ordained ministry of the Church of England'. Since this matter was being hotly debated in and out of the General Synod, the Church Union did not want ordained women brought in by the back door.

This, of course, would have happened. The Church Union was not aggressively hostile to the process of covenanting but it refused to let its mind be governed by its heart. The attempt to organise a covenant from the centre faded away and it has been left to local councils of churches to make their own arrangements. Surprisingly in some areas Roman Catholics have been in the forefront of covenanting services but are still precluded from intercommunion by papal authority.

So far disagreements within the Church of England had been about interpreting or adjusting what was already within its formularies and ministry. There now arose a more serious challenge to its Catholicity from the proposal to introduce the new element of a female priesthood into its constitution. Since this form of ministry could not be found in the Gospels, or New Testament, in tradition nor in the early Fathers, it was clear that it would be resisted strongly by those who valued those authorities. The debate became complicated because it took place against a background of social changes which had their roots in the days before the First World War. Since sex was involved, people inside and outside the Church became emotively involved, and opponents of a female priesthood were accusing of being unfair to women. To make the debate even more difficult, the later stages were carried out at a time of the radical biblical theology mentioned earlier in this chapter. As we shall see this virtually removed the teaching of Our Lord as an authority for deciding the matter. If 'the history of Jesus is reduced to the history of the church's understanding of him' — to use John Robinson's words again — then the tradition of sound teaching which the Catholic Church has followed from the beginning is removed and it is every man for himself.

It is possible to look back to the early years of this century and see a creeping barrage of feminism overwhelming one outpost after another until it finally reached the churches. Even before the First World War, women were making their voices heard in societies like the Student Christian Movement. The 1914–18 War began to mobilise women to keep the home fires burning while men were being slaughtered in great numbers abroad. This gave them an independence they had never had before. Between the wars it became the rule rather than the exception for women to go out to work, and the Second World War confirmed their importance in running the nation. Not only did they assume positions of responsibility in civilian posts but they took their place in the Armed Forces. In some places they shared the dangers of the menfolk when, for example, they manned gun sites or organised rescue work in the Blitz. After 1945, therefore, they sought and were given most of the authority which once belonged to men. Sex discrimination found its way into the statute book.

Until about twenty five years ago this unisex life style touched the churches only lightly and the Church of England not all. There had been poorly paid church workers and deaconesses for many years but few would have suggested that they should be given higher status. In 1916 Canon Lacey wrote in the *Church Times*, 'The scheme of the ladies who desire ordination has for a long time been familiar to me; I have never found occasion to do anything but laugh at it.' That remained the prevalent Anglican point of view except for a few liberals like Canon Raven who espoused many an unlikely cause. An exception was the ordination of a deaconess, Florence Li, as a priest in the Second World War when Hong Kong was isolated and a prison. The bishop ordained her to minister the sacraments in Macao. When the emergency was over she was persuaded to withdraw into lay life.[5] This precedent was remembered, however, as the women's movement everywhere, and especially in the United States, made headway. It should be said that feminism in the States developed into such an extreme dogma that some women thought it degrading to have to run a home and bring up children.

In time this development produced a feminist theology in which God was reckoned to be a woman and prayers to him were adjusted accordingly. No longer was it merely a matter of who should minister in his holy house.

Meanwhile the post-war years were difficult enough for the Church without the introduction of further complications and it is hard to see Archbishop Geoffrey Fisher, as a pillar of the Establishment, having strong views on the subject. However, the issue was discussed in the Fifties and when Michael Ramsey became Archbishop of York he was asked if he had any objections to women 'ministers'. He said the question ought to be fairly considered. On the one hand Christianity had enhanced the status of women and yet Christ had only chosen men as his apostles. As the Church on earth has the analogy of the family, the priest is like the father in the family. He said that he was prepared to have a good look at the possibility of change, knowing that God does reveal new truths to us after lapses of time. He saw, however, the importance of viewing the issue in relation to the cause of unity, with Methodists, Roman Catholics and in the links with other Anglican provices overseas.

Owen Chadwick notes in his biography of Michael Ramsey that in his early years at Canterbury he saw no possibility that women could become priests.[6] This was on traditional grounds. The Church had always insisted on males as priests. If there had to be change it could only be done by an ecumenical council of the whole Church. Chadwick writes that in his later years Ramsey thought it could happen, though not in his time as archbishop. This was because at the 1968 Lambeth Conference he saw that opinion was shifting in this direction. The conference asked all the Churches to study the ordination of women to the priesthood and to report the result to the Anglican Consultative Council which had been set up as a kind of mini-Lambeth to monitor any urgent needs of the provinces. Lambeth agreed that theology gave no clear guidance for or against a female priesthood, but one of its committees wanted a clear statement that there was no theological objection to the ordination of women. This demand was opposed and amended to something more inconclusive.

In fact, the Church of England's Church Assembly had discussed a report *Gender and Ministry* in 1963 and wanted reasons to be given for withholding the priesthood from women. A Commission was set up, but made no judgment and merely issued considerations, which was a convenient way of shelving an awkward matter. In fact the Church of England was about to be split over the Anglican/Methodist reunion scheme and to throw another explosive proposition into the middle would have been enough to blow this Church apart. In 1968, however, a report, *Women in Ministry*, said that the Church must resolve the matter of the ordination of women before a further definition of their ministry could be made. The Church Assembly agreed that women lay readers could take services and preach as their male counterparts were doing. They began to take an increased part in worship.

In 1971 the Anglican Consultative Council met at Limuru, Kenya, and at the Bishop of Hong Kong's request raised the matter. As was said earlier, Hong Kong was the only diocese to have experience of a woman priest and had not regretted it. The bishop asked for guidance. An Australian woman member of the Council asked for a practical answer to the question whether a woman might be ordained priest. A non-Anglican observer from Uganda, John Mbiti, drew attention to the fact that in some parts of Africa, women were the leaders of society and might more appropriately be priests. Ramsey, unhappy about this move to ordain women, voted against the resolution which, nevertheless was carried by a very small majority. The ACC was not the proper place for this kind of debate which should have taken place in a full synod of the whole of Anglican communion. Against Ramsey's advice the Bishop of Hong Kong ordained to the priesthood two women in November 1971. Far away, down under in New Zealand, women were ordained in 1974, followed by Canada in 1975. All this threw the Episcopal Church in America into chaos because a number of liberal bishops wanted to go the same way. In 1974 three retired bishops and a bishop from Costa Rica uncanonically ordained some women in Philadelphia. This opened the floodgates and soon women were being priested throughout the Anglican dioceses of the States, causing intense disunity. Not content with this, Bishop Spong, called a liberal subversive by John Peart-Binns in his biography of Graham Leonard, already had his sights on a woman bishop. This took some years to achieve but finally happened. Meanwhile Ramsey was wrestling with the problem at home. Chadwick notes that he said he was not against women priests but could not take the step without reference to other Churches. He found himself facing secular pressures when a bill about discrimination against women was debated in Parliament. Some peeresses, like Baronesses Summerskill and Gaitskell, who had no religion but only a concern for women's rights could not understand why the Churches should be exempt from the bill. All this made Ramsey glad to retire before the issue became too acute in England. This he did in 1974 and so was not president of the General Synod when it voted in 1975 that there were no theological objections to women priests. He had been succeeded by Donald Coggan who welcomed all the Anglican bishops to Lambeth in 1978. He himself was keen on the ordination of women and found himself joined by a number of fellow bishops who had actually done the deed. It should be pointed out that the Episcopal Church in America has such an abundance of bishops that they are able to flood Lambeth.

At this point Graham Leonard took the lead in opposing this trend. He had been the suffragan bishop of Willesden when he had effectively opposed the Anglican/Methodist reunion scheme and there were those who hoped he might be chosen for London when Stopford resigned in 1972. However he was passed over and was sent, some thought into exile, to Truro and here he employed his many talents for the benefit of that lovely and unusual diocese. He found himself at Lambeth in 1978 and organised bishops whom he knew were opposed to the ordination of women. There was little this group could do completely to stave off further moves to extend a female priesthood, but it was able to make important modifications to the final resolutions on the subject.

These resolutions were debated in the General Synod in November 1978 and here Graham Leonard was able to offer more effective leadership. Later,he was to give his reasons for opposing the ordination of women. Peart-Binns quotes a statement he made in 1986:[7]

'I believe it undermines and questions the way in which God himself has taught us how to speak of him and know him. I do not believe it was by accident but by God's deliberate choice that he chose to reveal himself in a patriarchal society and became man in Christ, as a male. The highest role ever given to any human being was given to a woman, Mary, when she responded to God's call to be the mother of Christ. We cannot disregard these facts to suit our ideas today.

'Secondly, the Church of England claims to have continued the ordained ministry as given by God and received from the universal Church. I do not believe it has the right or power to alter it fundamentally without destroying that claim.

'In my judgment, the whole approach (and the arguments) of those who press for the ordination of women questions and undermines the revealed nature of the Christian faith, as given by God, not devised by man.

I quote all this in full because they are basically my views and those of many Anglo-Catholics. Some of the latter would want to emphasise the importance of keeping in line with the rest of Catholic Christendom, but might not take such a firm stand on divine revelation in the Scriptures. But it has been said of Leonard that he judges contemporary thought by divine revelation rather than judging biblical revelation by the extent to which it matches contemporary thought. It will be clear from what I have written in an earlier chapter that I have the same respect for the revelation of God which Jesus gave us.

So the scene shifted from Lambeth to Church House, Westminster and Leonard summed up the situation as follows:

'The Church of England is still free to make its decision and this decision will have a considerable effect on the rest of the Anglican Communion.

'The Church of England must consider the effect in the Anglican communion and on ecumenical relations.

'The position of opponents must be openly and honourably faced.

The arguments in principle can still be put but they will have to be considered in the context of why it should not happen in England rather than on the bare principle of whether it should happen anywhere.'

He also noted that there was evidence that ordained women were not finding it easy to find employment in parishes. He said that there had to be sound theological teaching in our parishes without which pragmatism would win the day.

In his speech in the Synod he made it clear that he did not appeal to Rome, or Constantinople or Geneva but, as an Anglican, to scripture and tradition and reason, tested by scripture.

The full motion before the Synod asked for legislation to remove the barriers to the ordination of women to the priesthood and their consecration to the episcopate. The voting was:

Bishops 26 for, 10 against; Clergy 87 for, 113 against; Laity 110 for, 65 against.

Battle was now joined. A Movement for the Ordination of Women (MOW) came into being and campaigned with great energy. Among its leaders were the bishops of Southwark (Bowlby) and Manchester (Booth-Clibborn), supported by pamphlets from Salisbury (John Austin Baker) and Lincoln (Phipps). Later the Bishop of Bristol (Rogerson), took over the leadership of MOW. Monica Furlong, a journalist, was the moderator. Other bishops began to stand up and be counted as supporters of the movement.

It has been said the Catholics as a party were slow in organising opposition. Although the majority opposed it, a few thought that a female priesthood might belong to Catholic renewal. Generally they were dazed by the situation and, having lacked sound teaching for many years, did not know how to take their stand upon that biblical revelation which was the mainstay of Graham Leonard's approach to all church matters. The Church Union, however, remained steady in its opposition and under its president, Eric Kemp, now Bishop of Chichester, quietly made it possible for the Catholic Group in the Synod to enable sound theological argument to be heard. When Leonard retired in 1991, Eric Kemp became the leader of the opposition. He had been on the other side in the Anglican- Methodist debate and had that scheme been successful the Church of England would have found itself caught up in a female priesthood through its Methodist connection.

In 1981, however, Graham Leonard was translated from Truro to London where his leadership of Catholics became even stronger. He was quickly called upon to deal with an unwise incident in his new diocese where a woman priest from America, Elizabeth Canham, at the invitation of the Dean of St Paul's, Alan Webster, a leading supporter of MOW, celebrated a furtive Eucharist in his Deanery. Leonard took firm action over this illegal act and received much sympathetic support. Nevertheless MOW continued to go forward and increasingly invaded the business of the General Synod. In November 1984 in a packed house a motion was debated, asking for the standing committee to bring forward legislation to permit the ordination of women to the priesthood, and this was carried in all houses on a simple majority. This victory for MOW was not unexpected and it was known that a later stage would need a 67% percentage.

At this point it might be asked what the attitude of the Pope and the Roman Catholic Church was. Considerable advance toward understanding on most issues had been made in the ARCIC discussions and many Anglicans were hopeful of a better recognition of their status. The Vatican II aggiornamento had made many changes, as we have seen, among which was a greater place for women in the life of the local church. If Pope Paul VI had remained in office who knows what further adjustments there might have been? But it is clear from a booklet, *Women Priests: Obstacle to Unity? Documents and Correspondence, Rome and Canterbury, 1975–1986*,[8] that no encouragement was given for an Anglican move to ordain women. Despite a reasoned letter from Archbishop Runcie in 1985, the reply from Rome was 'No,' and it was made clear that it would become an obstacle to further unity between the churches. The Eastern Church was just as adamant. All this made Anglo-Catholics the more eager to defeat any moves to make women priests.

They were not so concerned, however, at the proposal to make women deacons, which received the royal assent at the end of 1986, because they hoped this would satisfy the women and they would not want more. The Bishop of London, anyway, for years had been in favour of a perpetual diaconate. Although it was clear that women had never been ordained to the priesthood in the Catholic church, the same could not be said of women as deacons and therefore he could not oppose the move on principle. Some Catholics did not agree with him. Two suffragans, Conrad Meyer of Dorchester and Brian Masters of Edmonton refused to ordain any women. Conrad Meyer took early retirement rather than be involved with such ordinations. In retrospect, it must be said that these two were right. There had been no proper theology of the diaconate worked out and some women continued to see it as another rung on the ladder toward the priesthood and episcopate. More seriously they were now included in the House of Clergy and although their numbers were restricted in the 1985–90 Synod, this did not apply in 1990 when more were elected on a priesthood ticket. This weakened the opposition in that house. Women deacons were now promoted in the dioceses to the limit of their authority and some were put in charge of parishes. This was done on the excuse that there were not enough men.

There was a shortage because in recent years vicars had been forced to retire at 65, or, at the latest, 70. Many would have gone on longer in the tradition of 'once a priest, always a priest'. A bureaucratic Church of England took a different attitude. In fact, there has been no shortage of celebrants for the Eucharist and many priests, relegated to the sidelines, have felt the loss of a regular altar very keenly. The opponents of a female priesthood, however, did have one success in July 1986 when the General Synod could not find a two thirds majority to allow women priests ordained abroad to minister in this country, even for limited periods. It was a hard fought battle led by the Archdeacon of Leicester, David Silk, who pointed out that the proposal was really prejudging an issue which had by no means been decided in this country. He was strongly supported by two laymen, John Gummer, who was a member of the Government as well as being a devoted Anglo-Catholic, and Oswald Clark, a solicitor. These three were later joined by Canon George Austin from the St Alban's diocese, who roundly attacked church authority on a very broad front for its liberalism. In a rare moment of generosity toward this enemy the Archbishop of York offered him the archdeaconry of his diocese. This high office has not diminished his opposition.

At the same July Synod the report, *The Ordination of Women to the Priesthood: the Scope of the Legislation*, was debated. This caused great alarm to Catholics because it seemed as if it were taken for granted that it was only a matter of time before such a proposal was successfully passed. Graham Leonard again took the initiative, and invited all who believed that the ordination of women to the priesthood would imperil the doctrinal position of the Church of England to write to a priest in Oxford giving their names to be included in a register. Quickly 20,000 names were recorded. An Open List of 2,000 clergymen who opposed the ordination of women was printed, and this steadily grew to 4,000.

The next stage of the debate moved to 1987 when the bishops spelled out the safeguards which would need to be brought into any legislation to allow women to be ordained to the priesthood. By the July Synod in York the bishops issued a code of practice to deal with those who could not accept women priests. As one Synod member notes, 'Up to that point the matter had been somewhat theoretical but now it became clear what opposition was going to cost and acrimony began to creep into the proceedings.'

At this stage a pressure group of mainly Catholic priests, and some Evangelicals, formed a movement called Cost of Conscience. Before that, female opposition to the ordination of members of their sex surfaced in a movement called WAOW, Women Against the Ordination of Women, and this too has gained great support and influence. Mention should be made of Dr Margaret Hewitt, a prominent member of the General Synod, whose energetic efforts for the Catholic cause enabled this society to be formed. Unfortunately she died of cancer before the debate was over, but there were outstanding women to take her place.

Yet another society was formed to oppose the MOW. This was called the AAM or Association for the Apostolic Ministry and was a largely theological approach by Catholics and Evangelicals, organised by the Church Union. Evangelicals had been slow to take action, mainly because they were deeply divided. Some leading memebers of their party, like Donald Coggan in the past, and David Sheppard, Michael Turnbull, Gavin Reid and Colin Craston in the present, have been strong supporters of the ordination of women. But others like Roger Beckwith and Canon John Pearce have opposed it, chiefly because it would give women an oversight in church worship and affairs which is contrary to Scripture.

The Cost of Conscience movement began by organising a conference at Keble College, Oxford which was so successful that others took place elsewhere. Generally it has sought to be practical about the consequences of priests being forced out of their Church. It has not only looked at financial aspects of the situation but has debated arrangements for alternative episcopal oversight. It has been made clear that bishops who ordained women to the priesthood would put themselves out of communion with those who had remained faithful to the traditional apostolic ministry. There has been no thought of taking refuge in Rome, but of seeking a solution within the Church of England. It has proposed that congregations who were opposed to women priests should no longer pay quotas to their diocese. This in the end may decide the issue for the time being, because the Church of England at present is short of funds.

It would also find it difficult to compensate those who had been forced to leave.

On a straight majority but with considerable opposition the Synod of 1985–90 sent a draft measure forward and then referred the matter to the dioceses. Voting figures on the ordination of women in dioceses and deaneries were not ready until 1992 when a new Synod had been elected. Although 38 dioceses were in favour, yet some had only narrow majorities and, if a two thirds majority had been required, approval of the proposals would have been gained in only 21. Seven dioceses, Blackburn, Chichester, London, Truro, Portsmouth, Europe and the Forces, voted against. Deanery voting showed even greater division and it became clear that if the General Synod voted for the measure, bishops would have to deal with great disunity. There were signs that some were unwilling to do so.

As I write this, yet another vote has been taken in the Synod on the draft legislation to admit women to the priesthood. For this a straight majority was required. This was given but it was clear that when a two thirds majority is needed, the House of Laity might not give it in November 1992. That would end the debate for the time being. Perhaps it is fitting that the laity should be the final jury in this very divisive motion. However, many think that the subject will only lie dormant until the next Synod, but by then legislation will have to begin afresh.

Those who have campaigned for the ordination of women have maintained it was necessary for the good and the growth of the Church. Anglo-Catholics throughout the world have disputed this. Evidence may be sought from those Anglican provinces which have already ordained women priests, some a number of years ago, to see what benefit has been gained. It is difficult not to conclude that disunity and chaos have resulted. This is seen especially in America where the Episcopal Church has splintered into several continuing churches and where court cases abound to decide the right to church property. A female priesthood has sparked off such a wave of liberalism that the traditional values and doctrines have all but disappeared. A considerable drop in church membership has been reported. The Church in Canada has similar problems. A growing church of continuing Anglicans exists there which maintains a traditional faith and practice in an almost catacomb-like style. I have before me a report from New Zealand which shows that from 1978 there has been an accelerating decline in Anglican church attendance, and this belies the hope that a female priesthood would rejuvenate the Church. The report also says that in important centres of church life, like for example St John's Theological College in Auckland, orthodox belief now has ceased to exist. Some teachings are barely recognisable as Christian. The prayer book has been revised on liberal lines. The psalms have received anti-Semitic treatment so that words like Sion and Israel have been removed. The Church in Australia is engaged at present in a damaging legal controversy and the Church of Ireland has not carried all its members along with it. Altogether this is not a happy picture and it is little wonder that Anglo-Catholics in England are fighting hard to preserve its own Church's unity. There are many non-party church people who do not want this female priesthood. This is the greatest crisis the Anglican Church has faced and it is not possible to see what the end will be. I have outlined the controversy in the same way as I did for the Anglican/Methodist reunion scheme because I believe it brings to a climax the uneasy situation which Anglo-Catholics have faced since 1833. If the theme of this book is marginality there can be no more extreme example than what is happening now. Catholics are even being pushed out of the margins. This might have happened over a united Anglican/Methodist Church when there was a prospect of a continuing Anglican Church. Such a crisis was avoided, but it is difficult to see anything but a splintered Church of England if the ordination of women is pushed further.

As will appear from the earlier chapter, I was much involved in the earlier controversy. I have had to watch the present one from the sidelines. When it was gathering speed I was hard at work in the classroom. Now in retirement I have watched the debate with increasing alarm and bewilderment, the latter because it has seemed madness to split a church which was engaged in ten years of intensive evangelism.

As I have listened to the debate from the margins, several conclusions have formed in my mind. The first is that behind it all has been a motivation to keep in line with social development. The place of women in society has improved, therefore it is claimed that this must also be shown in church life. With a woman prime minister and women invading every post of authority, the argument has been advanced that the Church should allow its women to be priests, bishops or even archbishops. This would help raise the status of woman through the world! Such arguments are tempting until one realises that the Church is not just another organisation, but a family established by Jesus Christ himself with a way of life which can be recognised as of God and not as of men. Sacraments are such because the Lord ordained the words, the minister, and the outward form. If we were following social custom should we not change the outward sign of the eucharist to tea and biscuits which, certainly in this country, are more normal than bread and wine? Most Christians, however, are simple people and can only understand the sacraments, especially the Eucharist, as means of holiness because they are revealed as such in the Gospels.

This brings me to another conclusion. This debate about women priests has taken place against a background of poor theology. In his history of Christianity in this century Hastings has pointed to the '60s as being a time when the authority of the Bible and the Church were rejected as irrelevant and outdated and when secularisation and demythologising took over. Most of the bishops and clergy who took part in the measure to ordain women were brought up in that kind of climate. They were taught that the formation of the Gospel writings took place in later generations of Christians and therefore were mainly their creations. A logical conclusion which follows from this is that if a later generation can put together its own experience of the living Lord in the Church, even later ones may do the same. So the conclusion passed by the General Synod in 1975 that there were no fundamental objections to women's ordination could easily be reached, because its members were not taking seriously the Gospels as reliable witness to the Lord's intentions for his Church. This kind of theology, however, is not the final story. As I said earlier, a more modern school of bible scholars is now seeing the Gospels as a product of a very early catechetical school in Jerusalem and therefore excellent authorities for guiding the Church in every generation until the end of time. This new school is still establishing itself and I would hope that any action to ordain women would be based on a more balanced biblical theology. If the Gospels do tell us about Our Lord's provisions for his Church then, in humility and obedience, those in search of holiness must observe them.

This debate has made Catholics examine how women can be better employed in the Church. One strong reason why women have sought the priesthood is that they felt themselves called to serve God more fully. Perhaps the answer may be found in what I said in the chapter on sound teaching. There I stated that there were three duties of both laymen and priests, kingly, priestly, and prophetic. Each assumed an importance in different situations. When the Church faces massive unbelief, apathy and ignorance, the prophetic or teaching office assumes an overall priority. It is useless to multiply the celebrants if nobody wants their Eucharists. So the lapsed and ignorant have to be taught back into the Church. For this devoted and professional teachers are required. I have seen from the classroom the shortage of RE teachers. This could be remedied if the women who feel they have a vocation from God could find it in the privilege of teaching. This is no soft option. The office of a Christian teacher today is much harder than that of the priest in the parish. Women, therefore, might well put their own ambitions aside for the time being and reconsider what God wants from them for the revival of religion in this country.

This is not a second-best solution thought up to divert women away from their object. It is part and parcel of the lesson which Catholics have understood from the beginning of the Oxford Movement. They taught first and then worked out other problems later. Sound teaching has always been the requirement for spiritual progress and this is desperately needed today. If more dedicated women could see their vocation in this light, our Church might be renewed and not divided.

References

1. Hastings p.662
2. Quoted Hastings p.650
3. Hastings p.643
4. Proposals for Covenanting: Some Considerations (CLA 1981)
5. Carpenter: Fisher p.659 seq
6. Chadwick W.O. *Michael Ramsey* pp.278 seq (Oxford 1990)
7. Peart-Binns: *Graham Leonard* pp.216 seq (DLT 1988)
8. Catholic Truth Society 1986

Chapter Twenty

Celebrating the Faith of
Marginal Catholics

The Anglo-Catholic movement began in the margins of the Church, and continued in the margins, and at the end of my story, finds itself so much on the edge that it may not be contained much longer. A small group of friends in an Oxford common room in the early part of the nineteenth century provided a marginal prelude to a cause which would in time influence the whole Church of England and beyond. An open list of several thousand clergymen who oppose the ordination of women and who are threatened with exclusion from their Church might be considered a suitable epilogue to a period of church history.

But is it an epilogue? Two recent writers on Anglo-Catholicism whom I mentioned at the beginning of this book suggest that it is. Francis Penhale writes in *Catholic In Crisis*, 'The future of Anglican Catholicism is uncertain. It is shrinking, divided and ageing. The current weaknesses are deep within its culture and institutions and will not be changed by rhetoric alone.... One hundred and fifty years after its beginnings Anglican Catholicism has run into some of the classic problems of the religious protest movement. It has become routinized and sclerotic: social change has removed large sections of its original constituency and it has failed to find a new one.'

Another study, *Anglo-Catholicism, A Study in Religious Ambiguity*, by W.S.F. Pickering, also mentioned earlier, lists all the signs of decay and decline in the movement;

many famous churches closed, congresses no longer viable, the collapse of various publishing houses such as the Dacre Press and the Society of SS Peter and Paul, failure to raise funds for Pusey House. He mentions divisions over matters like Vatican II, moral teaching, the charismatic movement, the reunion schemes and the ordination of women. He quotes Alan Wilkinson's essay, *Requiem for Anglo-Catholicism*, in the magazine *Theology* in 1978 and says that no theologian answered nor did hackles rise. 'None had the stomach or heart to reply – all assurance as to what Catholicism is about, or wants to achieve, seems to have vanished. The 1930s, as we have shown, was totally different, with the publication of a great deal of fairly learned polemic. Anglo-Catholicism was worth fighting for.' Pickering puts down the decline and fall of the party to not developing or moving on as the Roman Catholic Church has done.[1] It has become 'fossilized' because for a long time Anglo-Catholics have played for safety above everything else. It is fair to say that like Penhale he is unwilling to write off Anglo-Catholicism, but he certainly paints a gloomy picture. Both writers owe much to the movement and want it to succeed, but both agree to treat it as a bit of social history which has had its day. There are others who have not been so charitable and who would willingly see it expelled from its mother church.

As I read such jeremiads I am reminded of a story of a group standing round the bed of an ailing man – his wife, his doctor and his vicar. 'I think he's dying', said the doctor. 'I'm afraid you're right', said the priest. The man sat up and said, 'Oh no, I'm not'. At this his wife spoke up, 'Now just you lie down again. Parson and doctor know best.' However, my experience as a Catholic in the Church of England makes me see the situation differently, and the writing of this book has confirmed my optimism. I am on the side of the patient.

No doubt it is possible to look at the subject from different angles, and the two authors mentioned above write as sociologists. History and social factors may well have affected the course of the movement, but I believe it is first and foremost a spiritual phenomenon. My own experience inspires me to see it as part of man's search for holiness. For this reason, my first chapter dealt with the simple needs of religious man and I have tried to show how Anglo-Catholics have satisfied them and are still doing so. Because there is a persistence of religion in what appears to be a completely secular society, there will be a continuing need among some for what Catholicism offers.

Origen, an early Christian Father, writes that the main aim of all rational creatures is to become like God. He says this is not so much a discovery of the philosophers as something derived from Holy Scripture. For does not the book of Genesis illustrate this when it describes the original creation of the human race in the words, 'God said, "Let us make human beings in our image and likeness"'?[2] The human race received the dignity of God's image at the beginning of its creation, whereas the perfection of God's likeness is reserved for the end. Human beings must achieve perfection by imitating God in his works. The possibility of perfection is there right at the beginning by virtue of the image.' Origen's words explain why through the ages human beings have reached out toward the source whence they came. It is as if a small ship or boat, finding itself in the middle of an ocean, wants to be tied up safely again in its home port. In the first centuries after the resurrection of their Lord, Christians saw that by baptism they had entered into this desired relationship, and they sought to preserve it by their church life in sacraments, worship, prayers, and discipline.

Thus they found themselves in two kinds of life: living in ambiguity, to quote Pickering's words about Anglo-Catholicism. They were members of the world but also belonged to the heavenly city. In a letter to a man called Diognetus, an early Christian writes that the difference between Christians and the rest of mankind is not a matter of nationality, language or customs. 'They pass their lives in whatever township − Greek or foreign − each man's lot has determined; and conform to ordinary usage in their clothing, diet and other habits. Nevertheless, the organisation of their community does exhibit some features that are remarkable, and even surprising. For instance, though they are residents at home in their own countries, their behaviour is more like transients; they take their full part as citizens, but they also submit to anything and everything as if they were aliens.... Though destiny has placed them here in the flesh, they do not live after the flesh; their days are passed on earth, but their citizenship is above in the heavens.'

Here is real ambiguity, two kinds of life styles, which those who seek true holiness follow. In time those magical days of the early Church passed, and Christians became earthbound when membership of Christ's family became a formality. However, the revelation of God through Jesus which made the spirituality of the first Christians so enthusiastic, became encapsulated in a basic profession of belief. This deposit of faith (depositum fidei) which was worked out by Councils and the early Fathers, covered the Creeds, ministry, worship, tradition and Scripture. Bishops were responsible for handing on this depositum intact by ordaining and confirming fresh generations of faithful priests and laity. On this foundation an ideal of holiness could be pursued by those who wanted it.

There were eras when this vision faded, but there remained a few for whom the search for holiness remained imperative. They sought to sweep aside worldly impediments, to seek union with God and to become holy. In the very troubled world of the fall of the great Roman Empire, St Benedict established a school of the Lord's service and gave it a rule to lead it to holiness. Some centuries later, when the love of God had again grown cold in the world, as a Collect puts it, St Francis of Assisi renewed the vision.

Inspired by men like these, popular piety could blossom. Late medieval Catholicism in this country has been considered by historians as decayed and decadent. Recently Eamon Duffy, in a book I mentioned in my first chapter, has shown that this was not so. Englishmen were fervent in their practice of their faith and were assisted by a skilled programme of instruction. As the spirituality of the early Church had taken its strength from the celebration of the Lord's resurrection at the Eucharist, so villagers thronged the altars for Mass in the years before the Reformation.

'As kneeling congregations raised their eyes to see the Host held high above the priest's head at the sacrifice, they were transported to Calvary itself, and gathered not only into the passion and resurrection of Christ but into the full sweep of salvation history as a whole.... The body of Christ, greeted as "journey-money for our pilgrimage, solace of all our longing", was the focus of all the hopes and aspirations of late mediaeval religion. The sacrifice of the Mass was the act by which the world was renewed and the Church was constituted, the Body on the corporal was the emblem and instrument of all truly human embodiment, whether it was understood as individual wholeness or as rightly ordered human community.'[3] This was no perfunctory act of worship. Duffy shows how people were taught to pray the Mass both as individuals and as members of the community. Local custom and even superstition could be found mixed with Christian practice, but there is no doubt that the person of Our Lord in his suffering and glory was the main inspiration for the religion of the time. This the ordinary citizen could take part in and understand.

Duffy shows in the second part of his book that the Reformation swept all this away and left the average Englishman stranded. Arid years of Anglican church life followed in which Morning and Evening Prayer with long sermons took the place of a mass with which even the most illiterate person had been able to identify. There were oases of holy living, such as that found at Little Gidding and also with Wesley and the Evangelicals, but none found general acceptance within the nation. Evangelicals, however, deserve a further mention for they were part of the solution for a revived spiritual life and influenced two of the first Tractarians, Newman and Pusey. This party taught that the image of God in man had not been defaced but effaced and that, since man was basically evil, he could do nothing for his own salvation. He could be justified only by faith, which was God's free gift to his chosen. A man needed the drastic process of conversion before he could be suitable for God's service. Such beliefs were worked out at different levels and in their extreme form could be very unattractive. Newman and Pusey, though, seem to have experienced a more moderate form of Evangelicalism in which a search for holiness was worked out under the eye of an overwhelmingly transcendent God. Who knows where their spiritual journey would have ended, if they had not come under the influence of John Keble? Yet they seem to have retained something from Evangelical teaching and this legacy continued to break through in their later life.

Meanwhile, the leaders of the Oxford Movement, Keble, Pusey, and Newman, all of them outstanding scholars, were engaged in the academic exercise of uncovering the true nature of the Church of England. They used their talents to show that their Church at the Reformation had incorporated that deposit of faith which had been the hallmark of Catholicism since the early centuries. Newman argued that the Prayer Book was the 'depository' of the teaching of the Apostles, while the Thirty Nine Articles were 'polemical' and, except that they embody the creeds, are mainly protests against certain definite errors.

On the foundation of this rediscovered deposit of faith a Catholic spirituality could again be built. In this John Keble had the best organised approach to holiness, as his search was based on what one may call the great Anglican experience which he had learned from his father, also a priest. This included the martyrdom of Charles I who had died rather than compromise the faith and order of the Church of England; the devotion of the Caroline divines and the non-jurors; and the sacramental piety and pastoral example of the seventeenth century priest, George Herbert. It was all summed up in the Book of Common Prayer.

Geoffrey Rowell writes: in *The Vision Glorious*:
'If the way of holiness, enabled by the grace of God given most especially in the sacraments, was the way by which God made himself known, then the worship of the Church was the means by which men and women were led upon that way. For an Anglican that meant the Prayer Book, though the Prayer Book seen against the background of the Church of the Fathers. For the ordinary Christian believer, Keble wrote "in all great things the Prayer Book is really the voice of the ancient Church."'[4] Thus, he gave to his fellow pioneers of Anglo-Catholicism a view of the Prayer

Book which they did not know existed, and this was the text book which an increasing number of disciples used to teach the Church of England back to its apostolic dignity. Holiness could be gained not by a once for all conversion, but by a daily realisation of the mystery of God revealed by Jesus and continued in the life of the Church. For Keble, too, the whole world was full of the grandeur of God and words were inadequate to express this mystery. As Rowell says, Keble was aware of the deficiencies of the Prayer Book, but despite this, the order of the Eucharist could show Christ's self-offering and enable all to share in it. For him, the Eucharist was the centre of man's search for holiness, for his sanctification, and this meant it should be celebrated with increasing reverence. The ceremonial of the early years of the Catholic movement was simple, but the lesson was not lost that if a sense of the holiness of God was essential for man's aspirations, then nothing but the best was good enough when man came before him in worship. The overwhelming greatness and justice of God meant a complete interior experience for evangelicals: for the Catholic it meant a continual self-offering through the sacrifice of the Mass, celebrated with a ceremonial which taught the awareness of God.

From the earliest days of the movement, the Tractarians sought the approval of bishops for what they were doing. 'Exalt our Holy Fathers the bishops, as the representatives of the Apostles, and the Angels of the Churches; and magnify your office, as being ordained by them to take part in their Ministry', wrote a Presbyter to his fellow presbyters and deacons of the Church of Christ in England in the first of the *Tracts for the Times* in September 1833. To recover the sanctity of their calling, Anglican clergy needed to have bishops who also understood their high position within the Catholic Church. As the Tractarian movement grew in strength, it continued to need the kind of episcopal authority which had preserved that same Catholic Church through the ages. The bishops of the Church of Christ in England, however, were not ready or prepared to be exalted beyond their position in the House of Lords. The Tractarian leaders, especially Newman, hammered away at their task. In 1835 Newman wrote:

'Increase the number of our Bishops. Give the people objects on which their holier and more generous feelings may rest. After all, in spite of the utilitarianism of the age, we have hearts. We like to meet with those whom we may admire and make much of'.

Ker comments on these words:

'It must have surprised the bishops of the established Church to hear that the "sight" of their persons was certain to bring out the "purer and nobler feelings of our nature" and a 'flame of devoted and triumphant affection". It is doubtful if they had ever seen themselves in this light'.[5]

Newman finally gave up this unequal struggle and joined the Church of Rome. As the years went by, Anglican bishops emerged from the House of Lords to take their spiritual duties more seriously. With certain notable exceptions, however, they have never fully come to terms with Anglo-Catholicism. If they ceased to persecute their Catholic priests by the end of the last century, they have been reluctant to take sides with them in this century. They have been wary of being pushed into ceremonies of which they were uncertain. Between the wars there were some great diocesan bishops who tried to be fair-minded; these gained the respect of their Catholic clergy. In recent years, however, they have been lost in the bureaucracy of the General Synod and with a few exceptions have meekly carried out the resolutions of this body.

The relationship, therefore, between episcopacy and Anglo-Catholicism has seldom been a happy one. Catholics for this reason have been criticised for an ambiguity by which they regarded bishops as essential guardians of church order and yet have had at times to disobey them. Pickering writes:

'So here is the ambiguity for Anglo-Catholic priests: bishops are necessary functionaries for their very existence, yet vows of obedience made to them may be ignored. Bishops were thus seen as functionaries – as impersonal machines making valid priests. All they did and said was of no consequence. They were near to being a thorn in the flesh.'

Newman could not come to terms with this ambiguity, Keble and Pusey did. As Keble said of the church of England, 'It works'. In his Assize Sermon he gave a fuller answer. 'The Anglican Church is the representative in England of the whole Church Catholic and Apostolic, a society to use the biblical phrase, built upon the Apostles and prophets, Jesus Christ Himself being the chief corner stone.' Its authority is the authority of Christ, handed on by Him to the Apostles and their successors. This Apostolic Church is a greater thing than the Church of England, although the Church of England is assuredly a true part of it, and it is to this wider Church that a man's loyalty is ultimately due. Keble's solution to the problem has been followed by most Anglo-Catholics since Tractarian days. As I noted in my chapter on the ritualist priests, they were too busy in their slum parishes to worry overmuch about the problem of authority.

As I study church history, however, I notice what little impact bishops made on the daily life of parishes after the deposit of faith had been agreed at the early councils. As I said earlier in this chapter, it then became the duty of a bishop to see that this *depositum* was implemented in his diocese. He did this through the priests he ordained. It was obviously impossible for him to do it personally in ages when both travel and other forms of communication were difficult. In his *History of the Later Middle Ages*, John Dickinson writes about the difficulty of getting children confirmed by a bishop and quotes David Knowles, the monastic historian, as saying that thousands upon thousands must have died unconfirmed.[6] This neglect was due both to the slowness of travel and also to the many secular duties which a bishop had to carry out. Most parishes, therefore, would not have seen their bishop except at an ordination or the consecration of a new church. Duffy's compendious work on the pre-Reformation church makes no mention of an episcopal presence in parish life. After the Reformation, bishops took a greater interest in what was going on in the parishes but this was to make sure that the new religious legislation was being obeyed.

By the beginning of the nineteenth century, bishops were mostly concerned with their political duties and had lost touch with their parishes. Yet, when according to the requirements of their Church of England they ordained priests, they handed on the Catholic deposit of faith enshrined in the Book of Common Prayer. Like their predecessors of earlier ages, they were, as a senior diocesan described it to me a short time ago, facilitators of the age-old Catholic faith. If this depositum should be changed by the Church, its bishops would forfeit the allegiance of their priests and laity. This is the problem posed by the present debate on women priests. It would become no longer a question of the bishop's personal ideas and beliefs but the quality of faith he was communicating.

There was a change of priorities when Anglo-Catholicism moved out of the academic circle of Oxford and established itself in poor city parishes. The simple reverence of the Tractarians gave way to the ritualism of later generations. In fact, ritual was the chief way that people in slum parishes could be taught something of the holiness of God that they were meant to share. Criticism has been levelled at the Catholic movement because it aped Roman Catholic worship. It seems to me, however, that once the full implications of following the Prayer Book in the search for holiness were realised, it would not be long before the provisions of the ornaments Rubric would be brought into use.

It has already been noted that rites and ceremonies and lavish illustration of the Christian faith in art of all kinds were essential for parishioners of the later Middle Ages. They parted with these at the Reformation only after a hard fight, as Duffy shows in the second part of his book, *The Stripping of the Altars*. A momentum of popular piety then stopped and was replaced by a religion which was out of the reach of the lower classes. In order, therefore, to put these in touch with their Church again it was necessary to speak to them in a language they could understand. The ritualists set about this by reintroducing the ornaments and vestments which had been swept away at the Reformation. The Eucharist again became the main act of worship. The slogan, 'It's the Mass that Matters', reappeared in popular instruction. Confession was also taught. It was used by those who were surrounded in the slums by temptations of the fiercest kind and gradually found its way into the lives of Anglo-Catholics at large.

For this, the state of the Roman Catholic Church in England was not a good model to follow in the early years of the Oxford Movement. What Newman called The Second Spring, however, was not far away and after 1850 Roman Catholic immigrants, both priestly and lay, swept into Britain. Anglo-Catholic priests were then able increasingly to learn from them in both liturgical and pastoral matters. But both before and after this 'second spring', there was a strong anti-Catholic feeling in Britain which at times could verge on the hysterical.[7] This bias has continued to the present day. In a newspaper article in January 1993 a church correspondent, Clifford Longley, talks about 'the pernicious fog of anti-papism'. He writes:

'"No Popery" has been called the residual religion of the English – all that is left when positive belief evaporates'.

It is therefore, against this continuing anti-Roman prejudice that both the past and future of Anglo-Catholicism must be assessed. When opposition to this movement was aroused, 'No Popery' became the slogan, and persecution in different forms followed. There were martyrs for the cause, like Dolling, Mackonochie, Tooth, and Walke. Notable ministries were impeded, but not destroyed. A distinctive pastoral activity came into being which communicated the Catholic faith to many who otherwise would have been without it. Because this could not be done by Roman Catholic clergy, I can only conclude that there is still a future for Anglo-Catholicism.

The work of the Oxford reformers among the lower classes was the more difficult because popular piety had been lost in this country for several centuries. The ground has never been made up and today the same missionary situation awaits Catholics as in the last century. It has become more acute and new techniques must be found to bring people back into the Church. My chapter on The Gospel to our Neighbour should be read in this context. I believe that the Christian community which can develop a lay apostolate, based on sound teaching, will take the lead in evangelism. The Church Union once had it in its grasp and then let it go.

Our country is also worried about crime, wrongdoing, indiscipline, and falling standards. Thinking people are beginning to take the idea of evil seriously again and are concerned that the Church ignores the problem. From its earliest days, the Catholic movement in the Church of England revived the sacrament of penance and expected its members to have a rule about self-examination and confession. This habit has all but disappeared in many parishes, but sin is on the increase and seems to afflict the clergy as much as the laity, perhaps more so. Within the last few years I wrote to my diocesan about the moral difficulties of the clergy which were surfacing alarmingly around the country. I suggested that it might be helpful if every priest was encouraged to have a spiritual director who could keep in touch with his problems under the seal of the confessional. I received no answer to my letter but within six months, six lay psychiatrists, some without church connections, were appointed within the diocese to act as consultants. For me that sums up the lack of understanding which has followed marginal Catholics from the beginning. The story of the Church of England over the last one hundred and fifty years might have been different if its bishops had taken hold of the Catholic quest for holiness.

I have given sound teaching a prominent place in this book. This has been the prime concern of the Anglo-Catholic movement. Always it has fought bad teaching and unsound scholarship. At the end of the last century my parents learned their faith from booklets of simple instruction and I was similarly fortunate in the literature I was able to read in the years between the wars. The Anglo-Catholic congresses which began in 1920 were no mere displays of strength but were means of instructing the faithful. The publications of the Society of SS Peter and Paul, Faith Press, A.R. Mowbray, W. Knott and the Church Literature Association continued that tradition. Today this contribution to the Church is more needed than ever. The teaching of the Oxford Movement was founded on revelation as found in the Scriptures and interpreted by tradition and the Fathers. If Anglo-Catholics want to survive they must have the same foundation for their spiritual lives. It is therefore urgent that Catholic ordinands should have a balanced, professional education in the Bible and should persevere with this study after ordination.

A search for holiness, a concern for sin and repentance, an emphasis on sound teaching, a pastoral and missionary zeal, a willingness to suffer for the Faith: these attributes of the Catholic movement add up to a vital ingredient of any church life. The Church of England would be an empty shell without them.

A few months ago Catholic societies joined together for a celebration of faith in the Wembley Arena. The massive hall was packed with thousands of bishops, clergy and people. The sermon at the concelebrated solemn Mass was given by the Archbishop of Sydney, an Evangelical. He preached on the text from the letter of Jude:

But ye, beloved, building up yourselves on your most holy faith, praying in the Holy Spirit, keep yourselves in the love of God, looking for the mercy of our Lord Jesus Christ unto eternal life.

The first fathers of the Oxford Movement would have said Amen to that.

References

1.   Pickering p.267
2.   Origen Principles 3.6
3.   Duffy p.91
4.   Oxford 1983 pp.34 seq
5.   Ker Newman p.115
6.   Dickinson The Later Middle Ages p.166 (A and C Black 1974)
7.   Colley: Britons (Yale 1993) Chapter One

Chapter Twenty-one

Over the Edge

When I began this book more than a year ago it seemed unlikely that the measure for ordaining women to the priesthood would be passed in the General Synod, and that the debate would be carried over into the next synod in five years time. As the final vote at the November 1992 meeting approached, it was thought that it would fail in the House of Laity, because at the earlier July meeting a significant number had shown themselves against the measure. The October 1992 newsletter of the Cost of Conscience movement summed up this belief, 'Opinion seems to be that the measure will fail to get the required two thirds majority in at least one and possibly in all three houses of the Bishops, Clergy, and Laity, but the margin is likely to be close'. Many parish priests pinned their hopes on this forecast. The verdict was indeed close, by two votes in the House of Laity, but the vote went in favour of women priests. This has had a devastating effect on many priests in their parishes. They are faced with the likelihood of being without employment in two years time, and with the knowledge that the compensation offered will be inadequate. More than that, their devoted service to their people will now be cut short and there is no doubt that many lay people will leave the Church in anger. As we have seen in this book, Catholic priests have had a fine record in ministering to their flocks, especially in poor parishes, and this has not escaped the attention of many fair-minded people, inside and outside the Church.

We might enquire, after the event, why the measure succeeded at the last fence. Since the whole debate was

269

broadcast live on TV, it is possible to have a picture of what happened. The case for ordaining women has always rested very much on emotion, feminist principles, on secular example, and on the hope for an improved church life. All these strands can be detected in the Synod debate. Another impetus came from the Archbishop of Canterbury who 'put his job on the line'. His decision to take one side of the argument and to dismiss all counter arguments was irregular. On such a divisive and important issue he should have been neutral, during the debate at least. The emotive approach of the measure's supporters in the end defeated the more theological approach of the opposition and undoubtedly won over some of the laity.

In my earlier chapter on this subject, I pointed to two decisive factors in this controversy. The first was the vote in the General Synod in July 1975 that there were no theological objections to women priests. Only in an age of liberal biblical theology could this judgment have been made for there is no support for such a priesthood in the New Testament. This point has been argued already and I will not repeat it. The trouble has been that even Anglo-Catholics have neglected bible study and only Graham Leonard really made a stand on this ground. The second factor was the decision to accept women deacons in 1986. This allowed women deacons who supported the ordination of women to vote in the House of Clergy which, up to that point, had mustered enough opposition to a female priesthood.

We should be clear what has happened. The synod of a church which claimed to be part of Catholic Christendom has voted to change the deposit of faith which has come down intact from the early Church and which was retained in England at the Reformation. A female priesthood has not been part of this depositum which can be changed only with the assent of the world-wide Catholic Church. The Church of England, therefore, has voted to be Non-conformist as far as that universal Church is concerned.

At times the Church of England has flirted with Protestant Churches. In 1841 it set up a joint bishopric with the Lutheran Church in Jerusalem but this collapsed within forty years. The Anglican/Methodist scheme would have thrown it open to Non-Conformity if it had been accepted in 1969. It has survived attempts to change the Prayer Book in Parliament. In all these crises, Anglo-Catholics have voiced their dissent. Now they find themselves in a totally impossible situation. One newspaper summed up their dilemma by noting in a leading article that by the Synod vote the Church of England had destroyed its claim to be part of a wider Catholic Church, had flouted biblical teaching and ruined prospects of reunion with the rest of Catholic Christendom. These are matters which are the life blood of Anglo-Catholicism and its members *cannot* (and will not) accept them.

Readers of this book may conclude, as I have done, that the Church of England is back in the same position as it was in 1833 when popular understanding saw it as a mere department of the state, to be adapted to current social demands. It was this concept which the Tractarians denied and, in time, changed. It seems that we have returned to square one. Has the Catholic call to holiness, founded on God's holiness, been finally defeated by British Pelagianism which trusts in man's ability to save himself? If so, we have ample evidence in national life that this optimistic philosophy has failed to withstand the onslaught of modern evils. The Church might have been unable to do much about this, but it has at least kept aloft within Catholic Christendom the torch of God's revelation to the world.

What then, is the future for Anglo-Catholic priests who find themselves abandoned by most of their bishops? First, they should reflect that they have never had episcopacy on their side, and yet from the margins have distilled into the rest of their Church a spirituality which has been received from the past and developed in the present. They will, however, need bishops to enable the growth of the Church to continue through Confirmation and Ordination. Twelve bishops voted against the measure and they must play a significant part in the future of a continuing traditionalist body. A serious problem will be the training of future priests. This is, in fact, already arising because there is a proposal to close some of our theologial colleges, including Mirfield which has so far refused to train women. One solution might be to extend my lay apostolate strategy to include the local training of priests.

Should Anglo-Catholics stay within their Church and like the Oxford reformers work again for the renewal and revival of Catholic life? Would this be possible if alternative episcopal oversight were provided? There are three main objections to this. First, it would mean staying within a church which was no longer Catholic. As a parish priest asked, 'How do you teach your Confirmation candidates that they belong to the One, Holy, Catholic and Apostolic Church when it is no longer true?' Secondly there is no guarantee that alternative episcopal oversight would continue and that traditionalist parishes would not in time be overrun. Lastly and by no means least, how could Catholic priests be governed by a General Synod which has already drastically voted to alter the ministry and no doubt would not hesitate to approve women bishops within a few years? What would be the status of the men and women these women ordained? The lesson from abroad, also, is that a package of liberal theology follows the ordination of women.

Another solution is a church within a church. This would be a continuing church or an independent province. The history of such churches, however, has not been encouraging, as the episode of the non-Jurors attests. This could be only a temporary measure, therefore, and a larger parent body would have to be found. So some sort of recognition might be sought from the wider Catholic Church.

For those seeking merely a personal solution, individual submission to Rome is an answer. Some have already taken this road. This is not an easy choice for a married priest who wants to continue his ministry. Those who have been reordained have not usually been given positions of great responsibility. Before any course of action is taken, however, Our Lord's parable about the king planning to go to war with another, might be recalled. He was well-advised to sit down and consider whether he had sufficient troops for the venture. This, then, should be the first step for those who cannot accept the ordination of women. The question should be asked: How many priests are still prepared to pay the cost of conscience? Two or three years ago 3,000 priests signed an Open List indicating that they could in no way accept a female priesthood. Are these still standing firm or are they melting away? If the opposition is not strong, in vain will concessions be sought from the main body of the Church of England. As I write this final chapter, I have before me a communique from the Forward In Faith organisation which states that they have over 3,400 priests on their lists and thousands of laity. The number is rapidly expanding each day. From personal knowledge, in some dioceses nearly half the clergy will have nothing to do with the ordination of women. If this trend continues, it is a force to be reckoned with both by the Church and by Parliament. This appears to be the best argument for an alternative Anglican Church.

The danger of being a mere ghetto, however, awaits such a separated church. If its members were just taking refuge from something they did not want, then the future would be bleak. A programme of mission and teaching, therefore, must be worked out quickly. Both have been part of the Anglo-Catholic tradition and both are needed desperately in this country. I believe that any church which can offer sound teaching inside and outside school would received a general welcome. There is great anxiety, for example, that children are not receiving sound Christian religious education in school. Catholics need to rediscover the Bible and especially the Gospels as the foundation of their message.

There are considerable problems in a realignment of Anglicans. Priests, for example need to be paid wherever they are employed. At present the scale of compensation for those who cannot accept the ordination of women is inadequate and further negotiation will be needed. At this juncture, conditions of employment in the secular field should be examined. If an employee here has his work drastically altered, he can take his employer to court on the ground of constructive dismissal.

Since the General Synod has now voted to change radically its ministry, it could be maintained that a priest will find himself operating in a different kind of body from the one in which he was ordained. The goalposts have been moved after the game has started and this is proving unacceptable to at least one third of Anglican clergy. It would seem fair that they should continue to received stipends if they are working within the framework of the traditional Anglican ministry. Parliament might well take that line also.

My book ends with the Church of England in great confusion and the outcome uncertain. If the future of Anglo-Catholicism were part of my subject, I would delay publication for a few years. My purpose in writing, as I stated in my author's note, however, was to give a history of the Oxford Movement and to show how it transformed the Church of England. If I have been successful, my readers may well be alarmed that such a force for spiritual good should now be pushed out of the margins and over the edge of the Established Church.

I finish with a letter which was sent recently to the press by Fr Ian Ker, the biographer of Newman: 'Like Newman's departure in 1845 the Synod decision is really a triumph for liberals. Without the Anglo-Catholics, will the Conservative Evangelicals be able to resist the total liberalisation of the Church of England? More than 100 years ago, Newman feared the Church of England would become "so radically liberalised ... as to become a simple enemy of the Truth", as it seemed only a "matter of time, how long the Anglican church retains any part of the Faith".

If that "spell" which Newman thought prevented Anglo-Catholics from recognising the true reality of the Church of England has finally been broken, he would hope that the Roman Catholic authorities will now look as sympathetically as possible at the practicality of establishing, as has been done in the United States, a special rite within the Roman Catholic Church for former Anglicans.

When the possibility of an Anglican Uniate Church was mooted in 1876, Newman could only welcome "any means of drawing to us so many good people who are shivering at our gates" '.[1]

As this book approaches publication, the Roman Catholic bishops of England and Wales have given a warm welcome to those who can no longer remain in the Church of England and have laid down guide-lines for a change of allegiance. I hope I have shown that Anglo-Catholics will not enter the gates of Rome empty handed. They will bring courage in a quest for holiness, a concern for sound teaching and a passion for mission. All are essential qualities for the conversion of this country to the Christian faith.

References

1. Daily Telegraph, 18 Nov 1992

Index